C000245934

# The Art of
# Social Theory

# The Art of
# Social Theory

..............................................................

..............................................................

*Richard Swedberg*

PRINCETON UNIVERSITY PRESS
Princeton and Oxford

Copyright © 2014 by Princeton University Press

Published by Princeton University Press, 41 William Street, Princeton,
New Jersey 08540

In the United Kingdom: Princeton University Press, 6 Oxford Street,
Woodstock, Oxfordshire OX20 1TW

press.princeton.edu

Jacket art © Dmitrii Vlasov/Shutterstock. Jacket design by Pamela Schnitter.

All Rights Reserved

ISBN 978-0-691-15522-7

British Library Cataloging-in-Publication Data is available

This book has been composed in Garamond Premier Pro and Univers LT

Printed on acid-free paper. ∞

Printed in the United States of America

10 9 8 7 6 5 4 3 2 1

For Mabel

# Contents

................................................................

# The Art of
# Social Theory

# Why Theorize and Can You Learn to Do It?

Why is it important to know how to theorize in social science? And is it a skill you can learn—and perhaps also teach? Some interesting light was cast on these questions in the very strange way in which a crime was solved in the summer of 1879. The victim of the crime, and also the person who solved it, was philosopher and scientist Charles S. Peirce.

The crime took place on a steamship called *Bristol*, which was traveling between Boston and New York. At the time Peirce was thirty-nine years old and had just accepted a position as Lecturer in Logic at Johns Hopkins University. He was also working for the US government on the Coast and Geodetic Survey.

On Friday, June 20, 1879, Peirce boarded the boat in Boston. He would arrive the following day in New York, where he was going to attend a conference. When he woke up in his cabin the next morning he did not feel well. His mind was foggy, so he quickly dressed and took a cab from the harbor to the Brevoort House, a well-known hotel on Fifth Avenue where the conference was held.

After he arrived at the hotel, he discovered that he had forgotten his overcoat on the boat as well as an expensive Tiffany watch, to which a gold chain was attached. Peirce was especially unhappy at the prospect of losing the watch, since he used it as an instrument; it also belonged to the government.

Peirce rushed back to the boat, went to his cabin, and looked around. But the watch and chain and the coat were nowhere to be found. Peirce thought that one of the stewards must have stolen his belongings, since they were the only persons who had had access to his cabin. With the help of the captain he soon had the stewards lined up for questioning.

What then happened is strange. Instead of questioning the suspects in traditional fashion, Peirce proceeded as follows:

> I went from one end of the row to the other, and talked a little to each one, in as *dégagé* a manner as I could, about whatever he could talk about with interest, but would least expect me to bring forward, hoping that I might seem such a fool that I should be able to detect some symptom of his being the thief. (Peirce 1929: 271)

But this did not help, and Peirce had still no idea who the thief was. He decided to try something else:

> When I had gone through the row I turned and walked from them, though not away, and said to myself. "Not the least scintilla of light have I got to go upon." But thereupon my other self (for our communings are always in dialogues), said to me, "But you simply *must* put your finger on the man. No matter if you have no reason, you must say whom you will think to be the thief." I made a little loop in my walk, which had not taken a minute, and as I turned toward them, all shadow of doubt had vanished. There was no self-criticism. All that was out of place. I went to the

fellow whom I had fixed upon as the thief, and told him to step into the stateroom with me. (Peirce 1929: 271)

When Peirce was alone with the man, he did not try to make him confess. Instead he made an attempt to persuade the man to give back the stolen items. Peirce had a fifty-dollar bill in his pocket, which he offered to the man in return for his watch with the chain and coat.

"Now," I said, "that bill is yours, if you will earn it. I do not want to find out who stole my watch. ... You go and bring me the watch, chain and overcoat, and I shall only be too glad to pay you this fifty dollars and get away." (Peirce 1929: 271)

The man said that he did not know anything about the stolen goods, and Peirce let him go. He now decided he had to try something else and contacted Pinkertons, the famous detective agency. He explained what had happened to the head of the New York branch, a Mr. George Bangs.

Peirce told Bangs that he knew the name of the thief and wanted someone from Pinkertons to follow the thief when he got off the ship. "The man will go to a pawnbroker," Peirce said, "where he will get fifty dollars for the watch. When he pawns it, arrest him."

Bangs listened to Peirce and asked how he knew that this particular individual was the thief. Peirce answered, "Why, I have no reason whatever for thinking so; but I am entirely confident that it is so" (Peirce 1929: 273). Peirce added that if he was wrong, the man would not go to a pawnshop; and no harm would have been done by following him.

Bangs was not convinced. He told Peirce that his agency knew much more about thieves and criminals than Peirce did:

I am sure you have no acquaintance with thieves and are entirely ignorant of the species. Now we do know them. It is our business to be acquainted with them. We know the ways of every kind and every gang, and we know the men themselves—the most of them. Let me suggest this: I will send down our very best man. He shall bear in mind and give full weight to your impression. Only let him not be hampered with positive orders. Let him act upon his own inferences, when he shall have sifted all the indications. (Peirce 1929: 273)

Peirce agreed, and a Pinkertons detective was sent to the boat the very same day, where he questioned all the stewards. The detective soon found out that one of the stewards had a criminal record, and he had the man followed.

The individual Peirce had singled out as the thief turned out to have been the personal valet of the captain for many years. When the theft took place he had also worked on a different deck than where Peirce's cabin was located.

The detective followed the man with the criminal record, but this did not lead anywhere. Peirce asked Bangs what could be done next in this situation. Offer a reward of $150 to any pawnbroker who can give information about the watch was the answer.

Peirce followed the advice, and already the next day a pawnbroker reported that he had the watch. From the description that the pawnbroker gave of the man who had pawned the watch, Peirce immediately recognized the steward he had singled out as the thief.

Peirce now had his watch, but he still missed the coat and the gold chain that had been attached to the watch. To get back his remaining belongings he decided to go to the apartment of the thief, accompanied by a detective from Pinkertons.

When Peirce and the detective arrived at the place where the thief lived, Peirce asked the detective to enter the apartment and retrieve his gold chain and coat. The detective refused. " 'Oh,' he said, 'I could not think of it. I have no warrant, and they would certainly call in the police!' " (Peirce 1929: 275).

Peirce became annoyed and decided to do it himself. He climbed the stairs and knocked on the door of the apartment where the thief lived. A woman opened the door, and behind her was another woman. Peirce told the first woman that her husband had been arrested for the theft of the watch and that he had come to get his coat and his gold chain back. The women started to scream and said that he could not enter the apartment. If he did, they said, they would call the police. Peirce ignored them and stepped into the apartment.

At this point, the story takes another curious turn. Peirce describes what happened once he was inside the apartment in the following way:

> I saw no place in that room where the chain was likely to be, and walked through into another room. Little furniture was there beyond a double bed and a wooden trunk on the further side of the bed. I said, "Now my chain is at the bottom of that trunk under the clothes; and I am going to take it. It has a gold binnacle with a compass attached; and you can see that I take that, which I know is there, and nothing else." I knelt down and fortunately found the trunk unlocked. Having thrown out all the clothes—very good clothes—I came upon quite a stratum of trinkets of evident provenance, among which was my chain. (Peirce 1926: 276)

There was still the coat. When Peirce looked around for it, the woman said that he should feel free to look wherever he wanted.

But the way in which she said this made Peirce suspect that the coat was not in the apartment. He also noticed that the second woman had disappeared.

Peirce left the apartment and thought that the other woman might have been a neighbor. He knocked on the door opposite of the apartment where he had just been. Two young girls opened the door:

> I looked over their shoulders and saw a quite respectable looking parlor with a nice piano. But upon the piano was a neat bundle of just the right size and shape to contain my overcoat. I said, "I have called because there is a bundle here belonging to me; oh, yes, I see it, and I will just take it." So I gently pushed beyond them, took the bundle, opened it, and found my overcoat, which I put on. (Peirce 1929: 277)

What has so far been told about the theft of Peirce's belongings, and how he recovered them, might seem like an odd tale, showing how eccentric and willful Peirce was, but also that he had a certain talent as an amateur detective.

Peirce himself, however, interpreted what had happened very differently. He assigned great importance to the story and wrote it up during the spring of 1907 in the form of an article, titled "Guessing."

The episode, he said, was very instructive for scientists and could be seen as "a chapter in the art of inquiry" (Peirce 1929: 282). In a letter to his friend William James, he described what had happened as an instance of the "theory why it is so that people so often guess right" (Sebeok and Umiker-Sebeok 1981: 16).

Guessing, in Peirce's view, plays a crucial role in scientific research. It is precisely through guessing that the most important part of the scientific analysis is produced—namely, the explanation. What explains a phenomenon constitutes the centerpiece of scientific research, according to Peirce. It is correct that without facts to test the hypothesis or the idea, the guess is of little value. But without the hypothesis or idea, there will be nothing to test and no science at all.

The term that Peirce most often used in his work for the guess of a hypothesis is *abduction*. Human beings, as he saw it, are endowed by nature with a capacity to come up with explanations. They have a "faculty of guessing," without which science would not be possible in the first place (Peirce 1929: 282).

Science could never have developed as fast as it had in the West, according to Peirce, if people had just come up with ideas at random and tested these. Somehow scientists have succeeded in guessing right many times.

In the article titled "Guessing," Peirce also gives an account of a series of experiments that he and a student had carried out at Johns Hopkins on the topic of guessing. According to the article that resulted, which today is seen as a minor classic in experimental psychology, people have a capacity to guess right much more often than if only chance was involved (Peirce and Jastrow 1885).

The reason for this, the authors show, is that people pick up cues subconsciously, and then process these in ways in which science does not yet understand. They also established that people are better at guessing correctly under certain circumstances than others.

Is this also a skill that can be learned and taught? Peirce definitely thought so. It is also clear from his behavior in the episode with the theft that he had trained himself to observe and trust his own capacity to guess and come up with correct explanations. In fact, throughout his life, Peirce was deeply concerned with the issue of how to improve the capacity for abduction. He was especially interested in the practical ways in which people can train themselves to become better at coming up with solutions to problems and new ideas. With this in mind he also constructed a number of practical exercises.

This brings us back to this book, which is primarily aimed at those who want to learn the art of theorizing in social science. In fact, the one author who has inspired the main ideas of this book more than anyone else is Peirce, who was very concerned with this issue. It is, for example, his notion of science that underlies what follows—namely, that science is about observing a phenomenon, coming up with an idea or a theory why something happens, and then testing the theory against facts.

Most importantly, and again inspired by Peirce, I see abduction, or coming up with an idea, as the most precious part of the whole research process and the one that it is the most important to somehow get a grip on. It truly constitutes the heart of the theorizing process. Following Peirce, I also argue that an idea or a hypothesis is of little value until it has been carefully tested against data according to the rules of science.

What I have aimed for in writing this book is first to produce a practical guide. The book essentially contains tips on how to proceed for those who want to learn how to theorize in a creative way in social science. It also attempts to show how you can teach theorizing, or at least how you should approach this topic.

This is a tall order, and the book is by design as well as by necessity an experimental book. As a result, it contains more suggestions than prescriptions. Still, the hope is that the book will help to put theorizing—how to do it and how to teach it—on the agenda of today's social science.

The book has two parts, each of which consists of five chapters. The first part deals with the issue of what you do when you theorize in practical terms; the second with how to prepare and train yourself for theorizing.

In chapter 1, the project of creative theorizing in social science is presented. Here as elsewhere I will use the term *creative theorizing*, or an *abductive-oriented* type of theorizing, to distinguish the type of theorizing I advocate from that of others. I also discuss the need for a decisive break with some of the ways in which theory is currently understood in social science. This is followed by four chapters that describe how to theorize in a practical way.

Chapter 2 argues that creative theorizing in social science has to begin with observation. Chapters 3 through 5 describe how you proceed from the stage of observation to the formulation of a tentative theory. This part of the process I call *building out the theory*, and it can be described as giving body and structure to the theory.

First is the problem of naming the phenomenon you want to study and of developing concepts that can help you to nail it down and analyze it (chapter 3). In the attempt to produce a theory, you may also need to use analogies and metaphors, construct a typology, and more (chapter 4). No theory is complete without an explanation, and there are many different ways of coming up with one (chapter 5).

The second part of this book is devoted to the ways in which you prepare yourself for theorizing, and also how you teach students how to theorize. Heuristics are helpful in this and so are various practical exercises (chapters 6 and 7). It is imperative to know some theory to be good at theorizing, and how to accomplish this in a practical way is discussed in chapter 8.

There is also the question of the role of imagination and the arts in helping social scientists to theorize well (chapter 9). The general approach to theorizing in this book is summarized in the last chapter, which also contains a discussion of what I see as the inherently democratic nature of theorizing (chapter 10).

The book ends as it starts, with Peirce. I have included an appendix titled "How to Theorize according to Charles S. Peirce." The reason for this is that the work of Peirce is not as well known in social science as it perhaps deserves to be. This is especially true for the practical side of his work on abduction, which deals with *learning the art of theorizing*.

# PART 1

# How to Theorize

························································

## CHAPTER 1

# Starting Anew

> To think at all is to theorize.
>
> —Coleridge, *The Friend*[1]

Similar ideas to those of Charles S. Peirce on abduction and theorizing have been voiced over the centuries by a number of people, from scientists to artists. When Coleridge, for example, two centuries ago wrote that to think also means to theorize, he had little evidence to base his opinion on other than his own intuition as a thinker and poet.

Today, in contrast, the situation is different. Thanks to cognitive science and neurophysiology we know that people are born with a capacity to think; to create concepts, analogies, and metaphors; and to come up with explanations. In brief they are born with a capacity to think and to theorize (for example, Frankish and Ramsey 2012; Holyoak and Morrison 2012).

This capacity is used in people's lives, more or less constantly. It is also at work when theory is created in social science or any other science. It is a capacity that can be blocked or strengthened, given the social and cultural conditions that exist, as well as the will of the individual to push ahead and try something new.

## The Problems with Social Theory Today

An important reason for devoting a book to the topic of theorizing is that theory is currently not in very good shape in social science. One way to quickly get a sense for why this is the case is to compare the state of theory to that of methods. Since World War II methods have advanced very quickly. For many years students have also been able to take courses that give them a solid foundation in methods—and this goes for quantitative as well as qualitative methods. Nothing similar is available in theory or theorizing. More generally, social theory is currently not very innovative and has little to say on many important issues.

There are many reasons for the relatively backward state of modern theory in social science, and several of these are linked to specific practices. One has to do with the common tendency to carry out the empirical part of the research first, leaving theory to be added on afterward. The empirical material is either squeezed into some preexisting theory or labeled in some way.

Another common practice that is problematic is when the researcher is so convinced of the excellence of some theoretical approach that the topic is selected according to this theory. A problem with proceeding in this way is that the more one pays attention to the facts themselves, the more difficult it becomes to maintain the original idea. The result is a tug-of-war that resists any easy solution.

These are some of the current practices in social science that make it hard to create good theory. There also exist a few doctrines for how to conduct research that tend to block creative theorizing. *Empiricism* and the notion of *abstract theory* are two of these.

*Empiricism* is a doctrine according to which theory is clearly secondary to the facts, if necessary at all. Reality exists in the form of patterns and structures, and the main task of the social scientist is to capture these with the help of data. From this perspective, the task of theory is basically to summarize the existence of these patterns and structures.

Empiricism has a long tradition in several of the social sciences, such as sociology and political science. A recent version can also be found among those who work with Big Data. In their view the idea of developing hypotheses and then testing these will soon be seen as part of the past, when data were hard to come by and sampling was necessary. Today, with data sets where $n$ = all, the situation is different, and you can basically let the data speak for itself (for example, Anderson 2008; Mayer-Schönberger and Cukier 2013; but also see Conté et al. 2012).

Like empiricism, abstract theory comes in different versions. One that is nearly universally criticized is so-called grand theory, or the kind of theory that addresses the central problems of society but has next to no connection to empirical reality. Data are mainly used to illustrate the theory, and the analysis is about as nonempirical as it gets. This is a version of what has been called "'theoretical' theory," and it has been described as a theory that basically deals only with other (theoretical) theories (Bourdieu 1988: 774).

But there also exist other versions of abstract theory, such as the type of approach that has dominated mainstream economics during much of the twentieth century. In this type of research, the social scientist explicitly rejects starting out by observing empirical reality and instead begins with a theory. According to one proponent of this approach, you should start the research with "the combined postulates of maximizing behavior, stable preferences and market equilibrium, applied relentlessly and unflinchingly" (Becker 1976: 5).

## Theory versus Theorizing

The ways in which the word *theory* is currently being used in social science has led to much confusion about what theory is. As a result *theorizing*, or the process through which theory is produced, has also become hard to grasp. Like theory itself, theorizing has acquired an overtone of something that is abstract and useless, as exemplified by expressions such as "sterile theorizing" or that "one fact is worth a volume of theorizing" (Merton 1945: 472; OED 2000).

While theorizing is not very much discussed in the social science literature, articles and books on theory abound. But despite this fact, great confusion exists over what constitutes theory and what its task should be. In 1945 Robert K. Merton published an article on the way in which the word *theory* is understood in sociology; he found that it was used in no less than six different ways (Merton 1945). Half a century later an article along the same lines appeared in *Sociological Theory*; this time the author found seven different usages (Abend 2008; see also Camic and Gross 1998).

Since the basic approach of these two articles is more or less the same, I will present only Merton's list. Theory, Merton says, is currently viewed as constituting the following: (1) methodology; (2) general sociological orientations; (3) analysis of sociological concepts; (4) *post factum* sociological interpretations; (5) empirical generalizations in sociology; and (6) sociological theory (Merton 1945).

Merton's own definition of theory is well-known and often cited: "The term *sociological theory* refers to logically interconnected sets of propositions from which empirical uniformities can be derived." These uniformities, he specified, should be established via "empirically testable hypotheses" (Merton 1967: 39, 66, 70; compare Merton 1945: 472).

It is important to note Merton's emphasis on the role of verification for what in his view should be considered theory. As will soon be discussed, this also constitutes a key of sorts to what has happened more generally to social theory since World War II.

There are many problems with Merton's approach to theory, and in this book I will be using a different approach, as mentioned in the introduction. My view is very similar to that of Peirce and also to the standard view in science. Theory, as I broadly define it, is *a statement about the explanation of a phenomenon*. And theorizing, from this perspective, is *the process through which a theory is produced*.

## Context of Discovery and Context of Justification

One can also approach the topic of theorizing and its current situation with the help of the distinction between the context of discovery and the context of justification. Proceeding in this way also makes it possible to better understand why the topic of creative theorizing has been so little discussed in social science.

The terms *context of discovery* and *context of justification* were introduced in the early 1930s by philosopher of science Hans Reichenbach, and then diffused through Karl Popper's influential *The Logic of Scientific Discovery* (1935).

The expression context of discovery refers to the stage at which new ideas for how to explain a phenomenon are generated. The context of justification refers to the stage that comes after this, or when these ideas are given the form that they should have when they are presented to the scientific community.

Both Reichenbach and Popper were of the opinion that the philosophy of science is in principle unable to say anything of interest about what happens in the context of discovery. The reason for this, they argued, is that having good ideas is not something that can be analyzed with the help of logic and reason.

"The act of discovery escapes logical analysis," as Reichenbach put it (1951: 231). What takes place when ideas are generated cannot be understood with the help of science. It belongs at best, according to Popper, to "empirical psychology" (Popper 1935: 4–5).

The distinction between the context of discovery and the context of justification in the natural sciences was not something that Reichenbach had discovered; his accomplishment was to create a terminology that caught on. One can find the distinction, for example, already in the work of Peirce. Abduction stands for the context of discovery, and the generation of hypotheses and their testing for the context of justification. The distinction can also be found in the work of several other philosophers and scientists (for example, Schickore and Steinle 2006).

It is also important to point out that the distinction between the context of discovery and the context of justification was played out in a very different way in the social sciences and the natural sciences. An important reason for this is that theory had developed much more quickly in the social sciences before the 1920s than methods to test the theory (for example, Ogburn 1930; Bulmer 1984).

Especially after World War II, however, quantitative methods to test theory began to advance very quickly in social science and be generally accepted. Many sociologists now also began to argue that all theories had to be properly tested, using the new scientific (quantitative) methods.

The problem of generating new ideas, in contrast, attracted much less attention at the time, and was typically seen as belonging to the unscientific part of the research process. The result was a distortion not only of what theorizing stands for, but of theory itself.

## Theorizing Is Practical

Before proceeding any further, it is necessary to pause for a moment and say something about the way in which the terms *theory* and *theorizing* will be used in this book. The word *theorizing*, like the word *theory*, has over the years acquired associations to what is abstract and separate from action. This differs from its original meaning, as developed by Greek thinkers of the fourth century BCE, according to whom theorizing is practical in nature. To theorize, at this time, meant *to see, to observe*, and *to contemplate*.

That theorizing originally was seen as being practical as well as abstract in nature is reflected in the origin of the word *theōrein*, which is the Greek word for theorizing. This word, we are told, is "a compound of *thea,* the view or look of something; *horan,* to see a thing attentively; and the name *theoros,* the attentive observer or the emissary sent to observe foreign practices and to 'theorize' about them—that is, to construct rational explanations of the strange and unexpected" (Scaff 2011: 11).

There are two parts that are of special interest for our purposes in this account of the origin of the word *theōrein*. One has to do with the attempt in fourth-century BCE Greece to develop a new analytical way of thinking that was very different from what was then seen as the main goal of thinking—namely, to acquire wisdom. Heidegger has focused on this particular aspect in his attempt to reconstruct the original meaning of theory in Greek philosophy. According to Heidegger, to theorize and to create a theory originally meant to concentrate on a phenomenon, to stay with it, and in this way to try to understand it (Heidegger 1977: 116).

But there is also a second, very practical element to the meaning of the word *theorizing* in ancient Greece. According to recent scholarship, the word for theory, *theoria*, originally did not refer to a way of thinking but to a civic institution (see, for example,

Nightingale 2009). A Greek city would send an individual, or a *theoros*, on a pilgrimage abroad for the purpose of consulting an oracle or participating in a religious festival and then reporting back to his community what he had experienced. A secular version also existed, where the *theoros* traveled abroad more as a tourist or a researcher. In all of these cases, the traveler was reunited with his original community by giving an account of what he had witnessed.

Fourth-century BCE philosophers explicitly used *theoria* as an allegory or a symbolic narrative to explain what they meant by *philosophy*, and how they viewed the special way of thinking that this new term implied. The most famous account of such a *theoria*-journey to witness a higher reality can be found in the famous allegory of the cave in Plato's *Republic*: When the philosopher leaves the cave, he is at first blinded by the sun. But after a while he begins to see things as they really are, especially the Form of the Good. He eventually returns to the cave; and he now has difficulty in seeing in the dark. After a while, however, his eyes adjust. This time, however, he will see things in a different way, even if it is still *"seeing in the dark"* (Plato 1989: 211; emphasis added).

If we now leave the origin of the word *theorize*, which shows that it was seen as a practical activity of the mind, the next point to be emphasized is that theorizing is essentially an activity that you learn by doing. In this it can be likened to swimming or biking, two activities that you cannot learn simply by reading about them. The same holds true for the way in which people today learn methods in the social sciences.

That theorizing is a practical activity also means that what is needed to learn it (and to learn how to teach it) is knowledge of practical rules. This means rules that tell you what to do when you theorize, not abstract studies of theorizing from some objective and scientific perspective. Social science studies of creativity are, in other words, not very useful for this purpose, since they do not have as their goal to give practical advice.

The situation is similar with science and technology studies (STS). Their main contribution to the project of theorizing is to show that what goes on in the context of justification is not what we would expect from the logic of scientific research. The logic-in-use, in other words, is not the same as the reconstructed logic (Kaplan 1964).

Like studies of creativity, STS sometimes contain pieces of very useful information and even tips for the theorizer on how to proceed. But this is more of an extra bonus you get when you read these studies, rather than their main point.

But even if theorizing is a practical activity through and through, this does not mean that definitive rules can be devised for how to proceed at the different stages of theorizing. The reason is as follows. It is indeed useful to have some simple rules to follow when you *learn* how to theorize. Some rules of this type will also be presented in this book.

But at a later stage a skill in using these rules will develop, and at this point it is important to let go of the rules. Following the rules now will *block* the attempt to reach a higher level and turn the practice into a skill (for example, Dreyfus and Dreyfus 1986).

Wittgenstein provides another reason for not relying exclusively on rules (Wittgenstein 1953). His argument is that rules cannot cover all situations, and this is because they originate in situations where certain things are taken for granted (but not made explicit in the rules). When the rules are applied to new situations, in other words, they cannot provide guidance.

The upshot of this argument is that a too strong focus on following rules will stop the researcher from reacting adequately to the concrete situation. Max Weber came pretty much to the same conclusion, adding one more argument to the case against always following rules: "Indeed, just at the person who attempted to govern his mode of walking continuously by anatomical knowledge would be in danger of stumbling, so the professional scholar who attempted to determine the aims of his own research extrinsically on the basis of methodological reflections would be in danger of falling into the same difficulties" (Weber 1949: 115).

## Theorizing in the Different Disciplines

Theorizing is done differently in the various disciplines. The economists have their own way of handling theory, and so do people in law, archaeology, medicine, physics, and so on. To this can be added that there often exist different ways of theorizing within one and the same science, and that these ways also have changed over time.

The result of all this is a richness of ways in which to theorize. While some science may be strong in, say, the way that analogies are used, another may have developed an interesting approach to explanation. Very little of this material has been pulled together and discussed from the general perspective of theorizing in social science, but there is good reason to believe that much can be learned from it.

What needs to be created today is a distinct body of practical knowledge about theorizing and also a full-scale tradition of theorizing in social science. I have so far mentioned texts by Peirce and Weber, and there will soon be an opportunity to refer to the work of some other people who have been interested in this project, such as Karl Weick, James G. March, and Everett C. Hughes.

But, to repeat, most of the work on how to theorize in social science, in practical terms and in a creative way, does not yet exist. The material that does exist is also often difficult to locate and available only to those who are familiar with the ins and outs of the social sciences, philosophy, and so on. What is especially lacking are a number of helpful texts and exercises that can be taught in standard courses.

Even if the social sciences all draw on somewhat different traditions of theorizing, reflecting their different tasks, histories, and so on, an openness to the way that theorizing is done in the other sciences is much to be recommended. There is also plenty to be learned from theorizing in philosophy, physics, law, and many other sciences.

I would also add that you can learn from the arts, and the reason for this is that the arts constitute an area in modern society where much interesting experimentation and thinking is going on. What is happening in the arts is of much relevance to the project of theorizing in a number of ways, as I see it. Take, for example, the skill of artists in making novel observations and their eagerness to explore new means of expression. These and related issues are discussed in chapter 9.

## Theorizing as a Different Way of Thinking

In *The Rules of Sociological Method*, Emile Durkheim argues that it is the task of sociology to first establish what he calls "social facts" and then explain these. Social facts, according to Durkheim's definition, consist of different ways of thinking, feeling, and acting. After some time, these three different types of social facts are exteriorized in various ways; they also direct and constrain the way in which the actors behave.

Now the different social sciences all have their own ways of thinking, feeling, and acting, and these have by now hardened into accepted ways of doing things. One can also argue that doing theory the old-fashioned way represents a distinct way of thinking, acting, and feeling.

From a Durkheimian perspective, in other words, old-fashioned theory in social science can be described as a well-established social fact, exteriorized in the way that courses are taught as well as in the huge number of books and articles that have been produced on this topic.

Durkheim also teaches us that it will be hard to change the ways of thinking that comes with this type of theory, and that it exerts a coercive pressure on social scientists, pushing them to think in traditional ways. The new type of theorizing, as advocated in this book, is in contrast unstable, fluent, and not yet established.

The old type of doing theory in the social sciences belongs largely to a philosophical tradition according to which theory (and theorizing) should be formal, logical, and carried out in accordance to the principles of what is now seen as an outmoded epistemology in cognitive science (for example, Dreyfus 2009, chapter 3).

The new type of theorizing, as advocated here, would instead primarily draw on a plurality of forms of thinking, all of which differ from the formal, old-fashioned approach. What I especially have in mind are ways of thinking in the form of analogies, pattern recognition, diagrams, and the like. What goes under the names of *fast thinking* and *intuition* also belong here.

While the social sciences have paid some attention to these alternative and nonformal ways of thinking, the science that has done so in the most innovative and sustained way is cognitive science. I believe that a special place should therefore be assigned to cognitive science, in the attempt to create a new kind of theorizing in social science. What cognitive science has to say about the structure of concepts, the way analogies are used, and much, much more is far ahead of the social sciences, and indispensable to the project of theorizing.

## The Prestudy and Its Stages

How then is one to proceed, in order to learn how to theorize well and produce interesting theory? My suggestion will be presented and explained in detail in the next few chapters. It is important to note that this book is primarily directed at students of social science, at the undergraduate and graduate level. Hopefully it will also be of interest to social scientists more generally since it implies a change in the current view of what the research process should look like. I am essentially arguing for an expanded version of the research process, in which the theoretical element is explicitly included and given its own distinct place.

Students of social science are often taught to begin their research by producing a research design, in which they spell out the problem they want to study and how to go about this (the *research question*). A discussion of methods is part of a good research design. And so is a discussion of existing studies and relevant theory.

But proceeding in this way makes it hard to develop a new and interesting approach to the topic. Often the student hopes that something interesting will emerge as the research proceeds. Unless the student has a native knack for theorizing, however, this is not very likely to happen, and the reason for this is that the research starts with too few ideas.

To remedy this, I suggest that we proceed in the following way. We need to add a stage to the beginning of the process of inquiry, and make it part of the research process. The task of the researcher at this stage would be to come up with new ideas and to do so through an early and preliminary, yet intense, confrontation with data.

To make it easier to single out this early stage that should take place *before* the stage at which the research design is drawn up and executed, I suggest that we use a special name for it. The word I have chosen is the *prestudy*. In everyday English this is a verb that means to prepare. In social science the term gives associations to the pilot study and the exploratory study, but it has a very different task as it will be used in this book—namely to formulate the tentative theory that will be used in the main study.[2]

Introducing a term such as *prestudy* represents an attempt to give a distinct identity to the stage of the research project at which an early and creative form of theorizing can take place. From this perspective, the full research process or the inquiry consists of two stages, not one: the *prestudy* and the *main study*. The former takes place before the research design is drawn up; the latter is mainly the result of the research design and attempts to answer the research question. The prestudy and the main study belong together organically, even if it is useful to separate them for pedagogical reasons. Theorizing takes place in both.

Theorizing should from this perspective be allotted *a distinct and sizable space in the research process*. Theorizing is far too often done intuitively and only by those with a natural talent for it. This is a recipe for slow progress in social science. Similarly, theorizing is often done only while the main research is carried out or after it has been carried out. Also this makes it hard to produce good theory.

At the stage of the prestudy there is enough space for the researcher to experiment and theorize in a creative way, based on a brief but intense confrontation with data. At the stage of the main study the research design is drawn up and executed in an attempt to answer the research question. The theory that was developed during the prestudy can now be tested and developed in a methodical way—something that is not possible at the earlier stage. Whatever empirical value the theory from the prestudy may have will become clear only at this later stage, and after it has been properly tested against facts.

Theorizing, to avoid any misunderstanding, will and shall also take place during the main study. What happens during this stage is however a kind of theorizing that in some ways differs from the kind of theorizing that takes place during the prestudy. For one thing, it draws on a much better set of data. It can also be stretched out over a much longer time, giving more room for an iterative approach.

But to carry out a prestudy also has some consequences for the main study. Theorizing during the main study will be influenced by the theorizing that has taken place during the prestudy. It is also advisable to cancel the main study if the prestudy turns out to be negative, in the sense that no creative ideas have been produced.

It is important to realize that the risk you take, if you want to say something new, is always failure. Or to cite from "Science as a Vocation" by Weber: "the scientific worker has to take into his bargain the risk that enters into all scientific work: *Does an 'idea' occur or does it not?*" (Weber 1946: 136; emphasis added).

It is not advisable to always draw a sharp line between the prestudy and the main study. Once the student is well aware of the existence of these two parts of the research process, the situation changes. It now becomes necessary to develop a skill as a researcher, and to realize that the boundary between the prestudy and the main study is typically fluent for the accomplished researcher.

That the beginner should start out by following certain steps, and stop doing this when a skill has developed, is also true for what goes on in the prestudy. In a prestudy you typically begin with observation, then develop some concepts and perhaps a typology, and end up by formulating a tentative explanation. In this way, you build out the theory, providing it with a body and a structure.

---

The Two Parts of the Research Process or Inquiry in Social Science: The Prestudy and the Main Study

PHASE 1: THE PRESTUDY, OR EARLY THEORIZING

Observe—and focus in on something interesting or surprising to study.
Build out the theory (name the phenomenon; develop concepts, analogies, types, and so on to capture the process, pattern, and such involved).
Complete the tentative theory through an explanation.

PHASE 2: THE MAIN STUDY, OR THE PHASE OF MAJOR RESEARCH AND JUSTIFICATION

Draw up the research design based on the research question.
Execute the research design and theorize again.
Write up the results.

*Comment*: By including the prestudy as an organic part of the research process, a larger space is allotted to theory and theorizing. After having established what one wants to study through observation, one proceeds to give body and structure to the tentative theory in order to capture the process, pattern, and so on of the phenomenon in question. This is done through a process that has many elements to it, such as naming, constructing concepts, and coming up with an explanation. I refer to this process as *building out the theory*. The element of theorizing that goes into the main study is discussed in chapter 10.

---

The next few chapters contain a discussion of the key activities that make up the prestudy. Their purpose is to help the average student in social science to theorize in a creative way. The project of theorizing is not a utopian project that has as its goal to somehow turn every student into a pathbreaking social scientist. Its goal is instead to raise theory to the current level of methods. Just as students today can develop a competence in how to use modern research methods, so they should be able to develop a competence in creative theorizing.

# CHAPTER 2

...............................................................................................

# Social Observation

> Sherlock Holmes: "I have no data yet. It is a
> capital mistake to theorize before one has data.
> Insensibly one begins to twist facts to suit theories,
> instead of theories to suit facts."
>
> —Sir Arthur Conan Doyle, "A Scandal in Bohemia"[1]

In order to theorize well, as Sherlock Holmes explained to Dr. Watson, it is absolutely necessary to have facts. This chapter will elaborate on this point and also discuss what kinds of data are helpful to theorize well in social science. It is not, however, a chapter in methodology.

At the early stage of the research process the emphasis is on getting a good empirical sense of the phenomenon you want to study, in order to theorize it in a preliminary way. What is at issue is *not* to study it in the rigorous way that is necessary once the research design has been constructed and the main study is carried out. But again, without any data at all, it is impossible to theorize well.

Whether the main study will be statistical in nature or consist of a few case studies is of less importance at the stage of the prestudy. Getting a good sense for what you want to study through observation is as indispensable for the one as for the other. But it is also natural for scholars with different orientations to end up with different mixes of qualitative and quantitative data.

It must be emphasized that what matters at this stage is not only to collect data but also to collect *social data*. This means data about social life, about what happens between people who live in groups, communities, and societies. It is not a trivial task to be able to distinguish between data in general and social data. How to prepare for this—how to develop a good eye for what is social—will be discussed in the second part of this book. And so will the need to know some social theory when you theorize.

The way you observe at the early stage of the research differs from the way you do it later. What matters at this point is to get a real sense for the topic so that you can develop some good ideas, which may later be used to construct a theory. This means, among other things, that you have to open yourself up to what is happening, with all your senses as well as with your subconscious.

Durkheim's basic rule for how to observe is as valid for the prestudy as for the main study. This is that the social scientist must begin the research process by acknowledging that he or she does not really know anything about the phenomenon that is to be studied.

The kind of knowledge that you might have picked up here or there about some topic is superficial and of little value, according to Durkheim. It is absolutely crucial for the student of social science, he says, to realize his or her *"complete ignorance"* of what is to be studied (Durkheim 1982: 246; emphasis added). Or to phrase it in other words: *It is always different from what you think!*

The term that Durkheim uses to describe the kind of knowledge we all have before having studied something seriously is *preconceptions* (*prénotions*). It is basically a kind of knowledge that comes from living and operating in society. The rule for the social scientist is *"all preconceptions must be eradicated"* (Durkheim 1964: 31).

Durkheim's ideas about preconceptions are, to repeat, as valid for the prestudy as for the main study. They are also useful in that they make it easier for the social scientist to avoid the choice between empiricism and general theory. They do this by pushing the analysis beyond what exists on the surface, and this forces the social scientist to realize that a new conceptualization is often needed to account for the facts. It is precisely this that makes it easier to avoid falling into the trap of empiricism as well as general theory.

## Back to the Use of Theory in US Sociology

The danger of ending up with either the empiricist kind of social science or with the abstract kind of social science was early recognized in US sociology. This dilemma was, for example, very clearly presented by C. Wright Mills in a book that originally was to be called *Autopsy of Social Science* but that we today know as *The Sociological Imagination* (Mills 1959).

Mills's attempt to solve the dilemma consisted of two moves: letting loose imagination in the sociological enterprise and going back to the classics' view of social science as an attempt to deal with important social issues.

A very different attempt to solve the dilemma was made in the 1960s and 1970s by a small number of sociologists who tried to develop a new approach to theory, known as *theory construction* (for example, Zhao 1996; Willer 1996). Their main idea was to look at theory as if it was a method. Just as you need to be systematic and clear about the ways in which you collect data and process these (methods), you need to explain these in a systematic and clear way (theory).

A theory is not something given or just an idea, it was argued, you *construct* a theory. It has a number of parts that need to be fitted together in a special way. The result of looking at theory in this way implies a rejection of both empiricism and abstract theory. According to the advocates of theory construction, it leads to good, practical social science.

A few important works on theory construction were produced during these years, which are still very useful to study for those who are interested in theorizing. In sociology there is especially *Constructing Social Theories* (1968) by Arthur Stinchcombe. And if we broaden our view and go beyond sociology, there is *An Introduction to Models in the Social Sciences* (1975) by Charles Lave and James G. March.

From the perspective in this book, the idea of theory construction definitely represents a move in the right direction, and there clearly exists an affinity between the approach of creative theorizing and that of theory construction. Both argue that theory is not something that comes to you through intuition, nor is it something that should be restricted to a few star thinkers. It is instead something that needs to be carefully constructed, and you can learn as well as teach the skill to construct a theory.

But there also exist some weaknesses to the perspective of theory construction, and in my view these help to explain why it lasted only for about a decade in sociology and was then seen as a dead end (for example, Hage 1994; Zhao 1996).

One of these weaknesses has to do with theory contruction's preference for logical thought at the expense of most of what makes up ordinary thinking. This means among other things that the link to the subconscious was not understood and that the capacity to innovate could not be properly cultivated. One reason for this is probably that the theory construction movement developed its approach without any input from cognitive psychology.

As a result of this and some other reasons as well, which will soon be mentioned, there is something mechanical about the approach of theory construction. You essentially teach students to build a theory by fitting together prefabricated pieces, a bit like you put together something from IKEA. You need a certain skill to do this, but one that is quite different from the kind of theorizing that is advocated in this book.

One of these other weaknesses of the approach of theory construction has to do with the way it ignored the element of observation in theorizing and focused most of its attention on the stage of verification. From the perspective in this book, a lack of fresh empirical material makes it hard to go beyond the preconceptions that Durkheim speaks about.

When the process of research begins for the theory constructor, the first and the most important task is to produce interesting hypotheses of the type that can later be verified. Knowledge about the phenomenon you want to study is supposed to already exist. The key to successful research stands and falls with the number of interesting hypotheses that can be invented, and how well these are handled.

According to Stinchcombe in *Constructing Social Theories*, "a student who has difficulty thinking of at least three sensible explanations for any correlation that he is really interested in should probably choose another profession" (Stinchcombe 1968: 13).

In a similar vein Lave and March encourage the readers of their book to come up with as many hypotheses as they can for the phenomenon they are interested in, and to figure out how to discriminate between these through careful testing. But Lave and March do not tell the reader that it is necessary to observe something very carefully before you try to theorize it, and that you need to know quite a bit about a phenomenon in order to develop a theory about it. The reader is left with the impression that what fundamentally matters is to develop an agility in thinking and coming up with an explanation, rather than basing this on penetrating knowledge of what you are studying.

Both Stinchcombe and Lave and March ignore, to repeat, the element of early and deep observation in theorizing, and this means that they do not challenge what Durkheim calls *preconceptions*. Robert K. Merton, in contrast, was well aware that observation had been pushed aside when verification became a major issue a few decades into the twentieth century in social science. When you "exaggerate the creative side of explicit theory," as he wrote in an article from 1948, you end up by underestimating the "creative role of observation" (Merton 1948: 506).

Merton argued that on the surface of things, it would appear that the emphasis on testing hypothesis was indeed the correct way to proceed:

> With a few conspicuous exceptions, recent sociological discussions have assigned but one major function to empirical research: "testing" or "verification" of hypotheses. The model for the proper way of performing this function is as familiar as it is clear. The investigator begins with a hunch or hypothesis, from which he draws various inferences and these, in turn, are subjected to empirical test which confirms or refutes the hypothesis. (Merton 1945: 505–6)

But there exist many problems with proceeding according to this "logical model," Merton also noted, and these make it difficult to produce really good research:

> But this is a logical model and so fails, of course, to describe much of what actually occurs in fruitful investigation. It presents a set of logical norms, not a description of the research experience. And, as logicians are well aware, in purifying the experience, the logical model may also distort it. Like other models, it abstracts from the temporal sequence

of events. It exaggerates the creative role of explicit theory just as it minimizes the creative role of observation. . . . *It is my central thesis that empirical research goes far beyond the passive role of verifying and testing theory: it does more than confirm or refute hypotheses.* Research plays an active role: it performs at least four major functions which help shape the development of theory. It *initiates*, it *reformulates*, it *deflects* and it *clarifies* theory. (Merton 1948: 506; emphasis added)

Merton's diagnosis was right on target when he said that the element of verification—the testing of hypotheses against data—had become the central issue for many social scientists after World War II. But instead of drawing the consequences of his insight that social science research must start with observation, Merton wavered and cast his argument in terms of the contrast between how research is supposed to be carried out and how it is actually carried out. This made it hard for him to formulate a successful approach to theorizing.

The point that Merton did not make is that observation constitutes *the first stage of theorizing*; it is also an organic part of theorizing. The main purpose of observation at this early stage, he should also have added, is primarily *heuristic*—that is, its purpose is to help the social scientist to better understand what some phenomenon is really like.

It is important to emphasize that the notion of observation must be understood in a very wide sense at this stage of the research. There exist many different ways of making observations, not only in the social sciences but in society at large. To the extent that any of these can further the exploration and understanding of some phenomenon they should be used.

The main point of observation at this stage of the research is to get as much and as multifaceted information as possible about some phenomenon so that you can get a new angle on it. At the later stage, when your ideas are to be tested in a systematic and methodical fashion, it is enough to work with the more narrow range of what can be called "'hypothesis-testing' facts" (Stinchcombe 1978: 5).

But at the beginning of the research the information should come from a very broad range of sources. It can come from interviews, archives, newspapers, bar codes, autobiographies, data sets, dreams, movies, poems, music—pretty much from any source that has something to say about the phenomenon you are interested in.

Again, it is not at all necessary that this information should be gathered in a reliable manner—meaning by this, with the help of the best available methods. This goes for quantitative as well as qualitative methods.

If rule number one for this stage of observation is that things are not what they seem to be, rule number two is that you can use any data or information that will help you to go beyond the existing preconceptions. *Anything goes!*

To acquire information at this early stage represents a distinct and relatively independent stage in the theorizing process. To get the data you need will take its time, and it is important not to be impatient. It is also helpful to *not* start analyzing the material until you have learned quite a bit about the phenomenon you are interested in.

In the beginning of the research process, there exists a distinct temptation to either draw on the ideas you already have or to begin to analyze whatever you are studying very soon after starting to observe things. Both of these lead to mistakes. Wittgenstein's dictum for how to philosophize is also useful for this stage in social science: *"Don't think but look!"* (Wittgenstein 1953: 66e; emphasis added).

## Choosing a Topic to Observe

The first task when you want to do research is to pick a topic. The social science literature provides several suggestions for how to do this. You can, for example, choose something interesting, something that constitutes a problem, and so on. Since you can do good work and formulate a good research question only if the topic is well chosen, the issue of what to focus on is very important.

According to some scholars, you should choose a topic that is *interesting* and appeals to your curiosity. This makes intuitive sense, as does the idea that the kind of research we appreciate is research that we find interesting.

In an article by Murray Davis titled "That's Interesting!" it is argued that what makes us think that some studies are great is that they strike us as interesting (Davis 1971). The author also presents a theory why some ideas are seen as interesting and others not.

Something is seen as interesting, Davis suggests, because it breaks with what we expect to find. "All *interesting* theories, at least all *interesting* social theories, then constitute an attack on the taken-for-granted world of their audience. . . . If it does not challenge but merely confirms one of their taken-for-granted beliefs, [the audience] will respond to it by rejecting its value while affirming its truth" (Davis 1971: 311).

Some theories other than that of Davis try to explain why something strikes us as interesting. According to one of these, something is seen as interesting because it appeals to our sense of curiosity. Curiosity, in its turn, is often seen as a drive, like hunger or thirst. While we use food and drink to satisfy these two drives, we satisfy our curiosity by seeking knowledge (for example, Loewenstein 1994; Kang et al. 2009).

A second theory about what topic to pick holds that the scientist should choose to work on a *problem*. This view of things is quite common and has, for example, been advocated by Thomas Kuhn and Herbert Simon.

Calling something a problem (or a puzzle) means that while it resists an immediate solution, a solution is nonetheless seen as possible. The quality that a problem can perhaps be solved is important. According to Chomsky,

> we might distinguish "problems" from "mysteries," the former being questions that we seem to be able to formulate in ways that allow us to proceed with serious inquiry and possibly to attain a degree of understanding, the latter including questions that seem to elude our grasp, perhaps because we are as ill-equipped to deal with them as a rat is with a prime number maze. (Chomsky 1991: 41)

What constitutes a problem for a scientist is defined through normal science, according to Thomas Kuhn (1970). If you follow the existing paradigm, certain topics will be seen as problems to be solved. These will be searched out by scientists and pursued by them with passion. Herbert Simon similarly conceives of "the scientist as problem solver," to cite the title of one of his writings (Simon 1991b). Those who advocate that scientists should choose to study problems sometimes add that before a problem can be solved, it has to be formulated in a special way. "It is a familiar and significant saying that a problem well put is half-solved" (Dewey 1938: 108).

To this can be added that before you start working with a problem, you have to find one. It is sometimes noted that problem-finding not only precedes the stage of problem-solving, it is also considerably harder. "The experience of scientists," according to Merton, "is summed up in the adage that it is often more difficult to find and to formulate a problem than to solve it" (Merton 1959: ix).

Last is a third view of how scientists should select a topic to study. According to Charles S. Peirce, for example, the scientist starts out by observing things but is at some point *surprised* by something that he or she finds. The reason for the surprise is that it contradicts what the scientist expects to find, given the state of knowledge in his or her discipline (see also, for example, Dunbar and Klahr 2012: 706–7; Lombrozo 2012: 266).

In my view there are good arguments for following each of these three models for how to decide what to study and theorize: something interesting, a problem, and something that surprised you. There is also some overlap between them. Both what is interesting and what is surprising are, for example, the result of finding something else than what was expected. And when you are surprised by something, you have a problem to solve.

Since the view that you should study something that has surprised or startled you is the least known of the three approaches, I shall elaborate a bit on it. If you, for example, start out from Peirce's view, and try to translate it into practical tips or rules for how to proceed, you will get something like the following.

You begin the research by observing some topic you are interested in. While the search for facts at this stage is quite general, it should nonetheless be intense since the aim is to go beyond the current state of knowledge. At some point later in your research you will find something surprising, something that does not fit the current state of knowledge. It is *this* that should be studied.

The process of observation, from Peirce's perspective, consists of two stages: the first is broad but penetrating; the second is focused on the surprise and more intensive. It is important, in other words, not to pick your final topic until you have been surprised. If you follow this rule, you will study something that might lead to new knowledge.

But proceeding in this way also means that you typically have to discard quite a bit of the work you have done before the surprise. This can be quite difficult to do, but it is necessary so you will be free to exclusively focus on what caused the surprise. "It feels like cutting your feet and legs off," a colleague told me. But it is something that has to be done, because it is the second topic that will yield the most.

Finding a good topic is important, but it is not enough. You also need facts to study it—and this presents another problem. In the words of Robert K. Merton, what you now need to do is to locate some strategic research material (SRM). "By SRM is meant the empirical material that exhibits the phenomena to be explained or interpreted to such an advantage and in such accessible form that it enables the fruitful investigation of previously stubborn problems and the discovery of new problems for further inquiry" (Merton 1987: 10–11).

The two-stage process of observation that Peirce advocates is similar to Durkheim's argument about preconceptions. In both cases you start out with one view of things and have to wait to do the analysis until you feel that you have reached a deeper level (Durkheim) or found a new topic (Peirce).

To sum up, research can be triggered by a problem, by something interesting, and by something surprising. Regardless of what sets off the research, however, it is important to emphasize three things. First, the initial phase of observation should be carried out in a very free-ranging manner. Second, theorizing should be held off for a while. And third, the topic to study is not necessarily what you initially set out to analyze, but what after a while strikes you as being the most promising to pursue.

## Description and Observation

While *description* and *observation* by no means are synonymous, description occupies an important place in observation and therefore also in theorizing. Description is very helpful at this stage, since it allows you to gather facts without immediately linking these to a theory.

In many of the social sciences description is seen as inferior to analytic thinking and in general as unscientific and undesirable (for example, Abbott 2001: 121–22). Economists in particular have a low opinion of description, a topic that Amartya Sen addresses in "Description as Choice" (Sen 1980). In Sen's view description is an important as well as a difficult activity. The main reason for this is that it involves the choice of which details to focus on and which to leave out.

The typical attitude of economists toward description, Sen says, tends to lead to "confounding the nature of description as an activity and unnecessarily weakening the theoretical underpinning of many legitimate and useful activities in the social sciences" (Sen 1980: 368).

Among philosophers, it is perhaps Wittgenstein who has been the most interested in description (for example, Gert 1997). What you first have to understand, he says, is that there exist many different ways of making a description. Descriptions are "instruments for particular uses," and there is a difference between, say, describing your room and describing your mental state (Wittgenstein 1953: 290–91).

The kind of descriptions that Wittgenstein himself was most interested in were descriptions of words and how people use these, in which situations and with what intent and effect. By being extra sensitive to these issues, he believed, a number of difficult conceptual problems in philosophy could be solved.

While the interest of the social scientist differs from that of Wittgenstein, one can nonetheless follow his lead and make a special effort to observe very closely the way in which people use language and what they try to accomplish by doing so. Proceeding in this way allows you to tap into some of the most intriguing and complex aspects of social life.

Describing the ways in which words are used is essential for an understanding of the role of meaning in social life. It also draws your attention away from what is purely visual. In the terminology of modern anthropology, it leads to *thick description* as opposed to *thin description* (Geertz 2000).

The neo-Kantians argued that reality consists of an endless amount of details, and that you have to make a conscious choice if you want to be able to say anything at all. This was also the position of Max Weber, who in his methodological writings points out that it is "impossible in principle" to describe everything that happens (for example, Weber 1975: 173).

This position is by now well recognized. In order to move theorizing forward, however, a somewhat different message seems more important. This is that the more details you have, the better position you are in, especially when you try to theorize in a creative way. It is in the details that you will find the germs to the new theory.

It is also important to realize that the urge to push the details to the side and begin to generalize represents a temptation that should be resisted at the stage of observation. Detailed material is very useful when you try to theorize, and the reason for this, to repeat, is that it is typically untheorized. Of special interest among the details are so-called telling details. A *telling detail* is one that makes it easier to understand a phenomenon (for example, Pinch and Swedberg 2012).

## Fieldwork and Observation

Like description, fieldwork has a number of qualities that makes it useful for observation during the prestudy. Everett C. Hughes, who helped to introduce the idea of fieldwork into modern sociology, was well aware of its advantages in this respect. He spelled these out in what can be seen as his manifesto for how to do social research, "The Place of Field Work in Social Science" (Hughes 1984a).

According to this article, there is especially one quality to fieldwork that makes it important in this respect and that also makes it very useful for heuristic purposes. This is that it allows you to *see for yourself* (Hughes 1984a: 497).

The idea that the researcher should be in a position to check things out for himself or herself seems obvious enough, and something that any social scientist would want to do. If one looks at the history of the social sciences, however, it has taken a long time for the idea of fieldwork to be established. Anthropologists were the first social scientists to conduct fieldwork, and economists are currently in the process of discovering it.

In sociology, people like Weber, Simmel, and Durkheim never did any fieldwork, nor did they conduct any interviews themselves. The modern notion of an *interview*—a procedure during which both questions and answers are carefully recorded—did not have its breakthrough in sociology until after World War I (Platt 2002).

Fieldwork was introduced into sociology at about the same time and very much thanks to US sociologists, first by W.E.B. Du Bois and a bit later on a collective scale (that enabled the breakthrough) by the members of the Chicago School. According to Robert Park, its leader and also the teacher of Everett C. Hughes, it is crucial for social scientists to engage in firsthand observation.

What is meant by firsthand observation is clear from the following famous quote, summarizing Park's message:

Go and sit in the lounges of the luxury hotels and on the door-steps of flop-houses, sit on the Gold Coast settees and on the slum shakedowns; sit in the Orchestra Hall and in the Star and Garter Burlesk. In short, gentlemen, go get the seat of your pants dirty in real research. (Park in Bulmer 1984: 97)

Hughes points out that not only sociologists make observations but also reporters, and sociologists can learn much from them (Hughes 1984a). He does not mention comedians and authors of novels and poetry, but they also make very sharp observations. To paraphrase Wittgenstein, there exist many ways to make observations, and these need to be observed.

When you make an observation, Hughes says, it is important to "distance yourself," which roughly means that you need to position yourself vis-à-vis people in such a way that it becomes possible to make objective observations, as opposed to participating in their lives and looking at things from their perspective.

As part of this process the observer will also begin to transform the information he or she has picked up into objective knowledge about groups and institutions. This is when observation truly becomes what Hughes refers to as "social observation" (for example, Hughes 1984b: 317, 499; cf. Mills 1959: 70).

In his discussion of fieldwork Hughes also uses the expression "observation 'on the hoof' "—meaning the kind of observation that only the skilled social scientist can engage in. When you make observations on the hoof, Hughes says, you view things in terms of social patterns or institutions (Hughes 1984a: 504–5).

According to the dictionary, the expression *on the hoof* also has a second meaning, which is suggestive in this context and no doubt appealed to Hughes. It means doing something while you are also doing something else.

Observation often entails this double kind of behavior: the observer seems to be doing one thing, while he or she is actually busy observing. Double behavior also has the capacity to unlock your creativity; it is sometimes only possible to come up with a new idea, when your brain is busy with some other task.

In a similar spirit Howard Becker (who had Hughes as a teacher) mentions how he learned to make observations as a young boy in Chicago. He did this primarily by riding the subway for hours and hours, just looking at what was going on. Later he did the same thing, when he worked as a jazz musician (Becker no date).

While facts of all kinds may be of heuristic importance at the stage of observation, primary data of the type generated through fieldwork are special in this regard. One reason for this is that you know exactly how they have been produced; another, that they are untheorized, in the sense that they have not been filtered through the mind of some other social scientist. This makes it not only easier to theorize the data, it also makes it more likely that you will find something new.

## Statistics and Observation

At first it might seem that statistics would be useful only during the main study, because of the careful and methodical way in which a statistical study should be conducted. This, however, is not the case, and statistics can be part of what the theorizer draws on during the prestudy. This is true not only for descriptive statistics but also for more advanced versions.

During the early stage of the research, statistics can be used both for tentative explanations and for observation. Statistics are routinely used in social science for explanatory purposes, but as John Goldthorpe argues, they may also have a valuable function to play at the stage of observation. "It is important," he says, "that the use of rather advanced statistical techniques for ... purposes of what might be called sophisticated description should be clearly distinguished from their use in attempts at deriving causal relations directly from data analysis" (Goldthorpe 2001: 11).

What Goldthorpe advocates is not so very different, as it turns out, from Hughes. In "The Place of Field Work in Social Science," Hughes says that there exist two ways of bringing out the social dimension through observation. One is having a skilled observer on the scene. The other is when the social scientist takes a small fact and looks at it through the lens of a large number of facts (Hughes 1984a: 504).

It is also clear that at the stage of discovery you do not have to use statistics in the professional and methodical way in which it should be used in the main study. You can for example, make quick trial runs, use nonrepresentative samples, and in other ways just try to get a good sense for what is going on. The purpose at this stage is to generate ideas; and shortcuts can be taken.

To exclusively base your observation on quantitative data that others have generated should in principle be avoided, unless this is more or less impossible (for example, Heltberg 2011). The main reason for this is that statistics, like all computer-based observations, represents a kind of disembodied facts that are often hard to read (for example, Dreyfus 2009).

None of the senses of the researcher are very much involved when you work with other people's quantitative data, except for sight. The whole experience is as a consequence very cognitive and often leaves little room for the subconscious to pick up things. This can make for a narrow type of analysis, and it increases the chances of overlooking something essential. In this sense computer research is not so different from library research, which was the norm in sociology before fieldwork was developed.

One advantage in making your own observations is that you pick up a lot of things that are not particularly useful but that allow what *is* useful to become visible. Some of this information comes close to what Michael Polanyi calls "tacit knowledge"—

that is, knowledge that is necessary to execute some activity, but where the actors are unable to articulate what they are doing.

This brings us to the subconscious, which cognitive scientists have by now explored for many decades. They have among other things mapped out the extremely complex ways in which human beings record sounds and visual stimuli. The study of memory represents another area where interesting progress has been made, and which is of much relevance to theorizing in social science.

Exactly how social elements interact with the physiological processes that are involved in seeing, hearing, and remembering is not clear. Still, it would appear that knowledge of these processes is relevant for an understanding of the complexities of observation. The old idea in sociology that the social and the biological should be firmly kept apart is not useful any longer.

For this reason it is important that those who are interested in theorizing keep up with what is going on in cognitive science. It would be especially helpful for theorizers if a way was found to translate the insights of cognitive science into practical rules for how to become better at observation. It should be stated once more that what is of most interest to theorizers are practical tips and rules for how to proceed when you theorize.

What about introspection? Has the time also come to reevaluate the value of this way of proceeding? Introspection has by now been banned from the social sciences for a long time, and the main reason for this is that it made researchers rely on their own opinions rather than on facts.

That this is unacceptable is still a sound rule of course. But when it comes to theorizing the question is somewhat different, and what needs to be discussed is whether introspection can be useful for heuristic purposes. In my own view using introspection should be an option for the theorizer. Or to be more precise, and also supply the reason for this stance: *to carefully observe yourself,* and to do so for heuristic purposes, represents one way to get some ideas about the phenomenon you are interested in.

Take, for example, Peirce's description of himself when he looked at an impressionist painting of the sea. "As I gaze upon it I detect myself sniffing the salt-air and holding up my cheek to the sea breeze" (Peirce 1992b: 182). You can of course ask whether Peirce was correct when he said that this was the way he reacted to a painting of the sea. And for a quick and tentative answer—why not observe your own reactions?

Introspection in the form of self-observation can also be of help in establishing what meanings and moods actors invest their behavior with. One problem with meanings and moods is that it is very difficult to get into the head of the people you observe. Meanings and moods also tend to change and disappear. And again, one way to bypass this problem is to observe yourself (for the centrality of meaning, see, for example, Weber 1978; for the centrality of mood, see, for example, Damasio 2003).

But a better way to proceed, of course, is to somehow get into the mind of the people you observe. According to Weber, it is through the process of understanding that we are able to somehow enter into the mind of other people, and this understanding is typically either rational or "emotionally empathetic" (Weber 1978: 5). When someone behaves in a rational way it is relatively easy for the analyst to understand what is going on in the actor's head (Weber 1978: 4–7). A person is perhaps trying to solve a simple problem in arithmetic, and we immediately understand the way of reasoning that this involves.

When it comes to empathy the situation is more complex. Still "the more we ourselves are susceptible to such emotional re-actions as anxiety, anger, ambition, jealousy, love, enthusiasm, pride, vengefulness, loyalty, devotion, and appetites of all sorts, and to the 'irrational' conduct that grows out of them, the more readily can we empathize with them" (Weber 1978: 6). Note that Weber is here reminding us that understanding is directly linked to self-observation.

The role of memory was mentioned earlier apropos the advances of cognitive science, and something also needs to be said about its importance for observation at the stage of the prestudy. Memory is crucial for ongoing activities, in that you cannot act at all unless you have calibrated what you are about to do with the help of memory and experience. This means that exploring memory has to be part of observation. What do people remember; what do they forget? What do people want to remember; what do they want to forget (for example, Wickelgren 2012)?

Just as observation means paying attention to memory, it also means paying attention to history. According to Tocqueville, who did quite a bit of observation on the hoof when he traveled around in the United States, we are all linked to the past through invisible threads (Tocqueville 2009). History connects what individuals do now to what they did in the past.

The category of history goes well beyond memory, even if it also includes it. The problem for the theorizer, at the stage of observation, is to somehow see how paying attention to the past will make it easier to discover what is happening just now. This is also a reason why it is helpful to know something about the way that historians theorize (for example, Bloch 1964; Iggers et al. 2008).

## The Role of Earlier Social Science Studies and Theory

Some readers may by now have become impatient and ask, what about the role of earlier studies by social scientists on the topic you are observing? And what about your training and years of experience? Are these not important, and do they not sharpen as well as guide our sense of observation, especially social observation?

The answer to both questions is a clear "yes," but I have wanted to first of all emphasize the importance of trying to see things in a new light. And to do this, it is helpful to proceed in unorthodox ways and to be as open as possible to new observations.

To get a good sense for a new topic you clearly need to be familiar with earlier studies. There are many and obvious reasons why this is the case. They may contain data that are relevant for understanding your topic. They may contain useful concepts and theories. It is also with their help that you are able to decide what is known about a topic and what is not.

A caveat, however, is in place. This is that is that it is easy to become overly influenced by the existing research on some topic. And this can inhibit your creativity. For these reasons, it is helpful to try to find a way of both keeping the existing literature at a distance *and* having access to it.

Since this may sound vague and contradictory, let me give an example of a successful way of doing this. It was devised by Tocqueville, who was extremely inventive when it comes to gathering data and analyzing them (for example, Swedberg 2009).

When Tocqueville traveled around in the United States in 1831–32, he gathered as much primary material as he could, but he also avoided reading studies of the United States by his contemporaries. The reason for this, he said, was that he did not want them to influence his view of the country before he had developed his own analysis.

Still Tocqueville also wanted to know what these other studies contained already at this stage. His solution was to ask his traveling companion, Gustave de Beaumont, to read them and tell him if they contained something he ought to know.

When we do our research most of us do not have such a helpful and competent traveling companion as Tocqueville did. But there may be other ways of dealing with the existence of earlier studies so that they do not block our creativity. It goes without saying that these studies have to be worked through and referred to in the final study. The question is *when* to carefully work them through.

Studies on the topic you are interested in, but that have been written by scholars outside your own discipline, can be reviewed without much harm at an early stage. The reason for this is that they usually operate with different concepts and approach things in a different way. And this can have an invigorating effect on your imagination.

So much for studies by other social scientists. But what about the role of your training as a social scientist and general knowledge of social science for making observations? The answer is that both of these are indispensable for good work. They also confirm the well-known dictum that only scientists who are well prepared are in a position to make a discovery.

The more you have developed what Hughes calls a "sociological eye," the more you will be able to single out what is social about a phenomenon (Hughes 1984b). And the kind of methods you are used to working with will also influence the way in which a phenomenon is looked at and understood.

The need to be well trained in theory, in order to be good at theorizing, will be dealt with later in this book. And so will the topic of the close relationship between theory and method in the research process. Before addressing these two issues, however, it is important to address a different topic—that is, to discuss the process of theorizing in a more narrow sense, something that will be done in the next few chapters.

........................................................................................................

## CHAPTER 3

# Naming, Concept, and Typology

> The true method of speculation is like the flight of an
> airplane. It starts from the ground of particular observation;
> it makes a flight in the thin air of imagined generalization;
> and it again lands for renewed observation, rendered acute
> by rational interpretation.
>
> —Alfred North Whitehead, *The Function of Reason*[1]

Once the stage of social observation is over, it is time to start working with the empirical material and, in the narrow sense of the term, to theorize it. In the terminology of this book, the theory will now be built out and provided with a structure and a body.

According to Peirce, what should now take place is "that process in which the mind goes over all the facts of the case, absorbs them, digests them, sleeps over them, assimilates them, dreams of them" (Peirce 1906: 4–5). And this should continue, Peirce also says, until one has come to the very end of the theorizing process, which means coming up with an explanation.

Peirce's emphasis on absorbing the material and working it into your mind is no doubt essential, so that you will know the material in a truly intimate way. But as opposed to what Peirce argues, there is quite a bit more to do in terms of working with the material before you can proceed to the stage of the explanation.

What now needs to be done are the following tasks, which help to build out the theory: to come up with a name for the phenomenon you are studying; to develop some concepts that will help to analyze it; and perhaps also to develop a typology. In the next chapter some further ways to build out the theory, before you can proceed to the explanation, will be presented. They include the use of analogies, metaphors, and patterns.

These different ways of proceeding when you theorize are sometimes lumped together under the heading of *induction*, which is usually defined as the act of generalizing based on particular instances. This terminology, however, is confusing and not very helpful if you want to learn how to theorize. It is also clear that what most scientists do when they say that they simply use induction is much more complex than just generalize based on individual facts and observations.

It should also be pointed out that each of the different ways of working with the empirical material that comes after the stage of observation and makes up most of the prestudy plays, as it were, two roles. The first is to move the theorizing process forward in the direction of a tentative theory, centered around the explanation. This is very important.

The second role is less obvious but just as important to the task of successful theorizing. This is to move the theorizing process forward through discovery. This can be described as the *heuristic function* of the different moves that are part of the process of theorizing.

The second role is so important that it is worth formulating it as a rule: *All of the elements that are part of theorizing should also be used for heuristic purposes.* You should not only name to name, construct a concept to have a concept, and so on. Trying to find a good name can also make you discover aspects of a social phenomenon that so far have remained hidden—and so can the attempt to construct a concept, and so on.

Note that as the theory develops, you may want to go back to the stage of observation. The reason for this is not only to confirm what you suspect but also because you may now be looking for something different or for some additional information. The process of theorizing is in principle as iterative at the stage of the prestudy as in the main study.

At a general level, you might say that the stage that comes after the stage of social observation should be dominated by speculation. To use a term such as *speculation* may seem odd and old-fashioned, and it is true that speculation is rarely used in today's social science.

But speculation does have a place in science, including social science, and the reason for this is that without it little new can be created. Speculation stands for the kind of thinking through which something that has not yet been discovered can be discovered. It points to what lies beyond what so far has been understood. In brief it is indispensable if you want to say something new.

In his definition of speculation Ian Hacking emphasizes the element of play that goes into it. "By speculation," he says, "I shall mean the intellectual representation of something of interest, a playing with and restructuring of ideas to give at least a qualitative understanding of some general features of the world" (Hacking 1983: 212–13).

But speculation is multifaceted and has many other aspects besides playfulness (for example, Parisi 2012). One other element that is often mentioned is guessing (for example, Peirce 1929). Other aspects include a lack of practicality, and that the theorizer-speculator lets go of reality and allows his or her thoughts to roam freely.

There also exists a literature in cognitive science that is relevant for an understanding of speculation, which will be discussed in the next chapter. It deals with the ways in which people use analogies, metaphors, patterns, and the like when they think. By now it has been well established in cognitive psychology that human beings do not think in the formal way that has been advocated by Western philosophers, from Plato and Aristotle to modern analytic philosophy. Speculation, as it turns out, is not so far from the common way of thinking, just as theorizing itself is not so far from everyday thought.

By going through the procedure of building the theory out a number of times, a skill in theorizing is developed. Before looking in more detail at the different steps that need to be taken, however, it should be repeated that the theorizer not only has to develop a skill in how to theorize (which is the subject of part 1 in this book) but also has to do so from a social science perspective (which is discussed in part 2).

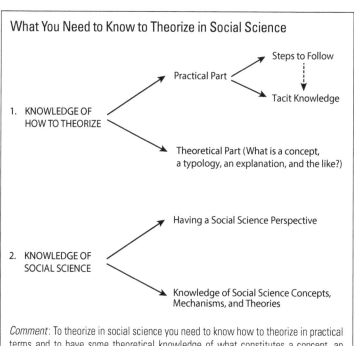

What You Need to Know to Theorize in Social Science

1. KNOWLEDGE OF HOW TO THEORIZE
   - Practical Part
     - Steps to Follow
     - Tacit Knowledge
   - Theoretical Part (What is a concept, a typology, an explanation, and the like?)

2. KNOWLEDGE OF SOCIAL SCIENCE
   - Having a Social Science Perspective
   - Knowledge of Social Science Concepts, Mechanisms, and Theories

*Comment*: To theorize in social science you need to know how to theorize in practical terms and to have some theoretical knowledge of what constitutes a concept, an explanation, and the like. Since what is at issue is theorizing in social science, you also need to have acquired a social science perspective and have some knowledge of social science concepts, mechanisms, and theories.

## Naming

Once the observation of some phenomenon has proceeded to the point where the preconceived notion has begun to fall apart, naming becomes an issue. *Dysnomia* refers to things that are called by their wrong name, and this is precisely what characterizes the situation at this particular stage. There is a new reality, but an old name.

If you continue to use the old name, there is a risk that the new phenomenon will slip through your hands. To give something a new name essentially means to give it a new identity. It also makes it easier to see a phenomenon. Hence the importance of *naming* in social science.

Note that what in everyday language is referred to with one word often turns out to be very complex and better conceptualized as several phenomena. This means that several names may be needed to capture what is going on.

There exist different approaches to naming in social science. You can, for example, use existing words or invent new ones. Max Weber took the position that it is usually best to use existing words. "If we are not to coin completely new words each time or invent symbols, like chemists or like the philosopher Avenerius, we must give every phenomenon to which no term has yet been accorded the nearest and most descriptive words from traditional language and just be careful to *define* them unambiguously" (Weber 2001: 63).

As an example of this Weber mentions what he calls "innerworldly asceticism" in his work. He also notes that most scientists dislike new terms, unless they are of their own making.

You can invent new words by, say, using Latin or Greek, or just by giving a twist to some word in your own language that already exists. Examples of this are terms such as *akrasia, colligation,* and *quantomania.* A variant of this approach is to find some obscure or forgotten term and introduce it as a social science term. This is quite common, as indicated by terms such as *anomie, charisma,* and *habitus.*

You can also just take an existing word and invest it with a new meaning or take two words that everyone uses and tie them together. This is the origin of such well-known social concepts as *stereotype, role,* and *social distance.*

Peirce was a stern advocate of the strategy of using new words when you create a concept. Philosophers should in his view not use everyday terms, and the reason for this is that philosophical terms must be "distinct and different from common speech" (Peirce 1998b: 265). As examples from Peirce's own work, one can mention such terms as *retroduction, interpretant,* and *phaneroscopy.*

In general Peirce was fearful of the popularization of philosophical terms, something that in his mind would inevitably lead to a distortion of their meaning. One way to counter this, which he himself sometimes engaged in, was to create terms that are "so unattractive that loose thinkers are not tempted to use them" (Ketner 1981: 343).

This is the origin, for example, of Peirce's term *pragmaticism.* He did not very much like what William James and others had done to pragmatism, and this was one way of drawing a line between his own view and that of others. Was it a successful strategy? Not very much, it seems, since Peirce is known today as one of the founders of pragmatism.

Peirce also believed that by choosing a new name, you would be in a better position to control its meaning than if you just chose an existing term. To some extent this is probably the case, even if it also seems that all social science terms tend to lose some of their freshness and original meaning after a while.

It is also true that it is a mistake to introduce too many new terms in an article or a book. The reader will soon lose patience if too many new terms are introduced. What matters, I would argue, is to draw attention to what is new in your work, not to create a whole new terminology.

By using common language for the term, it also becomes easier to communicate with the general public. It introduces "the possibility that the people we study will also be our readers," to cite one of the rare articles devoted to question of naming in sociology (Hughes and Hughes 1952: 132).

To what has just been said, it should be added that you can run through a number of potential new names in your mind, not just in an effort to find the right one, but also to discover something new about the phenomenon you are interested in. This is the heuristic function that was mentioned earlier, here applied to naming. Each name has a series of meanings and associations; and these can be interesting to explore.

## Concept

The skillful use of existing concepts as well as the creation of new ones are both essential parts of theorizing. They are also activities that people engage in all the time, more or less automatically. In this they are just as much part of human existence as thinking in general. And again it is important to learn how to use and further develop this common capacity in a conscious way for purposes of social science theorizing.

The use and creation of concepts is important at many points in the process of theorizing—for example, when a typology is constructed or an explanation is put together. But it also holds a crucial place in the process when you try to nail down the phenomenon you are interested in, and this is what will be discussed now.

Once the stage of observation is over and the phenomenon has been named, the name often needs to be turned into a concept. Some additional concepts may also be needed to get a firm grip on the phenomenon.

Turning some phenomenon into a concept means, for one thing, to make it more rational. Instead of using a word more or less automatically, an attempt is now made to scrutinize it and try to decide what is essential to it. Peirce, for example, describes a concept as "the rational purport of a word or a conception" (Peirce 1998a: 332).

Introducing a rational element into the analysis of a phenomenon can take many forms, such as making it more abstract and removing accidental elements from it. This can be done successively, and each step can provide a different angle on the subject.

Creating a definition is another way to proceed in constructing a concept, and the notion of *concept* is closely related to that of *definition*. At some point in dealing with an existing concept or creating a new one, it is usually important to define the concept.

This does not mean that all concepts necessarily have to be defined, and inflexibility on this point may lead us astray. "A word like 'cause' cannot be defined, but is still indispensable to most scientists," according to Raymond Boudon (1995: 561). "Thus, many words cannot be defined and are still normally used in scientific language."

There exist different types of definitions, and at an early stage of theorizing a working definition may be the most helpful. It is often recommended that the theorizer creates his or her own definition by stating what he or she means by the term (a *stipulative definition*), rather than trying to establish the existing use of some term (something that may be helpful for other purposes). It can also be argued that a definition should be *deictic*—that is, the circumstances and conditions under which it is valid should be specified.

Just to state what is to be defined (*definiendum*) and how to define it (*definiens*) can lead to new ideas. Definitions are also useful, for reasons of clarity and precision (for an introduction to the topic of definitions, see, for example, Robinson 1950). As helpful in this regard one can mention the definitions that accompany Weber's presentation of the basic concepts of sociology in chapter 1 in *Economy and Society* (Weber 1978).

It is important to realize that there are several steps to the process of creating a concept. To begin this process by creating a definition is usually not the best way to proceed, and there are many reasons for this. For one thing, the notion that you are pretty much finished with a concept, once you have produced a definition, is wrong (for example, Goertz 2006: 3–5).

The idea that you can somehow produce a definitive definition is also erroneous. When a word is defined, as Wittgenstein has pointed out, the problem is basically shifted to other words. "What should we gain by a definition, as it can only lead us to other undefined terms?" (Wittgenstein 1958: 26).

Most importantly, a rush to creating a definition may be a rush to judgment. The reason for this is that a concept, like an explanation, can rarely be formulated at the beginning of the research process. It is often not possible to create a concept until the research is well under way.

An example may be helpful. In *The Protestant Ethic and the Spirit of Capitalism* Weber begins with a description of the spirit of capitalism, not with the concept. This is a deliberate move on his part, and he tells the reader that you cannot begin an investigation with "a conceptual definition" (Weber 1930: 48).

According to Weber, you should start with "a provisional description," and "such a description is . . . indispensable in order to clearly understand the object of the investigation. . . . The final and definitive concept [in contrast] cannot stand at the beginning of the investigation, but must come at the end" (Weber 1930: 47).

Before you decide on a concept, you can let your imagination run free, in order to come up with creative ideas (for example,

Weber 1949: 94). But once this has been done, you need to tighten up the analysis, and for this you need concepts.

The concept, Weber also points out, is "one of the great tools of all scientific knowledge" (Weber 1946: 151). It allows you to proceed in the research. It does this through its capacity "to establish *knowledge of what is essential*" (Weber 1975: 213).

In one of his writings Weber describes the discovery of the concept:

> Plato's passionate enthusiasm in *The Republic* must, in the last analysis, be explained by the fact that for the first time the concept, one of the great tools of all scientific knowledge, had been consciously discovered. Socrates had discovered it in its bearing. He was not the only man in the world to discover it. In India one finds the beginnings of a logic that is quite similar to that of Aristotle's. But nowhere else do we find this realization of the significance of the concept. (Weber 1946: 141)

In the section that follows on this mini-history of the concept, Weber describes how the idea emerged in early Greek philosophy that if you could only find the right concept for some phenomenon, the problem of its true meaning would be solved. This idea was to have a profound impact on Western thought, and the tendency to look for the one true concept, in which all the different manifestations in reality of some phenomenon can be found, still haunts social science.

Weber writes as follows:

> In Greece, for the first time, appeared a handy means [viz the concept] by which one could put the logical screws upon somebody so that he could not come out without admitting either that he knew nothing or that this and nothing else

was the truth, the *eternal* truth that never would vanish as the doings of the blind men [in Plato's cave] vanish. That was the tremendous experience which dawned upon the disciples of Socrates. *And from this it seemed to follow that if one only found the right concept of the beautiful, the good, or, for instance of bravery, of the soul—of whatever—that then one could also grasp its true meaning.* (Weber 1946: 141; emphasis added)

Most of the rest of what Weber has to say about the way to use concepts in social science can be found in his discussion of the *ideal type*, a term that he had picked up from a colleague and invested with his own content.

Weber mainly discusses the ideal type from a philosophy of science perspective, and what he says on this topic is often hard to penetrate (for example, Bruun 2007). In what follows I will not attempt an interpretation of this material but instead focus on another task—that is, to spell out the practical consequences of using ideal types when you theorize, according to Weber.

An ideal type, Weber says, is a concept created by and for the social scientist. It can be described as a "mental construct" or a "mental picture" (*Gedankenbild*). This means, among other things, that it is not the same as reality and therefore cannot express all of reality. It is essentially created by the social scientist through a combination of two mental operations: a synthesis of what is known about a phenomenon, and an "analytical accentuation" of its key features (Weber 1949: 90, 93).

An ideal type has a number of practical functions, and one of these is to provide terminological clarity and precision. Since reality is endlessly rich and contradictory, it is of importance that the ideal type is clear and coherent. That an ideal type fulfills these criteria is helpful when you theorize and especially important when the results of the research are presented.

The most important function of an ideal type, however, is something else, and it is precisely this quality that makes it particularly well suited for theorizing during the stage of the prestudy. This is to be *heuristic*.

The ideal type, Weber repeatedly says, is a "heuristic tool," and this means that it should primarily be used to discover new aspects of a phenomenon (for example, Weber 2012: 116, 132). The ideal type "is *a tool*, never an end" (Weber 2012: 126).

The ideal type can be heuristic in a number of ways. One of these is to help the researcher come up with hypotheses. An ideal type, Weber says, "is no 'hypothesis' but it offers guidance for the construction of hypotheses" (Weber 1949: 90).

The one way in which an ideal type can be heuristic, which I have personally found to be the most useful, is the following. One of the purposes of an ideal type, Weber says, is to "serve as a harbor before you have learned to navigate in the vast sea of empirical facts" (Weber 1949: 104). This means, as I understand it, that when you begin to study a complex phenomenon, it is very useful to have an ideal type at your disposal. Once you have reached the point where you know in which direction to look, it is time for step number two. This is to focus on the significant differences (if any) between the ideal type and empirical reality, and to try to account for these. At this stage the initial ideal type has fulfilled its function and can be discarded.

If you want to study Japanese feudalism, for example, you may begin the research by using an ideal type of Western feudalism or alternatively, if no such ideal type exists, by creating one. With its help, you will then be able to focus in on certain aspects of Japanese history, while ignoring others, and in this way get your bearing. If you discover significant differences between the concept of Western feudalism and Japanese reality, you will then have to account for these empirically, and possibly also create a new concept, perhaps of Japanese feudalism. If not, you can keep the original ideal type.

Herbert Blumer has suggested that the function of all social science concepts is to "sensitize" the social scientist to the empirical richness of reality, and this position has a certain affinity to what Weber says (Blumer 1954). A *sensitizing concept* helps the researcher to see new things by sharpening his or her senses. It is not a *definitive concept*, and no such concepts exist in social science, according to Blumer.

Let us now leave the ideal type and return to the problem of how to create a concept in the first place. What I first want to discuss is the situation when a social science concept grows out of some existing term in an accidental manner. In this case, which is common, the meaning of the concept will often fluctuate and be imprecise.

As an example I will use the word *mobbing*, which today is an accepted social science term (Agevall 2008). This word was first used in 1969 by a Swedish medical doctor who was upset over the harassment that his adopted son had to put up with. In talking about mobbing, he made an explicit analogy to Konrad Lorenz's theory of the inborn aggression of animals, and how violence is sometimes directed by a group of animals against one of their own.

The word immediately struck a chord with the Swedish public. And as the term *mobbing* started to bounce around in the media its meaning was extended to a number of other phenomena. The term was, for example, given a legal meaning; it was also given a psychological interpretation. The latter was done through a popular book by psychologist Dan Olweus that appeared in 1973, and it moved the meaning of the term *mobbing* from the arena of the group to the individual, and from animal aggression to human behavior.

While Olweus mainly had schoolchildren in mind when he talked about mobbing, a decade later another Swedish psychologist extended its meaning once more. This time the actors were adults and the situation the average workplace, where some people try to freeze out or otherwise hurt and harass a fellow employee. Today the social science term *mobbing* also includes this latter type of behavior. Its current meaning, in other words, is more or less the sum of its accidental history.

But social science concepts can also come into being in a more deliberate way. One that is quite common is that a term that has been used for some time in social science is transformed into a full-fledged concept at a later stage. With Robert K. Merton we may call these terms *proto-concepts*. He has also described how these differ from full concepts in an instructive way.

*Proto* means the earliest form of something, and "a proto-concept is an early, rudimentary, particularized, and largely unexplicated idea" (Merton 1984: 267). "A concept," in contrast, "is a general idea which, once having been tagged, substantially generalized, and explicated can effectively guide inquiry into seemingly diverse phenomena." While proto-concepts, Merton says, "make for early discontinuities in scientific development," fully developed concepts "make for continuities by directing our attention to similarities among substantively quite unconnected phenomena" (Merton 1984: 267).

As an example of how a proto-concept can be turned into a full-fledged concept we can take the notion of social mechanism. The term *social mechanism* can be found in a number of early works by social scientists. But it was not much discussed in these, nor was it turned into something like a full-fledged theoretical concept. This did not happen until much later (for example, Hedström and Swedberg 1997).

Another example of a proto-concept that is hopefully in the process of becoming a full-fledged concept is that of theorizing. In sociology, the word *theorizing* made its first appearance around 1900, but as a search in JSTOR shows, it has had to wait for more than a century to be put forward as a full-fledged social science concept (Small 1896: 306; Swedberg 2012).

It is not clear through what kind of cognitive processes a concept is constructed, and how you consciously go about constructing one. Hopefully we will know more in the future, thanks to cognitive science. In the meantime and provisionally it can be argued that when you go from observing something to turning it into a concept, it is possible to proceed in at least two ways: you *abstract*, and you *generalize*.

When you abstract, you remove details or, to use a metaphor, you move upward and try to create different levels. When you generalize, in contrast, you mainly move sideways. You do this by incorporating other phenomena, and finding things in common between your phenomenon and these phenomena.

A sign of someone being an imaginative social scientist, according to C. Wright Mills, is precisely "the capacity to shuttle between levels of abstraction" (Mills 1959: 34). Everett C. Hughes meant something similar when he said that a social scientist should also be able to see "likeness within the shell of variety" (Hughes 1984a: 503).

To run up and down the ladder of abstraction, and also to be able to stretch a concept through generalization, is something that you can learn through training. It is also an activity that certain individuals excel in. Among philosophers, Kierkegaard is in my view unsurpassed when it comes to the ease with which he forms new concepts and handles their different levels. Reading through such sparkling texts as *Repetition* or *The Present Age* is not only instructive but also very inspiring when you are trying to create a concept.

It is also possible to err in various ways when you run up and down the ladder of abstraction, something that has been especially discussed by Giovanni Sartori and a number of political scientists inspired by his work (for example, Sartori 1970; Collier and Gerring 2009). A very helpful view of such notions as *conceptual stretching*, *conceptual traveling*, and the like can be found in the work of Gary Goertz (for example, 2006).

According to Goertz, you can extend the scope of a concept by reducing the number of central features associated with it, and vice versa, you can limit its scope by adding features. A concrete example may make it easier to understand Goertz's argument. You can define the concept of peasants in a very general way, as say "rural cultivators" (1). You can then specify by adding that they live in "peasant villages"(2); that they show "high levels of rural social subordination" (3); and that they "control/own land" (4) (Goertz 2006: 73).

Goertz also points out that different theories have used different combinations of these features in their analyses of peasants. Advocates of the moral economy approach, for example, tend to define peasants as rural cultivators (1) who live in peasant villages (2) and who show high levels of social insubordination (3). Marxists would probably want to add that peasants also control or own land (4).

One point that Goertz is very careful to make is that depending on how a concept is defined, you will end up with different populations. Merton has expressed the same idea, but also pointed out what this means for observation: "concepts, then, constitute the definitions (or prescriptions) of what is to be observed" (Merton 1945: 465).

From a theorizing perspective this means that you may want to play around with different definitions and see what happens when you do this. This is also one reason why an iterative element is part of early theorizing. You start by observing things and then proceed to concept formation, and having done this, you may need to go back to observation if your concept is such that you need more data to figure things out.

There also exist different ways to proceed when you want to operationalize a concept, and Goertz suggests that you should always try to minimize the distance between the definition of a concept and its operationalization. What Goertz does not say, but is perhaps implicit in his approach, is that by playing around with different ways in which to operationalize it, you may also discover some new aspects of a phenomenon.

In fact, in Goertz's important work on the construction of concepts, he pays next to no attention to the way in which you create totally new concepts or, more generally, to the way in which you deal with concepts in the context of discovery. This is somewhat disappointing since it is clearly Goertz's ambition to cover all the major aspects of the use of concepts.

This does not mean that Goertz's work is not useful for the way in which concepts are to be dealt with, in the context of discovery. On the contrary, a good knowledge of his work is essential for what takes place during this process.

Through a small sleight of hand, it is also possible to turn some of Goertz's insights in a heuristic direction. Take, for example, his insistence that when you map out the meaning of a concept, you should also decide what its opposite is. If you study war or revolution, you need to figure out what nonwar and nonrevolution mean. And when you try to figure out the opposite of something, you may end up with some new and interesting ideas. By proceeding in this way, you easily move into new and interesting territory.

So far in this discussion I have mostly talked about creating new concepts, but it is more common when you theorize to use existing concepts or a mixture of new and old concepts. You can either use existing concepts, without changing them at all, or you can tweak them a bit, like Weber often does. You can also use existing concepts as building material for new concepts, something that terms such as *class struggle*, *status contradiction*, and *greedy institution* are a reminder of.

The skillful use of existing social science concepts presupposes that you already know quite a few concepts, so you have something to draw on and play around with. Some works are very rich in interesting concepts; and some knowledge of these is therefore helpful (see also chapter 8).

One work in sociology that it is full of concepts is Weber's *Economy and Society* (Weber 1978). This is especially true for its first chapter, which contains what the author considered to be the basic concepts of sociology (chapter 1, "Basic Sociological Concepts" [*Soziologische Grundbegriffe*]). Weber carefully defines each of these concepts, and also tries to link them together, either in groups or by relating them to his central concept of social action.

While one may agree or disagree with the way in which Weber defines these basic concepts, this chapter is still very useful for anyone who wants to have a number of solid social science concepts at his or her fingertips. You can also add to your store of concepts by looking at the next three chapters in *Economy and Society* (chapter 2, "Sociological Categories of Economic Life"; chapter 3, "The Types of Legitimate Domination"; and chapter 4, "Status Groups and Classes").

Also Georg Simmel's sociological writings are full of useful concepts, but these are of a more intuitive and artistic character than those of Weber. Simmel rarely defines a concept, nor does he try to relate his concepts to each other. This may lower their value from one perspective, but it also makes it easier to take them over and make them into your own.

Simmel was well aware of this particular quality of his concepts and actually cultivated it. Just before his death, for example, he wrote in his diary that his ideas are not so different from money that you inherit and with which you can do whatever you want: "My legacy will be like cash, which is distributed to many heirs, each transforming his portion into a profit that conforms to his nature; and this profit will no longer reveal its derivation from my legacy" (Simmel 1919: 121).

Simmel's writings also illustrate the point that it is useful to be familiar not only with works that contain a number of carefully constructed concepts but also with social science literature, which is full of ideas. Works such as, say, *The Wealth of Nations* and *The Prince* contain plenty of ideas that can easily be turned into modern social science concepts.

Of contemporary works in sociology that contain many interesting concepts, I have especially found the works of the following authors useful: Robert K. Merton, Erving Goffman, and Everett C. Hughes. Merton's work contains many more concepts than most sociologists are aware of, and these have been as carefully crafted as those of Weber. The works of Hughes and Goffman are, in contrast, more like those of Simmel: very suggestive and easily made into your own.

What makes it difficult to discuss the nature and use of social science concepts in a more satisfying way than what so far has been done in this chapter has much to do with the unclear status of the concept in modern science. What I am referring to is the important research that has been carried out by cognitive scientists since a few decades back, according to which the so-called classical view of the concept is wrong (for example, Smith and Medin 1981; Murphy 2002).

By *classical view of the concept* is meant the theory, which originated in antiquity and was famously advocated by Aristotle, that a concept covers a certain class of objects and has clear boundaries. Sometimes this is also called an *essentialist definition* of the concept, and it means that it is possible to enumerate all the necessary and sufficient conditions for a concept (for example, Goertz 2006).

The problem with this approach is that people do not use concepts this way, according to cognitive scientists. Instead, they may use concepts as a kind of standard, which means that they see some phenomenon as being fully part of some concept, and others as being less so (the so-called prototype view). A robin, for example, is often seen as more of a bird than is a penguin or an ostrich.

People's concepts are sometimes also centered around concrete examples, again in a way that goes counter to the classical view. If you grew up with a German shepherd, this type of dog may well be the archetypical dog for you (the so-called exemplar view). In all brevity, according to cognitive science, there exists quite a bit of ambiguity and lack of permanence in the way that people use concepts in their everyday lives.

Little effort has been made to spell out the consequences of this new view of concepts for the formation of concepts in social science (for an exception, see, for example, Collier and Mahon 1993). It is, however, clear that one would end up with a new kind of social science concept if one followed the nonclassical view (for example, Goertz 2006; cf. Ragin 2000).

Goertz has suggested that under certain circumstances, it can be useful to use nonclassical concepts in social science or what he calls "family resemblance concepts," following Wittgenstein. He defines these as concepts that fulfill some necessary conditions but no sufficient conditions. Social scientists, for example, often define the *welfare state* as a state that fulfills some but not all of a number of conditions. A welfare state may be defined as a state that provides, say, two of the following three items: old-age pensions, health insurance, and unemployment compensation.

As I see things, it is definitely useful to know that it is possible to use two kinds of concepts: (1) those that fulfill both necessary *and* sufficient conditions (the classical view); and (2) those that fulfill some necessary conditions but no sufficient conditions (the family resemblance view). What is not so clear, however, is that the latter type of concept captures what is radically new and different with the view of concepts that can be found in Wittgenstein and in cognitive science.

You can, of course, make the argument that it is important to stay with the old view of social science concepts, even if it is true that people in their everyday lives use concepts in a different way. The reason for proceeding in this way would be that it is much more difficult to meet such criteria as clarity, economy, and lack of ambiguity when you use the view of concepts in cognitive science.

As an example of the traditional way of defining a concept one can take Weber's concept of "social action" in *Economy and Society*. The term *action* is defined as behavior in which the actor has invested meaning, and the term *social* as action oriented to the behavior of others (Weber 1978: 4). Or we can use another example, this time from *States and Social Revolutions* by Theda Skocpol. According to this work, "Social revolutions are rapid, basic transformations of a society's state and class structure, and they are accompanied and in part carried through by class-based revolts from below" (Skocpol 1979: 4–5).

Regardless of how this issue is decided, it is true that the new view of concepts in cognitive science invalidates once and for all the notion that you can somehow distill *the* true interpretation of a concept from the ways in which it is used. This is simply not possible, as Wittgenstein was the first to establish.

This view, Wittgenstein explains, is very much similar to the way in which we sometimes try to teach children the meaning of words (Wittgenstein 1953). We point at an object, say an apple, and then pronounce the word *apple*. To this view of seeing things Wittgenstein counterposed his own theory of language games.

The meaning of a word or a concept depends on the ways it is used or, more precisely, on the language games in which it is part.

Take, for example, the word *democracy*. When two ordinary persons discuss democracy it has one meaning; as part of a constitution, a second meaning; and as part of a social science analysis, a third. Or take *love*, which can mean the same as *agape*, what you feel for your dog, or that you have zero points in a tennis game—all according to the context and how the word is used.

Other examples of language games, to cite from *Philosophical Investigations*, are the following:

> Giving orders, and obeying them
> Describing the appearance of an object, or giving its measurements
> Constructing an object from a description (a drawing)
> Reporting an event
> Speculating about an event
> Forming and testing a hypothesis
> Presenting the results of an experiment in tables and diagrams
> Making up a story and reading it
>
> (Wittgenstein 1953: 11e–12e)

As this list makes clear, each language game demands its own specific meaning of words and expressions, something that means that the theorizer has to be extremely sensitive to the context, in order to understand the meaning of a word.

The current view in cognitive science of the unstable nature of a concept may also help to explain why it is so hard to fix the meanings of social science concepts and keep them stable once and for all. It is not only that the world changes, and with it the meaning of words. Social scientists will also use concepts in the nonclassical way when they talk, write, and think.

What is referred to as the *clarification of concepts* has attracted quite a bit of attention over the years in social science. Committees for this purpose have, for example, been created in political science, sociology, and so on. These have typically published statements about the way that certain concepts should be defined. Little else seems to have been accomplished.

This should not necessarily be seen as an argument against having this type of committees. But their task may need to be changed. What is especially needed is conceptual clarification of a more fundamental type—namely, attempts in a Wittgensteinian spirit to clear up the various problems that are often created through the use of concepts in social science research (Wittgenstein 1953).

As mentioned earlier new social science concepts may lose their original meaning after a while—another complication to keep in mind. This is probably due to a number of causes. One way that this may come about, for example, is through the diffusion of social science concepts into common language, via newspapers, television, and so on. As examples of this one can mention concepts such as *charisma* and *serendipity* (for example, Merton and Wolfe 1995).

Another way in which new social science concepts may lose their original meaning is through the way in which they are used by other social scientists than the ones who originally invented them. Peirce was particularly concerned with this issue and created an "ethics of terminology" to deal with it (Peirce 1998b; cf. Oebler 1981). Peirce argued that a scientist who uses a concept in any other way than its original meaning, "commit[s] a shameful offense against the inventor of the symbol and against science, and it becomes the duty of the others to treat the act with contempt and indignation" (Peirce 1998b: 265). So far, no one has tried to implement Peirce's ideas.

The unstable nature of the concept also affects attempts to operationalize it. For a concept constructed according to the classical view, there will presumably be less room for different measures than when a concept of the family resemblance type is involved. It is difficult to say much more on this particular issue, even if it would seem that the impact of the new view of the concept will affect operationalization also in other ways.

But the topic of operationalization raises some other issues as well that are important to mention. One of these has to do with the way in which measures of operationalization are related to a concept in the first place. It deserves, for example, to be noted that the idea that a concept can be operationalized at all is a relatively new notion in social science (for example, Adler 1947). Another issue has to do with the different approaches to operationalization that can be found in quantitative and qualitative studies.

These two issues, as it turns out, are often related. Qualitative social scientists tend to be interested in concepts as such, and also in the way in which these are related to data. Quantitative social scientists, in contrast, spend much less time with concepts, and what especially interest them are indicators and their relationship to variables (for example, Abbott 1997).

An interesting discussion of these different attitudes can be found in a recent book by Gary Goertz and James Mahoney on the cultures that have emerged around qualitative and quantitative studies in social science. In *A Tale of Two Cultures* they write

> For qualitative scholars, the relationship between a concept and data is one of *semantics*, i.e., meaning. These scholars explore how data can be used to express the meaning of a concept. For quantitative scholars, by contrast, the relationship between variable and indicator concerns the

*measurement* of the variable. These scholars focus on how to use indicators to best measure a latent construct. (Goertz and Mahoney 2012: 140)

In practice, this means that quantitative scholars tend to downplay the role of concepts, which they basically equate with the way that these are operationalized. This is not very helpful when you try to theorize.

## Typology

As part of the process of creating a full tentative theory with the help of the empirical material, you may at this point use a *typology* or a *classification*. And just like concepts, these can be consciously constructed with the help of certain building blocks.

Typologies and classifications belong to the same family, with the former consisting of fewer categories than the latter. A classification also often attempts to be complete and cover all of the cases. While you begin to construct a typology by looking at a few cases, and then extend it to all of the cases, to see whether it fits and makes sense, you often proceed differently with a classification. Here you start with the whole population and try to divide it up into various categories.

Classifications, more than typologies, are used to bring order into the empirical material at an early stage. A good classification also has an internal structure, as opposed to a list that just consists of a number of items, one after the other.

Sometimes, of course, it can be very helpful *not* to have a structure and just list a number of items. A list can be very useful in its own right: to remind you of all the items of a special kind; their exact order; or the like. Lists and their uses are more complex than you would expect, as a reference to Wittgenstein's view on language games should make clear.

A classification can be used early in the research and then discarded, once you have a better view of what is going on. This is along the lines of Weber's suggestion that an ideal type can be used as a harbor, before you have learned to navigate on the sea of empirical facts.

But a classification can also be heuristic. According to a biologist who has helped to develop a new approach to taxonomy,

> Classifications that describe relationships among objects in nature should generate hypotheses. In fact the principal scientific justification for establishing classifications is that they are heuristic (in the traditional meaning of this term as "stimulating interest as a means of furthering investigation") and that they lead to the stating of a hypothesis which can then be tested. A classification raises the question of how the perceived order has arisen, and in a system in which forces and relationships are transitory one may conjecture about the maintenance of the structure. (Sokol 1974:1117)

While a classification may be of help in various ways, it does not represent the end of the process of theorizing. Much remains to be done, once a classification has been produced.

It is especially important not to confuse a *classification* with an *explanation*. Linnean botany initially represented a welcome advance, because it brought order into what at the time was a bewildering state in the study of plants. But Linneus's system of classification soon became an obstacle to further progress, since it was based more on a passion for logic and classification than on research (for example, Mayr 1982:171–80). Just like a concept should ideally be constructed in such a way that it can easily be linked up to a full theory, the same holds true for a classification. One way to proceed, in order to produce a classification of this type, is to explore its theoretical assumptions and also its associations. Behind most categories there is a set of assumptions, and in a really useful classification these assumptions belong together with other parts of the theory at a deeper level.

A typology consists of two or more types. Social science is, for example, full of so-called paired concepts, such as *Gemeinschaft-Gesellschaft* (Tönnies), lion-foxes (Pareto), cosmopolitan-local (Merton), and so on. The main value of this type of pairs is that they allow the researcher to clearly outline two subtypes of a phenomenon. In many cases the function of paired concepts is also heuristic: they point in which direction to go, but let the researcher decide exactly which path to follow.

Political scientists have tried to identify the building blocks of a typology, and in a recent overview of work along these lines, the authors write "A good typology . . . centrally involves identifying the overarching concept being measured, organizing the row and column variables, and establishing the cell types" (Collier et al. 2008: 167). Good typologies, it is added, should also be mutually exclusive.

A 2 × 2 table may help us to understand some phenomenon, by providing four subtypes. That this type of table is very useful has been noted by many social scientists. According to Arthur Stinchcombe, for example, "the fourfold table with types as entries in the cells is a standard tool of sociological theorizing" (Stinchcombe 1968: 46).

Another reason why 2 × 2 tables are useful, and even more so tables with a large number of cells, is that they invite you to try to fill in all of the cells. Doing so can make you realize that some cases are very rare but important, while others should be more common than they are, and so on. It also encourages you to try to name and develop all of the types.

From what has just been said it is clear that a typology can be used for heuristic reasons, even though this is usually not emphasized in social science discussions of typologies (for an exception, see, for example, Bailey 1973). According to a common argument, it is important that a typology should be used only if it can be justified on empirical grounds. Unless there is reason to believe that two or several phenomena differ sufficiently from each other on empirical grounds, the typology should not be considered legitimate (for example, Lazarsfeld 1962).

But this, to repeat, represents a misunderstanding of how to proceed at the stage of discovery versus the stage of justification. At the former stage, before the results have been reached, speculation should be the rule. And the task of speculation is not to stick too close to the ground. It is instead, to return to Whitehead's metaphor of the airplane that was mentioned at the outset of this chapter, to soar high into the air and make us see things that we otherwise would never be able to see.

..................................................................................................

## CHAPTER 4

# Analogy, Metaphor, and Pattern

> Those who have treated of the sciences have been either
> empiricists or dogmatists. Empiricists, like ants, simply
> accumulate and use; Rationalists, like spiders, spin webs
> from themselves. The way of the bee is in between: it takes
> material from the flowers of the garden and the field; but it
> has the ability to convert and digest them.
>
> —Francis Bacon, *The New Organon*[1]

How does the social scientist produce the sweet-tasting honey that Bacon refers to in *The New Organon*? One answer is that he or she must not only be good at observing, naming a phenomenon, developing concepts and types, and in this way begin to develop a theory. There also exist some other skills that are important to have, if you want to be able to analyze a phenomenon well.

The three skills to be discussed in this chapter are the following: using analogies, working with metaphors, and learning to recognize and read patterns. These skills are more general in nature than the ones that have been discussed so far, and they can also be of help at many different points during the process of theorizing. All three can, for example, be used when you observe as well as when you try to come up with an explanation.

But just as it is important to make clear that you can develop a skill in seeing patterns, and in coming up with useful analogies and metaphors, it should be emphasized that at the stage of discovery these skills can also be used for heuristic purposes. Analogies and so on can be used to capture something that is hidden and so far has resisted analysis.

Using analogies and metaphors as well as pattern recognition also represent three ways of thinking that differ from the classical way of reasoning. One of their strengths is precisely that they are able to proceed in ways that formal logic cannot. Another is that they are helpful in coming up with new approaches to things. They are especially helpful when used in combination with patient and methodical reasoning.

Analogies, metaphors, and pattern recognition have all been used in a wide array of disciplines, from archaeology and biology to economics and law. This means that there exists plenty of experience to draw on for the theorizer. As in so many other areas of creative theorizing, however, this material is currently not very much known or discussed, something that is a reminder that much remains to be done before social science theorizing is in good shape.

The one science that by far has shown the most interest in studying analogies, metaphors, and patterns is cognitive science. One of its insights is that these are all part of the way in which human beings normally think. That this is a fact will naturally also affect the ease with which they can be used for some special activity, such as social science theorizing. In being part of the cognitive repertoire of human beings they are similar to the skills that were discussed in earlier chapters, such as naming, using concepts, and so on. And just as these, they need to be consciously adapted to the particular purposes of social science research and theorizing.

But there also exists quite a bit of disagreement in cognitive science about the nature of analogies, metaphors, and pattern recognition. Some scientists argue, for example, that the analogy represents *the* key to the way that human beings think. There is also quite a bit of debate about how to define analogies, metaphors, and patterns.

For all of these reasons I will interpret each in a broad way. When I discuss patterns, for example, I will also discuss the use of figures and diagrams. Here as elsewhere in the context of discovery, you do better to cast your net widely than to stick to a narrow definition.

## Analogy

Analogies can be used in several different ways in science (for example, Gentner 1982; Nersessian 2008). For one thing, they can be used in a fairly simple way—namely, to transfer the meaning of one phenomenon to that of another in order to get a better grip on the latter. But analogies can also be used in a more complex way. It is, for example, possible to link several analogies together in order to solve a problem. While both of these ways of proceeding are useful, the latter is probably better suited to difficult problems.

When an analogy is used in a simple way, one is reminded of its original meaning, which is *proportion* (in Greek and Latin). As an example, one can refer to the everyday experience of explaining something by referring to something else. In order to understand the financial crisis, think of the Depression; in order to understand the way that a nation state works, think of the way that a household works; and so forth.

In its more complex form, the analogy similarly helps to produce a new understanding, but it does so in a less mechanical fashion. What is involved here is either the use of repeated analogies, as in a chain, or the use of an analogy in a way that goes beyond a simple comparison of two phenomena. James Clark

Maxwell used analogies in both of these ways, and I shall return to his way of proceeding in a moment.

Several of the classics in sociology discuss the use of analogies, and they do so in a helpful and instructive form. Max Weber, for example, was very interested in the role of analogies in social science and often commented on their use by various scholars. He also traced the early history of the analogy.

The origin of analogical thinking, according to Weber, is to be found in magic (Weber 1978: 407). If you do A, and B follows, doing something similar to A—that is, something that is *analogous to A*—will result in something that is similar to B.

Analogies have also been used in legal thought for a long time, according to Weber. By subsuming a concrete case under a legal rule it was early understood that a solution could be provided. The use of analogies in law also inspired the idea of *syllogism* and in this way helped to introduce formal reasoning into philosophy.

Weber mainly writes about the analogy in his methodological writings, his sociology of religion, and his sociology of law (for example, Weber 1975; 1978: 787, 978). In his usual concentrated manner, he sums up the early history of the analogy in a few lines:

> Analogy has exerted a lasting influence upon, indeed has dominated not only forms of religious expression but juristic thinking, even the treatment of precedents in purely empirical forms of law. The syllogistic constructions of concepts through rational subsumption only gradually replaced analogical thinking, which originated in symbolistically rationalized magic, whose structure is wholly analogical. (Weber 1978: 407)

Thanks to Weber we have some knowledge of the history of analogical thinking. We also know that it was primarily used for conservative purposes (magic and law). Durkheim tended to look at the analogy in a way that is more in tune with the current view of the analogy in cognitive science.

Analogies are primarily used to produce new knowledge, according to Durkheim, both by individuals and scientists. In an early lecture he formulated his view of the analogy as follows:

> We cannot forget that analogy is a precious instrument for knowledge and even for scientific research. The mind cannot create a new idea out of nothing. Should we discover an entirely new being without analogue in the rest of the world, it would be impossible for the mind to grasp it; it could only be represented in terms of something else that the mind already knows. What we call a new idea is in reality but an old idea which we have touched up in order to accommodate it as exactly as possible to the special object which it must express. (Durkheim 1978: 55–56)

When he wrote this Durkheim was mainly concerned with the use of the analogy for heuristic purposes. In one of his later writings he also addressed the use of analogies when you want to prove your case empirically. Analogies could be used for this purpose as well, but their value was clearly limited:

> If analogy is not a method of demonstration in the true sense of the word, it is nevertheless a method of illustration and secondary verification which may be of some use. It is always interesting to see whether a law established for one order of facts may not, *mutatis mutandis*, be found to apply elsewhere. (Durkheim 1974: 1)

Also Simmel, another sociological classic, assigned an important role to the analogy in his sociological writings. In a program-

matic article on the nature of sociology he argued along the lines
of Durkheim that when you create a new science, it is very helpful to look for analogies between the new science and sciences
that already exist (Simmel 1959).

But Simmel's view of the analogy also differed from that of
Durkheim, and while Durkheim had a tendency to advocate the
simple use of the analogy, Simmel preferred the more complex
one. The purpose of using an analogy, he said, is not so much to
compare two phenomena, and through this comparison transfer
the meaning of one to the other. It is rather to compare two phenomena and, in doing so, discover something that is new in relation to both of them.

In a passage that is not overly clear, either in the original German or in translation, Simmel writes:

> The introduction of a new way of looking at facts must
> clarify the various aspects of its method by resorting to
> analogies taken from recognized fields of study. Nonethe-
> less, it is only the process (perhaps never completed) by
> which the new principle become realized, clearly defined,
> and legitimated as fruitful through concrete research that
> can purify such analogies of the confusion of material dif-
> ferences that in the beginning cover up *the decisive identity
> of form.* However, to the same degree that the process frees
> these analogies from their ambiguity, it makes the analo-
> gies themselves superfluous. (Simmel 1959: 336; emphasis
> added)

What Simmel seems to be getting at is that you need to proceed
in two stages in order to use an analogy effectively. You should
first carry out a simple analogy between two phenomena. You
should then press on and try to eliminate as much as possible of

the differences between the two phenomena, and in this way try to figure out what they have in common.

Simmel's term for what two phenomena have in common is *form*, and the main task of sociology was in his view to suggest and investigate *social forms*. Or to cast Simmel's way of proceeding in the language of Diane Vaughan, who is herself a strong advocate of analogical thinking in sociology: you want to go from looking for similarities to looking for "Simmelarities" (Vaughan 1998; cf. Vaughan 2014).

Before leaving the classics in sociology, it can be added that Weber's point that analogies can be used not only to produce novelties but also to block them finds ample support in the literature on analogies in legal science. In *An Introduction to Legal Science*, for example, Edward Levi states that the most common way to proceed in law is to reason from case to case. This is done in a three-step process in the following way: "Similarity is seen between cases; next the rule of law inherent in the first case is announced; then the rule of law is [analogically] made applicable to the second case" (Levi 1949: 2).

The result of proceeding in this way is not that law stands still, according to Levi, but that it moves ahead very slowly and avoids all leaps. What makes it possible to slow down change through the use of analogy is that there always exists a number of possible analogies to choose from, and no particular reason why one is inherently preferable over the others. When several laws can be drawn on in a concrete case, there exists what Levi calls "competing analogies" (Levi 1949: 5).

In discussing the negative side of analogies, at least in relation to discovery, one should also mention the fact that an analogy can be wrong. One way to spot a so-called false analogy in social science is by confronting the analogy with facts. This can be done provisionally in the prestudy, and later on, in a much more thorough and methodical manner, in the main study.

Knut Wicksell, one of the founders of modern economics, has laid out the strategy for how to deal with a false analogy in a clear way:

> As soon as we discover a similarity between two phenomena, we at once suspect a closer connection, and tentatively assume that they are also similar in other respects. This method of proceeding by analogy has not a high place in formal logic, but it is fundamentally the only one at our disposal apart from immediate perception; it is often deceiving, even usually deceiving, and it is then called false analogy. The difference between false and true analogy cannot be seen *a priori*, only *a posteriori* in accordance with the evidence of experience. (Wicksell 1958: 57–58)

As mentioned earlier the science that has shown the most interest in analogy is cognitive science. In its analyses the following terms are often used. In an analogy, you *map* what is called the *source* onto the *target* or what you want to better understand. In doing so, you *transfer* the meaning from the former to the latter.

Analogies may also refer to different aspects of two phenomena: their surface features, their structures, and their systems (for example, Gentner 2003; Gentner and Smith 2013). Analogies that refer to the surfaces of phenomena are often considered simplistic, while those that refer to their structures and systems are seen as more complex and useful.

In the work of Nancy Nersessian, which combines cognitive science with the history of science in an interesting way, it is suggested that many important scientific discoveries are the result of analogical thinking (Nersessian 2008). Her main example is Maxwell's attempt to create a mathematical representation of the electromagnetic field, something he did by conceiving it in terms of non-Newtonian dynamics. In doing so his main tool was the analogy.

Maxwell was very interested in analogies and often commented on them. He developed what he called a *theory of physical analogy*, and its key features can be summarized as follows. First, a good analogy deals with *relations*. Second, and this is the feature that Nersessian focuses on, the scientist should proceed *stepwise* and use several analogies in solving a problem. And third, the target should be something that lies beyond the comparison of the target and the source, what Maxwell calls the *form*.

The first feature of a good analogy, according to Maxwell, is that it compares the relation in one set of facts to the relation in another set of facts:

> Although pairs of things may differ widely from each other, the *relation* in the one pair may be the same as in another. Now, as in a scientific point of view the *relation* is the most important thing to know, a knowledge of the one thing leads us a long way toward a knowledge of the other. (Maxwell 1884: 354)

The second feature of Maxwell's theory of physical analogy is that you should not use just one analogy when you try to solve a problem, but several. Nersessian's term for these intermediary analogies is "bridging analogies." You first construct one analogy, which addresses part of the problem and also takes you part of the way to the solution. You then construct another analogy, which brings you still closer, and so on.

The third feature of Maxwell's theory of physical analogy is the idea that the solution will not be found by comparing the source and the target but has to be sought somewhere else. By taking this stance Maxwell was closer to Simmel than to Durkheim. What you are looking for, according to Maxwell, is what two phenomena have in common. Or, as he put it: "In an analogy one truth is discovered under two expressions" (Maxwell 1884: 348).

## Metaphor

It is often pointed out that the metaphor is a kind of analogy, and that there consequently exists no reason to discuss it separately from the analogy. This seems to be the dominant view in cognitive science as well. But there also exist some arguments against proceeding in this way, and given the importance of metaphors in science, including social science, it may be useful to devote a separate discussion to them.

Metaphors abound in everyday language, in the arts as well as in the sciences. Their power can be immense, as evidenced by the metaphor of the brain as a computer. This metaphor is generally seen as having helped cognitive science come into being. To see the mind in terms of information processing—as encoding, retrieving, and storing information—helped to open up a whole new set of research topics (for example, Gardner 1987).

The original meaning of the word *metaphor* is "transfer" (in Greek), and this meaning is also part of Aristotle's famous definition in *Poetics*: "Metaphor consists in giving the thing a name that belongs to something else; the transference being either from genus to species, or from species to genus, or from species to species, or on grounds of analogy" (Aristotle 2001: 1457 b 6–9).

According to Aristotle, a metaphor is especially useful to the poet, since it has the capacity to invest a sentence with life and surprise the reader. It can also make something visible and inspire to "new ideas" (Aristotle 1984: 2,1410 b).

The way in which a metaphor operates is through a kind of comparison. To metaphorize, as Aristotle phrases it, is to intuit a likeness: "A good metaphor implies an intuitive perception of the similarity in dissimilars" (Aristotle 2001: 1459 a 3–8).

Besides intuition, in order to produce a good metaphor you also need to be able to speculate. More precisely, speculation is needed to tie things together that do not seem to belong together:

> In philosophy it requires speculative capacity to observe the similarity even in very mutually remote things, as Archytas said that an arbitrator and altar are the same, as the injured party takes refuge in them both. Or if one were to say that an anchor and a pot-hook were the same; for both are the same thing, but differ by being set upward or downward. (Aristotle 1991: 1412 a)

An important advance in the analysis of the metaphor took place in the twentieth century, when the focus was shifted from viewing the metaphor as a single word to seeing it as part of a discourse. The impact and meaning of a metaphor, it was now suggested, derives from the encounter of two words that are part of two different discourses (Richards 1935).

This idea was further developed by philosopher Max Black, who argued that a metaphor does not just transfer the meaning from one word to another ("the substitution view"; Black 1962: 25–47). Its power is instead the result of two interacting sets of meaning ("the interaction view").

When two words interact, their associations get entangled, according to Black. To illustrate what happens, he uses the expression "man is a wolf." What makes us see human beings from a novel perspective, with the help of this metaphor, is not that the qualities of a wolf are just transferred to a human. Instead the metaphor allows us to single out and regroup some of features that we associate with human beings ("associated commonplaces"). According to Black, "the wolf-metaphor suppresses some details, emphasizes others—in short, *organizes* our view of man" (Black 1962: 41).

To be good at creating and using metaphors is a very useful skill for the theorizer since it helps you to come up with new ideas, just as Aristotle says. It would also seem that it does so in several different ways.

There is first the plain comparison of what you are interested in with something else. Black pushes this aspect of the metaphor to the side and considers it uninteresting since it produces nothing that is really new ("the substitution view"). But this view may well be a mistake, since it was precisely the close comparison of the mind to a computer that helped cognitive science to emerge. It was probably also this very quality of a metaphor— the close comparison—that Durkheim had in mind when he noted that "for the sociologist, biology became a veritable treasure trove of perspectives and hypotheses" (Durkheim 1978: 55–56).

But it would also seem that the metaphor, just like the analogy, can inspire to something that is radically novel and goes well beyond the item-by-item comparison. Black refers in his explanation of man as a wolf to the associations of words, and he suggests that these are somehow involved in the creative process ("associated commonplaces"). The idea that it is helpful to use the association of words when you theorize will be discussed in a later chapter.

Before leaving the topic of the role of metaphors in social science a mention can be made of the argument that modern political social science has become impoverished by its attempt to eliminate metaphors in an effort to be more scientific (Zashin and Chapman 1974; similarly for economics in, for example, McCloskey 1986; Klamer and Leonard 2004).

Given the heuristic power of the metaphor, it would seem that this argument may well be correct. What is at issue, here as in so many other discussions of theory, is a confusion between what is appropriate in the context of discovery and what is appropriate in the context of justification. The metaphor, like the analogue, is mainly important for discovery, not for verification.

## Pattern

Just like human beings seem to be born with a capacity to think in terms of analogies and metaphors, they also seem to be able to discern as well as generate patterns (for example, Sacks 2012). And just as you can develop your skill in using analogies and metaphors, it would seem that the same is true for learning to identify patterns, be they visual or nonvisual.

Social scientists often use the term *pattern* to describe what they have discovered and what needs to be further analyzed. Patterns, it is commonly argued, are part of the social order, the social structure, and so on. The skilled social scientist also knows how to detect patterns in statistical information.

But while the term *pattern* is commonly used, little effort has been made to take a close look at it, define it, and turn it into a full-fledged social science concept. It is rather used as a kind of background term, a concept whose meaning is taken for granted.

What then is a pattern? This is not an easy question to answer. It would seem that a pattern implies first of all repetition, not novelty—that the same thing occurs over and over again. But this is true only up to a point, because a pattern has to come into being; it may also change. Nonetheless, the social scientist primarily wants to capture what drives the repetition—that is, the rules behind the resulting pattern.

Second, a pattern has a holistic or an emergent quality. The actions that follow the rules result in the emergence of something else. This something else can, for example, emerge from a fractal pattern, which is self-similar and comes from a repetition over and over again of the same rules. But it can also be something that is radically different—say, when a society emerges from the interactions of individuals, along the lines of Durkheim, or when life itself emerges through autocatalysis (for example, Padgett and Powell 2012).

Simmel has compared his concept of social form to a geometric figure. Just as a circle does not exist in reality, he argues, neither does a social form (his term for a social pattern). As if to underscore the nonrealistic nature of his social forms, Simmel typically takes his illustrations of these forms—such as the stranger, the dyad, and so on—from the most diverse historical, geographic, and social contexts (for example, Zerubavel 2007).

The capacity to discern patterns in things is clearly part of a social scientist's heuristic arsenal. Like analogies and metaphors, it allows the social scientist to both observe new things and to get a handle on them.

What a mathematician has said about using patterns as a method of investigation, may also fit social science:

Whilst human perception is not as perfect as mathematical ideals, people need patterns as a means of creative expression across time and space, and as such patterns become devices, methods of investigating personal and social worlds. Pattern is both a noun and a verb but as a verb it is an active way of seeing the world, a process by which to take in and make coherent the random and often chaotic information the world has to offer. (Stewart 1998: 11; cf. Jefferies 2012: 125)

But it should also be pointed out that if you are a social scientist, to discover a pattern or to pattern something means not only that you are able to view something in the form a pattern. Since much of what goes on in society has already been cast in the form of patterns, this is often a process in two steps.

You first have to break up some existing pattern and then regroup the pieces into a new pattern. This is a difficult thing to do and can be likened to going from one *Gestalt* to another, as when the eye is confronted with the picture of something like a duck-rabbit and tries to switch from one to the other. One may also cast this process in terms of what Durkheim calls preconceptions (*prénotions*).

But how do you go about this? How do you reject the pattern everyone sees and find another? Benoit Mandelbrot, who had an uncanny talent for seeing visual patterns where others saw nothing, says that the answer can be found in very careful and repeated observation. He writes in his memoirs:

> [A colleague] wondered aloud what made me succeed where those seekers and so many others had failed. My answer distilled—once again—the already told story of my scientific life: when I seek, I look, look, look, and play with pictures. One look at a picture is like one reading on a scientific instrument. One is never enough. (Mandelbrot 2012: 258)

To pattern something also means that you are now able to discard quite a bit of information that was collected as part of observation. The capacity to synthesize or to pull out what is essential from a mass of empirical information enters at this stage; even if it is not clear how the capacity to synthesize is related to the capacity to discern patterns. It is nonetheless very useful for the theorizer to know how to synthesize; and since this capacity is rarely mentioned as being useful in social science research, it deserves a few words.

The idea that people have a capacity to synthesize brings to mind Kant's famous notion of judgment, especially a synthetic judgment. In *Critique of Pure Reason* and other works Kant introduced his concept of judgment, which refers to the capacity of the human mind to mentally organize material. In a so-called synthetic judgment, Kant says, you mentally organize what is empirical in nature; while in an analytical judgment you develop and organize what is already contained in a concept (Kant 1998: 130–33).

Since the days of Kant, the meaning of the term *synthetic* has changed quite a bit, as has the meaning of *analytic*. Nonetheless, the idea and technique of synthesizing can be of help in the process of theorizing, just as pattern recognition.

One example of this would be when you make observations during the prestudy, since this usually results in a mass of unwieldy information. An important task of synthesizing, in other words, is to order the material in some creative way, and thereby reduce the nearly infinite amount of data that you encounter in many empirical setting.

Exactly what happens when you make a synthesis is unclear. While it can take a long time to observe a phenomenon, it would seem that a synthesis can come about very quickly, just like pattern recognition. To synthesize, in short, may well be part of a person's inborn capacity.

There exists some work in cognitive science that looks at the speed with which a judgment (or a synthesis) can be made of new facts, so-called thin-slicing (for example, Carrère and Gottman

1999). Not only are experts able to make judgments extremely quickly, it would also appear that if they take more time to evaluate something, the errors will increase.

Figures, tables, maps, and other kinds of visualizations can also help you to discern a pattern, as earlier mentioned. While the conventional reason for the use of figures and tables in an article or a monograph is well known—they present the empirical material or the analyses in an effective and visually arresting way—less has been said about their use at the stage of discovery. Essentially they do the same job as synthesizing—that is, they help to reduce the complexity of the data and suggest the existence of patterns.

Maps have been seen as an important tool of social science for a very long time. In the Chicago School, for example, knowing how to make maps was seen as indispensable for the sociologist. More recent contributions include both technical advances, such as the Geographic Information System (GIS), and the notion of mental maps (for example, Milgram 1976).

Drawings can also be used to represent the overall argument, with the help of causal arrows or more complex notations. One type of drawing or figure that is especially useful for heuristic purposes, and which also has been much studied in cognitive science, is the diagram (for example, Nersessian 2008: 158–72).

An important reason for the attention that has been devoted to the diagram is that it allows the researcher to work through an argument with the help of images rather than cognitively (for example, Larkin and Simon 1987). It can also make you understand an extremely difficult argument very easily, as the Feynman diagram shows. In brief, a diagram facilitates thinking. It also seems that some people prefer to think with the help of diagrams.

For heuristic reasons, you may also try to draw a path diagram at an early stage of the research. By the simple procedure of representing the variables as nodes, and using arrows to connect the nodes, you can quickly try out different ideas and see how the variables are interconnected (for example, Firebaugh 2008: 15).

Charles S. Peirce greatly appreciated the use of diagrams in logic and also saw them as very helpful in developing new ideas. In one of his writings, he says that

> Diagrams have constantly been used in logic, from the time of Aristotle; and no difficult reasoning can be performed without them. Algebra has its formulae, which are sort of diagrams. And what are these diagrams for? They are to make experiments upon. The results of these experiments are often quite surprising. Who would guess beforehand that the square of the hypotenuse of a right-angled triangle was equal to the sum of the square of the legs. . . . All reasoning is experimentation and all experimentation is reasoning. (Peirce 2010: 24)

The diagram also favors heuristic thinking in that you do not know where you will end up when you start constructing a diagram and work your way through it. You just have to trust that somewhere along the way you will find what you are looking for. In this sense a diagram is similar to a model, at least to a model in its early stage.

But the model also has some features that the diagram lacks. This is a topic that will be discussed in the next chapter, which is devoted to the very last stage in building out the theory: coming up with an explanation.

## CHAPTER 5

# Coming Up with an Explanation

*Abduction* [or explanation] is the only kind of
reasoning which supplies new ideas, the only
kind which is, in this sense, synthetic.

—Charles S. Peirce, "Reasoning"[1]

The focus of this chapter is on how to come up with an explanation, not on the nature of explanation. The latter topic is of great
importance, extends well beyond the social sciences, and has resulted in a huge and difficult literature that is well worth studying in its own right. How to come up with a good explanation *in
practical terms*, and from the perspective of the person who is
doing the analysis, is less often discussed.

An explanation represents the natural goal of theorizing and
completes the process of building out the theory. This means
that the explanation is a very special part of the process of theorizing. For Peirce and many others, the basic value of a theory is
mainly to be found in its explanatory quality.

As a consequence it is important to push ahead when one theorizes during the prestudy and not stop before a tentative explanation has been produced. This explanation should be as solid as
possible, so that it can become part of the research design and constitute the basis for hypotheses (or their equivalents) that will be
tested in the main study. It is also common to work through a
number of possible explanations before the right one can be located.

Having said this, the following should be added. In some cases the theorizing process should be seen as successful even if you fail to come up with an explanation. Sometimes just seeing and/ or clearly identifying a phenomenon represents an important step forward. The same is true for coming up with a new concept, an interesting typology, and so on.

Some phenomena can also be more difficult to discover than to explain. Charisma and anomie are two examples of this; women's work is another. In each of these cases, there exist today huge research literatures and many rival explanations. But the most difficult thing was to identify and "see" the phenomenon in the first place.

It should also be pointed out that an explanation consists of two parts: (A) what should be explained, and (B) how to explain it. One can sometimes be misled to think that an explanation is exclusively about an explanation (B), but this is not the case. Without a clearly formulated A (*explanandum*), there will be no B (*explanans*).

At this point the reader should be reminded that what in everyday language is referred to with one name often turns out to cover several phenomena when it is studied carefully (chapter 3). A preconception operates in this sense like an umbrella term. This also means that one of these phenomena typically has to be selected and singled out for explanation, while the others are ignored.

The phenomenon that needs to be explained must be constructed out of the material from the observation, while irrelevant material is removed. Again, an example from Weber may help to clarify things. When a boulder falls down and splinters, the individual pieces will scatter in many directions. To study where each and every one of these splinters land plus how they are shaped is not of scientific interest. Instead you want to carefully construct what should be explained. In this particular case that would typically be the general trajectory of the boulder as caused by certain forces (Weber 2012: 42–43).

What matters for the social scientist is also to come up with explanations of *social* phenomena. This does not mean that one should divide explanations into two categories: those that can be used only in the natural sciences and those that can be used only in the social sciences.

A quick look at the type of explanations that have yielded important results in the social sciences shows that several of these have come from the natural sciences. Explanations often travel between the sciences, just like methods. They are sometimes borrowed when they produce new and interesting results, and ignored when they do not.

But the social sciences also have a special focus of their own—to explain social life—and this means that they study some phenomena that are different from those that the natural sciences are concerned with. What makes them different are primarily three items. First, the meanings with which the actors invest their actions often play a role in what happens. Second, the reality that social scientists study changes in ways that nature does not. And third, social scientists may influence what they study by being part of it. While this may also be the case in the natural sciences, it is of less importance there.

Granted that it is crucial for anyone who theorizes to come up with a good explanation, how can you train yourself to become good at this? In this chapter I will suggest two answers. The first is that you need to train your capacity to guess, and especially to guess right, as Peirce puts it. The second answer is that it is useful to know many different types of explanation when you are looking for an explanation.

## Abduction in the Form of Guessing Right

While Peirce is primarily known today as one of the founders of pragmatism, in this chapter I will look at his notion of *abduction*, or his theory of how to come up with an explanation from the practical perspective of the scientist. The reader will recall from the introduction that Peirce had trained his own capacity in this regard, and that he exercised it in his everyday life as well as in his scientific work.

With a bit of exaggeration one can say that figuring out the way in which scientists come up with new explanations constitutes *the* major theme in the research that Peirce pursued throughout his life. In any case Peirce deserves to be seen as a major figure in the history of explanation, and especially in the history of how to come up with an explanation from the practical perspective of the scientist.

"Abduction," Peirce writes, "is the process of forming an explanatory hypothesis" (Peirce 1934a: 171–72). As this quote illustrates, the emphasis is not only on the explanation but also on *the process of coming up with an explanation or how to get there.*

To Peirce, the explanation that comes from an abduction is just a possible explanation, never the final one. "Abduction merely suggests that something may be" (Peirce 1934a: 171–72). Until an explanation has been tested, he always insisted, its value will be uncertain.

What has been said so far about Peirce's concept of abduction is pretty basic and noncontroversial. From this point on, however, the complexity of this concept and what it refers to rapidly increases. One reason for this is that Peirce's thought evolved over time, with certain ideas being added, while others fell away or were changed.

Another reason for the complexity of Peirce's thought is that he felt that he was entering a totally new territory with abduction and that he needed to try out his ideas in different directions. I am "an explorer upon untrodden ground," as he once said when he discussed his work on abduction (Peirce 1932: 102).

Linked to this last reason is also the density and obscurity with which Peirce wrote. He viewed everything as related to everything else in the cosmology that he developed, and this made a special demand not only on his thought but also on his way of writing. Throughout his life he struggled hard to express his ideas in a clear way, but often with uneven result.

For all of these reasons Peirce's writings on abduction represent a challenge and have attracted a large number of interpretations (for example, Fann 1970; Paavola 2006). Nonetheless, very few of his commentators have been interested in the practical aspects of abduction or how you can increase your capacity for creative thinking, according to Peirce.

The term *abduction*, according to Peirce, comes from Aristotle, who used it in his logic. A translator, however, failed to interpret Aristotle correctly and chose a different term, *reduction* (for example, Ross 1949: 489).

But let us start from the beginning. When Peirce first began to use the word *abduction* instead of *reduction*, he saw it as a technical term in logic. In his later work he broadened its meaning to also cover the process of coming up with a scientific explanation.

Besides *abduction*, Peirce used several other terms for how the scientist proceeds in order to produce an explanation. One of these is *colligation*, a term coined by William Whewell that means linking facts together in a new way when you make a discovery. In Peirce's work one can also find the term *retroduction*, a word that reminds us that to explain a phenomenon means to look at what comes before the phenomenon.

*Hypothesis* is another term that Peirce used in this context. It emphasizes that an abduction is just a suggestion for an explanation, and that the explanation has to be tested against facts before it can acquire scientific value.

*Guessing*, finally, indicates that the scientist does not know how to proceed when he or she is looking for an explanation, but must somehow do so anyway. And *guessing right* indicates that the scientist is more often correct than you would think, given the fact that there exist an infinite number of theories that could explain any one phenomenon.

Peirce's theory of how to come up with an explanation acquires further complexity from the ambitious nature of his scientific projects. Sometimes he approached abduction from the viewpoint of pragmatism, at other times from his theory of semiotics. As mentioned earlier there also exists a link between abduction and Peirce's theory of cosmology.

In the appendix to this book the reader will find a presentation of how Peirce viewed the theorizing process in general, and the role of abduction in this. Here I shall instead focus on a neglected dimension of abduction. What I am referring to is Peirce's theory of abduction as a theory of *guessing* and *guessing right*, and especially how you can improve this capacity.

While Peirce at times spoke of abduction as something that just comes to you, like "a flash of insight" or "the bursting out of the startling conjecture," he typically viewed it as a process (Peirce 1934a: 181; 1935: 469). Coming up with an explanation was not the same as coming up with *the* explanation.

An abduction is "an act of *insight*, although of extremely fallible insight" (Peirce 1934a: 181). The scientist should try to guess at an explanation, but also be aware that most abductions or guesses are wrong. You guess, and you hope that you are right.

What especially fascinated Peirce with guessing was that it drew on some of the most mysterious qualities of the human mind. These had to do with the fact that scientists had guessed right so many times over the centuries, much more often than if chance alone had been involved. Any phenomenon could in Peirce's view be explained in any number of ways—so how come that scientists so often had gotten it right?

As the reader may recall, this issue was touched upon in the introduction to this book, in which the strange story was told of how Peirce retrieved some stolen items in the summer of 1879. In his article "Guessing," as well as in some other writings, Peirce also addressed the following issues: where does the remarkable power of guessing come from, and how can one improve one's capacity to guess right?

The answer to the first question is that Peirce, like Galileo, believed that human beings are born with a *Lume Naturale,* and that it is this natural light that allows them to divine some of the secrets of nature.

This light, Peirce also thought, was similar to the kind of instincts that animals are born with. Just as the chicken knows from birth what to pick up from the ground to eat, so human beings have an inborn capacity to somehow, and after many trials, come up with the right answer to scientific questions.

The reason for this remarkable capacity, Peirce believed, is that the skills human beings need to have in order to feed themselves and to reproduce themselves somehow also makes it possible for them to understand certain things that they otherwise would not be able to do.

Human beings, in brief, are part of nature and can therefore also sense its workings. "Nature and the mind have such a community as to impart to our guesses a tendency toward the truth, while at the same time they require the confirmation of empirical science" (Peirce 1992: xxv).

Exactly how this instinct for the truth and coming up with explanations works was unclear to Peirce. At one point, he suggested that what accounts for the progress in science is roughly the same as what accounts for the survival of certain individuals, according to Darwin. In other words, the abductions of a scientist can be viewed as equivalent to the individuals who make up each successive generation of a species in Darwin's theory. The hypotheses that have been able to withstand rigorous tests are the ones that have "survived" and that then became "the parents" of the next generation of hypotheses.

If this argument is correct, as Peirce believed it was, the question of how to become good at coming up with explanations has to do with becoming good at a certain type of guessing. You somehow have to learn to sharpen the capacity you are born with to come up with explanations.

The first step in this process is to become a specialist in whatever science you have chosen. Becoming good at guessing as a scientist is only possible, according to Peirce, if you are well prepared.

Another way for the scientist to sharpen his or her skill at guessing is to realize that you have a capacity to somehow guess right. Human beings, just as animals, have many more mental powers than they are aware of:

Animals of all races rise far above the general level of their intelligence in those performances that are their proper function, such as flying and nest-building for ordinary birds; and what is man's function if it be not to embody general ideas in art-creations, in utilities, and above all in theoretical cognition? To give the lie to his own consciousness of divining the reasons of phenomena would be as silly in a man as it would be for a fledgling bird to refuse to trust its wings and leave the nest, because the poor little thing had read Babinet [the French physicist], and judged areostation to be impossible on hydrodynamical grounds. (Peirce 1998: 443)

When you try to come up with an explanation, it is crucial to relax and let your subconscious do its job. If you try to push things and concentrate too hard on a problem, the result is not going to be good. "My own experience," Peirce writes in "Guessing," "is that self-consciousness, and especially conscious effort, are apt to carry me to the verge of idiocy, and that those things that I have done spontaneously were the best done" (Peirce 1929: 280).

Peirce was eager to show that his ideas about guessing were not idiosyncratic but perfectly sensible. As mentioned in the introduction, at Johns Hopkins he carried out an experiment to find out under which conditions people are good at guessing right and found that it had to do with people's subconscious (Peirce and Jastrow 1885). The practical conclusion that follows from this is that you somehow have to open up your conscious mind to your subconscious, so that you can access some of its contents.

At the time no one followed up on Peirce's experimental work on guessing. Today, however, the situation is different, and cognitive psychologists are likely to look at Peirce's ideas about guessing as perfectly natural. And as this research develops, it will be important to try to translate its insights into practical advice.

## The Many Types of Explanations and the Means of Approaching These

If being good at guessing and abduction represents one way of coming up with an explanation, knowing a number of different types of explanations represents another. Again, you need to be able to come up with a number of explanations in order to find the most adequate one.

Wittgenstein once noted that the problem with emphasizing causality is that it makes you think there exists only one explanation, when in fact there may be many. He writes,

> The insidious thing about the causal point of view is that it leads us to say: "of course, it had to happen that way." Whereas we ought to think: it may have happened like that—and also in many other ways. (Wittgenstein 1980: 37e)

Knowing many different ways of establishing causality makes it easier to break with the idea that the first explanation or the first type of explanation is the right one.

There exists a multitude of different types of explanations, from the ones that are used in everyday life to those that have been invented by scientists in various disciplines (for example, Lombrozo 2012). Everyday language has many words that are used to describe that something causes something else, and these can serve as an inspiration to think about the explanation of some phenomenon in new ways. "Causes," according to a political scientist, "bring, throw, hurl, propel, lead, drag, pull, push, drive, tear, thrust, or fling the world into new circumstances" (Brady 2008: 223).

The idea that an explanation always has to be directed at some person is also helpful in this context. In the formulation of a sociologist, "[an] explanation is a social relationship between people in which some phenomenon is explained to some person so they understand it.... A explains B to C" (Martin 2011: 333).

This is also true for scientific explanations, and again the emphasis should be on the plural, since there exist many different approaches here as well. As Weber, for example, points out: "The form in which the category of causality is employed by the various disciplines is quite different" (Weber 1975: 195).

Another authority, Ernest Nagel, distinguishes between four general types of explanation: genetic (historical) explanations, functional explanations, probabilistic explanations, and deductive explanations (Nagel 1961: 25ff.). Of these four, it is clear that today's social scientists find functionalist explanations unacceptable. While this may be a sound stance to take, there is also the heuristic argument. According to Weber (who was very interested in this type of questions), functionalist analyses are in principle "highly dangerous"—but also "indispensable" at an early stage of the analysis (Weber 1978: 15).

But there exist many more ways of explaining something than Nagel's four categories. This is especially the case if one broadens the category of explanation to also include the means through which you come up with an explanation. While these two—explanations and the means through which you can come up with an explanation—are in principle distinct, when you are searching for an explanation, they tend to come together.

## Experiment, Comparison, and Counterfactual

The experiment constitutes the archetype for how to produce an explanation, and its use in the different social sciences has increased quite a bit during the last decade (Jackson and Cox 2013). According to Weber, the experiment represents "the second great tool of scientific work," with the concept being the first (Weber 1946: 141). What makes the experiment so useful are two features: intervention and control. You add something, and you follow its effect under controlled conditions.

Social scientists often use short experiments, as in social or cognitive psychology. In the natural sciences, in contrast, experiments are often very long. In both the social and the natural sciences, however, one experiment is usually not enough. It is only through repeated experiments that a new piece of knowledge can be fully established. This means among other things that the topic of replication should be seen as part of the explanation (for example, Young 2009; Lucas et al. 2013).

Many first published findings in science are wrong, and there are many reasons for this (for example, Ionnadis 2005). One is that it is often not possible to rule out alternative theories just through one or a few experiments. A phenomenon can always be explained in a number of ways, and it takes time to go through and reject the various candidates.

This is where the so-called crucial experiment comes into the picture (for example, Lakatos 1974). This can be described as a very special type of experiment, constructed in such a way that it can decisively determine that one theory or hypothesis is correct and that alternative theories are wrong.

To carefully fashion the explanation also in social science in such a way that it can address different theories and eliminate all but one is crucial for the formulation of a solid theory. It is also something that has to be done, whether you work with an experiment or address a problem in some other way.

To go through and reject alternative theories is a necessary part of theorizing in social science, but it can only be done in a thorough and fully satisfying way in the main study. At the stage of early theorizing, however, to look at alternative theories also has a heuristic function. In casting around for alternative theories to explain some phenomena, you may find out something else about the phenomenon you are studying.

There also exist so-called thought experiments, in which the researcher plays out the experiment in his or her mind. These have been used as early as Galileo and also by philosophers, as illustrated by Rousseau's *Emile* and John Rawls's notion of *veil of ignorance*.

*Simulation* can be said to represent a modern version of the thought experiment and has by now been used in most of the social sciences. The value of simulations for establishing empirical proof in social science is debated. Perhaps, as Duncan Watts has noted, their main value is heuristic:

> Computer simulations are useful tools that can generate great insight. But in the end they are more like thought experiments, and as such are better suited to provoking new questions than to answering them. (Watts 2011: 98)

While control is one of the advantages with an experiment, the history of science also includes many examples when it was precisely the lack of control in an experiment that was decisive. A famous example of this is how Alexander Fleming discovered penicillin. By mistake Fleming let some cultures in his laboratory be contaminated by a fungus, and it was this that triggered his insight.

Robert K. Merton was fascinated by this type of accidental discoveries, a phenomenon he called "serendipity" (for example, Merton 1968: 157–65). He did not, however, think that serendipity was something you could cultivate. It is not as if you can court accidents. If you are lucky, you are lucky—that is all.

Also Herbert Simon has argued that the lack of control in experiments can lead to discoveries, but in a different way from Merton. According to Simon, ill-designed experiments can play a constructive role in science and there should be more of these.

In reflecting on the many experiments he himself had carried out during his career, Simon wrote in his autobiography:

> The experiments described up to this point all compare performance under two or more different conditions, by manipulating an independent variable. When I examine

my other experimental research, I find to my embarrassment that this fundamental condition for sound experimentation is seldom met. What have I been up to? What can I possibly have learned from ill-designed experiments? The answer (it surprised me) is that you can test theoretical models without contrasting an experiment with a control condition. And apart from testing models, you can often make surprising observations that give you ideas for new or improved models. (Simon 1991a: 383)

A bit further along in the book, Simon adds the following to his argument that it is not always necessary to control for something to make an experiment useful:

If the methodology troubles us, it may be comforting to recall that detailed longitudinal analysis of the behavior of a single solar system was the foundation stone for Kepler's laws, and ultimately for Newton's. Perhaps it is not our methodology that needs revising so much as the standard textbooks on methodology, which perversely warn us against running an experiment until precise hypotheses have been formulated and experimental and control conditions defined. Perhaps we need to add to the textbooks a chapter, or several chapters, describing how basic scientific discoveries can be made by observing the world intently, in the laboratory or outside it, with controls or without them, heavy with hypotheses or innocent of them. (Simon 1991a: 385)

The idea of using a *comparison* to come up with an explanation can be seen as a version of the experiment or, more precisely, as something that should be used when an experiment is not possible. Durkheim, who argued along these lines, called the comparison "an indirect experiment" (Durkheim 1966: 125).

To imitate the logic of an experiment as much as possible is something that many social scientists besides Durkheim have done. One may even speak of a continuum of sorts, all the way from the natural experiment over the field experiment, to the metaphorical use of the laboratory as in the notion of the city as a "social laboratory" (for example, Park 1929). The very logic of how to reach an explanation in social science may also mirror the attempt to compensate for the absence of the conditions that are necessary to carry out an experiment according to the books. A classic example of this can be found in the work of John Stuart Mill on causality, as adapted for use in modern social science. The way that social scientists use the method of difference, the method of concomitant variations, and so on, have their origin in this type of argument.

It is known today that there exist several problems with Mill's view of causality, and especially modern political scientists, who specialize in comparative politics, have contributed to the sophisticated use of comparisons in coming up with an explanation (for example, Box-Steffenmeier et al. 2008). Some of these insights have been transmitted to sociology via James Mahoney, who in the process has added many interesting ideas of his own (for example, Goertz and Mahoney 2012).

But a comparison cannot be used only to establish and examine the difference between two cases; it can also be used to establish similarities, and in this way help to produce an explanation. In sociology this is a common way to advance to an explanation, with Simmel being one of its masters.

To divide and conquer, for example, is a strategy that has been used in very different types of activities (for example, Simmel 1950: 162–69). And according to Everett C. Hughes, to cite another example, there exist interesting similarities between prostitutes and psychiatrists, in that both must be careful not to become too involved with their clients and their intimate problems (Hughes 1984b: 316).

Another tool, which similarly can be used to produce an explanation, and also for heuristic purposes, is the *counterfactual*. Like the comparison, it has been used in a number of sciences, all in somewhat different ways that are instructive to know about. Cognitive psychologists, for example, use counterfactuals, and so do political scientists, philosophers, historians, economists, and sociologists.

The counterfactual may at first glance look very much like an experiment. You begin with one state of things, but instead of adding something in order to see what will happen, you reverse the process and remove some factor that you think is important.

To look at a counterfactual as being similar to an experiment, in the sense that in the experiment you so to speak turn the key clockwise and in a counterfactual exercise, counterclockwise, has proved useful. It informs, for example, David Lewis's philosophical theory of counterfactuals (Lewis 1973). Via Lewis, this idea has also influenced statistical methods in social science (for example, Brady 2008).

What this way of thinking misses, however, is something that is clearly related to the existential condition of human beings. This is that you can only advance forward in historical time, not backward. The two movements are not the same.

This fact is one reason for the many interesting issues that the counterfactual raises. These range all the way from existential questions to questions of causality—and sometimes a mixture of both.

For an illustration of how the counterfactual can be used in social science to come up with an explanation, one can refer to Max Weber's ideas on the topic of "objective possibility" (his term for counterfactuals; Weber 1978: 10–11; 2012: 169–84). I will briefly summarize Weber's approach since it is not very much known outside of sociology.

According to Weber, counterfactuals represent a form of "imaginary experiments" and only make sense on the assumption that human actions are voluntary and not deterministic. Why would we bother about what to do, he asks, if our actions were determined? Being human means that there always exist different possibilities for how to act.

You construct a counterfactual, Weber says, in two steps. You begin by singling out the factor you think is of strategic value (say, factor X). This is called *isolation*. You then look at the remaining factors and determine if these add up to a *general rule of experience* (Weber 2012: 175). If this is the case, the counterfactual analysis can be carried out with a positive conclusion. The reason for this is that if factor X had been absent, the result would in all likelihood have been different.

Using Weber's model for how to proceed can lead to new perspectives. New insights can also be generated by taking a close look at the three examples that Weber uses to illustrate his ideas about counterfactuals.

The first is Bismarck's decision in 1866 to go to war. Since this started the process of German unification, the counterfactual question is: would Germany have united if Bismarck had not made this decision in 1866?

The second example is the Battle of Marathon, which took place in 490 BCE. If the Persians had won, they would have imposed their authoritarian culture on the Greek city states. The counterfactual is: what would Western culture have looked like if the Athenians had lost the Battle of Marathon?

Weber's third example is not historical but hypothetical. Assume that a young mother gets irritated and slaps her child. If she had not been irritated, would she have slapped the child?

Just by working through each of these three examples, you can get a sense for how a counterfactual can raise new questions, make the researcher look for new empirical material, and the like. To this can be added that while the well-known case of Bismarck and the unification of Germany fits the historical standard example of what-would-have-happened-*if*, the other two cases expand the current notion of the counterfactual in some interesting ways. The Battle of Marathon is not so much about a counterfactual historical event as about counterfactual historical culture. And the case of the irritated mother is about a counterfactual micro-event.

One can also argue that the Weberian approach to counterfactuals helps us to realize an interesting quality about counterfactuals in general. This is that they make us confront our intuitive feeling that what happened in some way *had* to happen. "Outcome knowledge," to cite two political scientists, "contaminates our understanding of the past" and may lead to "the creeping determinism" of hindsight (Tetlock and Belkin 1996: 15).

In sum, backward reasoning and forward reasoning when it comes to explanations should be the same thing, but they are not. Backward reasoning, in the form of a counterfactual, opens up new ways of looking at what has happened and why, and cannot be replaced by experiments or comparisons.

## Meaning, Statistics, and Social Mechanisms

It was earlier mentioned that the social sciences, as opposed to the natural sciences, need to be able to deal with meaning; and this also has some consequences for the way that explanations are constructed in social science. The first sustained attempt in sociology to insert meaning directly into the explanation was made by Max Weber in *Economy and Society*. Since he was very careful in his argument, it is instructive to see how he went about this task.

The basic role that meaning plays in a sociological explanation, according to Weber, is as follows (Weber 1978: 4). The meaning with which an actor invests his or her action (the typical actor, not an individual) is *not* the same as that which explains what happens. It is, however, one of the factors that does this.

As social action develops, the actions of many actors have to be taken into account in order to explain what is happening, and these other actors typically invest their actions with different meanings. There are clashes of actions and unintended consequences of social actions as well. The meaning of the individual actor, to repeat, is just one of the many reasons why some social action unfolds as it does.

Weber also suggests that two conditions have to be fulfilled in order for a social science explanation, which takes meaning into account, to be valid. The first is that there is a natural fit between the meaning and the action that accompanies it ("adequacy on the level of meaning"; Weber 1978: 11).

If the actor, for example, intends to greet another person, and walks toward this person with an extended hand, there is a natural fit between the meaning and the action. If the actor who intends to greet the other person instead turns around, sits down, or does something else that is unusual, there is no adequacy on the level of meaning.

Second, what the actor does should also have the intended effect, based on what usually happens in cases of this type ("causal adequacy"; Weber 1978: 11–12). If someone approaches you with an extended hand, and this is what the beginning of a handshake looks like, the action is causally adequate.

At this point of his argument Weber returns to the counterfactual model that was discussed earlier, and which is based on his writings on the philosophy of science. In *Economy and Society* the counterfactual argument is quickly summarized in the following way. One way of establishing causality is with the help of an "imaginary example" (Weber 1978: 10). The way you do this, the reader is told, is by "thinking away certain elements of a chain of motivation and working out the course of action which would then probably ensue, thus arriving at a causal judgment."

Weber also supplies his readers with a heuristic rule for how to come up with an explanation quickly. This is to start the analysis with the assumption that the actors behave in a rational way and then compare their actions to what happens in reality. If some discrepancy appears, Weber says, it must be accounted for through empirical research (Weber 1978: 6).

In Weber's model for how to include the element of meaning in a sociological explanation, statistics and probability enter in two ways. First, a causally adequate action is not deterministic; only probability is involved. Second, no exact probabilities can be established, since probability theory cannot be directly applied to social life, according to Weber. But just as loaded dice will tend to oscillate around certain values, depending on how much extra weight is involved and where the weight is located, so will this type of action (Weber 2012: 180–81).

Let me now leave Weber but stay with the topic of statistics. Even if the type of statistics that is used in mainstream social science today does not explicitly address the issue of meaning, it can be very helpful when you try to tease out a new explanation.

For obvious reasons, statistics is often indispensable when you construct an explanation (for example, Woodward 2009). The fact that statistics is probabilistic in nature and not deterministic also opens up statistics to analyses of meaning. The way that modern content analysis has developed illustrates this (but also see Biernacki 2012).

Just as Herbert Simon advocates the use of sloppy and hastily put together experiments, a quick-and-dirty analysis of a data set that is not in very good shape may still be of help in coming up with fresh ideas for an explanation. Simple correlations can similarly inspire to new ideas, even if they may not help to determine how two phenomena are related. It is, for example, generally acknowledged that democracy and economic development tend to go together, even if the exact relationship between the two is still unclear.

Some advocates of Big Data argue that correlation will soon replace causation and that the question of *what* will replace the question of *why* (for example, Mayer-Schönberger and Cukier 2013). While this seems doubtful, what we do know so far about Big Data is that very interesting and suggestive studies can be carried out with the help of correlation. Rather than interpret this as a sign that causation will soon become superfluous and that "the end of theory" is in sight, it can be seen as another indication of the heuristic potential of correlation (for example, Anderson 2008).

In modern statistics you essentially trace the effects of a cause, rather than try to find out what caused some special effect, which is how qualitative social scientists proceed. Just like in a counterfactual the exercise of going back and forth through an example can help to shake things up and make it possible to see things in a new light.

The current enthusiasm in some quarters for the idea of social mechanisms has much to do with the feeling that it is hard to explain what happens exclusively in terms of variables and correlations (for example, Hedström and Swedberg 1998). The very notion of mechanism also allows you to cast the cause as a process, something that is the sign of a sophisticated explanation (for example, Lave and March 1993: 40–41).

Just as we can literally see how a mechanism operates—say how a cogwheel locks into another cogwheel and makes it rotate—so many social scientists ideally want to be able to link the cause to the effect in an organic way in their analyses. The whole thing is in other words a bit like what Weber felt about Chicago, which he visited during his American trip in 1904. Looking at the city, he said, was like seeing "a man whose skin has been peeled off and whose intestines are seen at work" (Weber 1975: 286).

It can be added that the same ambition of seeing how cause and effect are linked together in a transparent manner is also behind the approach known as *process-tracing* (for example, Beach and Pedersen 2013). The word *process-tracing* lacks the attractive imagery of the mechanism, but the idea of conceptualizing the cause in terms of a process is similar.

## Models and More

There exist many other ways of coming up with an explanation than the ones that have been discussed so far. In such areas as law and medicine, for example, a number of interesting approaches to explanation have been developed over the centuries (for example, Hart and Honoré 1958; Groopman 2007).

More generally, there is also the *model*, or the attempt to construct an explanation with the help of formalization. Models are typically used in many of the explanations that have already been discussed, but they also deserve a discussion of their own.

At the stage of discovery, models tend to be more intuitive and less worked out than at the stage of justification. Still, one advantage of using a formal model when you theorize is that the assumptions are made explicit. Another is that models are economical, and a third, that they allow you to see all the consequences of making certain assumptions—including novel and surprising ones (for example, Chomsky 2004).

Models essentially reconstruct something *as if* it had happened in a specific way. In social science this means two things: much of the material that comes with close observation is disregarded, and an abstract process is postulated. According to one philosopher, models are "speculative instruments" (Black 1962: 237). As does a wedding, they bring together "disparate subjects." They also "reveal new relationships" and, "as with other weddings, their outcomes are unpredictable" (Black 1962: 237).

Stephen Toulmin, another philosopher, describes the advantages of using models as follows: "It is in fact a great virtue of a good model that it does suggest further questions, taking us beyond the phenomenon from which we began, and tempts us to formulate hypotheses which turn out to be experimentally fertile. . . . Certainly it is this suggestiveness, and systematic deployability, that makes a good model something more than a simple metaphor" (Black 1962: 239).

A quick mention should also be made of James Coleman's notion of sometimes-true theories when models are discussed (Coleman 1964: 516–19; cf. Cartwright 2011). There exist many complex social phenomena, according to Coleman, that cannot be captured in a single theory. By varying the conditions under which these phenomena exist, however, you can produce several models which are all true. They are all true *sometimes*— that is, under certain specified circumstances.

Coleman draws the following conclusion from this:

This term "model" . . . seems to have come into use precisely to characterize these sometimes-true theories. The term "theory" has the connotations of being ultimately true or false, while it is precisely characteristic of these sometimes-true theories or models that they are neither true nor false. (Coleman 1968: 518)

You can, however, also look at sometimes-true theories in a different way. You can use the strategy of varying the conditions for the model to be true as a way of figuring out what would be the best way to explain some phenomena. Maybe the sometimes-true theories will remain "models," but they may also turn into a "theory," in Coleman's terminology. Before you have studied some phenomenon, it is hard to know.

But even after you have come up with a satisfactory explanation during the prestudy, some tasks remain to be done. One is to see whether it is possible to expand the explanation also to other phenomena. Another is to make a quick check that some typical error has not been made.

The value of the explanation you end up with often increases if it can also be used to explain a number of other phenomena; and this is where generalization once more comes into the picture. The general rule is that the more phenomena that can be explained, the better the explanation. The more different these phenomena are, the more elegant the explanation also is. In social science this last point often means that while the structural element is the same, the content differs. The notion of structural equivalence in network theory is an example of this.

The reason for the check that some error has not been made is simple. Since a prestudy is not conducted according to reliable rules, the chance of making errors is much higher than in the main study. This goes for all of its stages, from observation to the tentative explanation.

Some useful information on what kind of errors to look for in the case of the explanation can be found in a field known as the *cognitive psychology of explanation.* Its main focus is the way that people come up with explanations and what these explanations look like. One of its insights is that people ever since childhood continuously generate explanations, as part of their attempt to understand things. This means, among other things, that they tend to produce explanations when there is nothing to explain.

People also tend to make systematic mistakes when there is a legitimate need for an explanation. Simple explanations, for example, are typically seen as more probable than complex ones. A cause that can explain several observations, is typically viewed as more probable and valuable than one that can only account for one observation. Adding a detail also tends to make an explanation more believable (Lombrozo 2006, 2007, 2012; Watts 2011: 132).

Some other errors that are often made during the prestudy will be discussed in chapter 6. I have nonetheless included a list of potential errors here, to make clear that checking for errors should be regarded as an integral part of the prestudy.

---

### A Checklist for Possible Errors in Early Theorizing

1. RELIANCE ON PRECONCEPTIONS OR COMMON SENSE
   What you "know" to be true may not be true.

2. BIAS FOR INDIVIDUAL VERSUS SOCIAL EXPLANATIONS
   It is easier to focus on the motives and interests of the individual than to think in terms of social emergence and social structure. Compare fundamental attribution error or the tendency to wrongly attribute the effects of the context to the individual.

3. SAMPLING BIAS
   It is easy to look only at what is interesting and in other ways introduce bias into the sample.

4. BIAS FOR SIMPLE EXPLANATIONS

A bias for simple explanations exists, at the expense of complex explanations.

5. CREEPING DETERMINISM

Despite a realization that the actors view the future as uncertain, it is easy to see what happens as inevitable.

6. AVAILABILITY BIAS

The ease with which something comes to mind influences your general view of something.

7. ANCHORING BIAS

Your view of some phenomenon is influenced by your starting point.

8. REPRESENTATIVENESS BIAS

Judgments are often based on a stereotype.

9. AFFECTUAL BIAS

Your emotional view of something affects your understanding of it.

10. THE HALO EFFECT

Your basic approach to something influences the way you view all of its aspects.

11. THE FALLACY OF COMPOSITION

What is true for a part is not true for the whole.

12. CONFIRMATION BIAS

You test only one and typically your favored hypothesis.

*Source*: For items 1 through 5, see, for example, Duncan Watts, *Everything Is Obvious* (2011); and for items 6 through 10, see, for example, Daniel Kahneman, *Thinking, Fast and Slow* (2011).

PART 2

Preparing for Theorizing

## CHAPTER 6

# Heuristics

> Anything is right that leads to the right idea.
>
> —Georg Polya, *How to Solve It* [1]

So far in this book it has been argued that you can learn to theorize by following certain steps: you observe, try to name the phenomenon, and so on. The time has now come to add that there is more to theorizing than this. You also need to develop a special skill in theorizing and you need to have some knowledge of theory in social science.

In the next few chapters I will try to show how this can be accomplished. In this chapter I will look at a useful tool for helping you to theorize in a practical way—namely, heuristics. In the next chapter, the focus will shift to practical exercises. The remaining three chapters will deal with such topics as what kind of social theory is useful to know, and how to train your imagination in dealing with it.

## The Importance of Heuristics for Theorizing

That taking a heuristic stance can be very useful has already been mentioned. When you theorize, it has been argued, you should not only use the individual steps to move forward—to create a

concept, a typology, and so on—but also to try to discover something new about the phenomenon you study.

But there is more to the topic of discovery than so. It is very
important to more generally take a heuristic stance when you
theorize. It is also very helpful to develop your own personal set
of heuristic rules.

The heuristic stance, or the attitude that theorizing is about
discovery, is to some extent inherent in the decision to theorize
in the first place. You constantly theorize in everyday life. Every
situation is somewhat different from all the others, and this
means that you quickly and instinctively have to adjust, improvise,
and try something that is a bit new in order to move forward.
When you theorize in social science this is even more the case.

And just as you soon develop a number of rules for how to handle new situations in everyday life, you will do the same when you
theorize. This chapter is about making this process more conscious, so you can develop your own personal set of heuristic rules.

A discussion of these and related questions can be found in a
special literature, which has its beginnings in antiquity but
which has flourished especially after World War II. The heuristics
literature was originally about natural science and philosophy,
but today it also includes social science.

For those who want to become good at theorizing, it is helpful
to know something about this literature. It raises questions that
go all the way from how very creative scientists have approached
problem-solving to the way that ordinary people tend to make
decisions in their everyday lives.

## A Modern Heuristics

The word *heuristics* has many meanings, something that is important to keep in mind when you discuss heuristics in relation to

theorizing. What you need, in all brevity, is a kind of heuristics that allows you to theorize well.

The most common interpretation of the word *heuristics* is that it means "discovery" and that it has its origin in a well-known episode in the life of Archimedes. Having solved a particularly difficult problem Archimedes ran through the streets of Syracuse, shouting "Eureka!" or "I have found it!" This supposedly took place around 250 BCE, as first reported two centuries later by Vitruvius (for example, Biello 2006).

But the word *heuristics* has other meanings as well. While some of the literature on heuristics is about making important discoveries along the lines of Archimedes, there also exists another and more recent branch that has a much more modest aim. This type of heuristics essentially tries to teach the average student, and not the potential star scientist, to develop an independent approach to solving problems. It is mainly this type of heuristics that will be discussed in this chapter; and I will try to show its relevance for theorizing in social science.

One way of looking at heuristics and the various forms it has taken over the years is to see it as being situated somewhere between two poles. One of these has to do with creativity, while the other is more about moving on, in your actions and in your analyses. While old-fashioned heuristics is close to the former pole and modern heuristics to the latter, they have each elements of both.

The transformation of heuristics from being the art of great discoveries to a modest tool for helping students with problem-solving is largely thanks to George Polya (1887–1985), a Hungarian-born mathematician and author of the classic *How to Solve It* (1945). Beginning in the early 1940s and keeping at it for several decades, Polya developed what he called a "modern heuristics," by which he meant a heuristics that was practical in nature and modest in scope.

Polya was mainly interested in mathematics, which means that his work is of extra interest to social scientists who use and/ or teach quantitative methods. It was especially the process leading up to the solution of a problem that fascinated Polya, "mathematics in the making" as he called it (Polya 1954: vii).

But there also exist many important aspects of Polya's work that speak to the nonmathematical social scientist. One of these is his interest in developing a general and everyday kind of heuristics:

> A great discovery solves a great problem but there is a grain of discovery in the solution of any problem. Your problem may be modest; but it challenges your curiosity and brings into play your inventive faculties, and if you solve it by your own means, you may experience the tension and enjoy the triumph of discovery. Such experiences at a susceptible age may create a taste for mental work and leave their imprint on mind and character for a lifetime. (Polya 1954: v)

Another aspect of Polya's work that is important to social scientists is his emphasis on the way that "heuristic reasoning," as he calls it, can be taught to the average student. It is primarily through practice and imitation, he says, that this can be accomplished:

> Solving problems is a practical skill like, let us say, swimming. We acquire any practical skill by imitation and practice. Trying to swim, you imitate what other people do with their hands and feet to keep their heads above water, and, finally, you learn to swim by practicing swimming. Trying to solve problems, you have to observe and to imitate what other people do when solving problems and, finally, you learn to do problems by doing them. (Polya 1954: 4–5)

According to Polya, there exist no specific heuristic rules, in the sense of rules that will lead to the solution of a problem if they are followed. What does exist, however, are certain "mental operations" that can help you to move in the right direction, and which can be taught to students (for example, Polya 1954: 171). These mental operations turn into useful "mental habits" after being used for a while (Polya 1954: 21).

Problem solving, Polya suggested, is essentially a process that can be approached in four steps. He also recommended that students ask three questions when they try to solve a problem.

The four steps are as follows:

1. You have to understand the problem.
2. You need to make a plan to solve it.
3. You have to carry out the plan.
4. After having solved a problem, you should look back at the solution and analyze how you went about it.

(Polya 1954: 5–23)

The first three steps—trying to understand a problem, making a plan for how to solve it, and following the plan—may or may not be useful for social scientists to keep in mind when they do research. Of special interest to theorizers, however, is step 4—namely, the need to go back and review the way in which you came up with the solution to a problem. By trying to figure out what you did right, you may be able to turn your hunch into a skill.

The three questions that Polya wants students to memorize and to think about when they try to solve a problem are the following:

1. What is unknown?
2. What are the data?
3. What are the conditions?

He has also provided a number of examples to illustrate how these questions can be of help.

In one of these examples the task is to find the diagonal of a rectangular parallelepiped, where the length, width, and height are not known (Polya 1954: 7–14). This means that the *unknown*, or what we are looking for, is the length of the diagonal (question 1). The *data* are the length, width, and height of the parallelepiped (a, b, and c; question 2). The *conditions* are sufficient to determine the solution in that if we know a, b, and c, we will also know the diagonal (question 3).

Translated into social science, you could say that it is always important to know what is unknown—that is, what you do not know. The same goes for what Polya says about the data. What is more problematic is the assumption that there exists one correct solution to every problem, at least when you try to say something new and move into unknown territory.

Polya also suggests that if the three questions do not help you to come up with a solution, you should try to approach the problem by circling around it, rather than attack it head on. Maybe there exists a similar problem that has already been solved? Only extremely talented people, according to Polya, can solve a problem that is unique. You can also try to use analogies, add to the problem, divide the problem into parts, recompose the parts, and so on (for example, Polya 1954: 116).

All of these tips are useful for the social scientist as well. It is also clear that you have to have a solid knowledge of your own discipline in order to know if any similar problems exist and how these have been solved. And since the different social sciences often deal with the same topics or problems, knowledge of what has been accomplished in the other social sciences can be helpful as well.

Polya also points out that there is an emotional aspect to problem solving, and that it is important to tap into one's subconscious (for example, Polya 1954: 93–94). When you are stuck and do not have the energy to work with the original problem any longer, switching to a related and similar problem allows you to deal with something that feels new and fresh. Sleeping may also sort things out in your mind and help you to come up with a solution.

It is always imperative to try to generate new ideas, Polya adds, because without ideas there will be no solution. It does not matter if the idea is small or confused, as long as you have one. He writes:

You should be grateful for all new ideas, also for the lesser ones, also for the hazy ones, also for the supplementary ideas adding some precision to a hazy one, or attempting the correction of a less fortunate one. Even if you do not have any appreciably new ideas for a while you should be grateful if your conception of the problem becomes more complete or more coherent, more homogenous or better balanced. (Polya 1954: 35)

It is finally important to train yourself in guessing and become "a good guesser" (Polya 1954: iv). Guessing is an integral part of heuristic reasoning and it should be taught as part of the instruction in mathematics. "Let Us Teach Guessing," as Polya called one of his articles (Polya 1950).

But not all guesses are useful:

[Only] guesses of a certain kind deserve to be examined and taken seriously: those which occur to us after we have attentively considered and really understood a problem in which we are genuinely interested. Such guesses usually contain at least a fragment of the truth although, of course, they very seldom show the whole truth. Yet there is a chance to

extract the whole truth if we examine such a guess appro-
priately. (Polya 1954: 99)

To this should be added that the bottom line for guesses is the
same for Polya as for everything else that is produced through
heuristic reasoning. This is that guessing is very useful in suggest-
ing an idea, but that an idea is not the same as a proof. "Heuristic
reasoning is good in itself. What is bad is to mix up heuristic reasoning with proof" (Polya 1954: 113).

## Social Science Heuristics

Polya's notion that heuristics is more about ordinary problem
solving than about making great discoveries has become popular
over the years. Herbert Simon is one of those who picked up on
this idea and developed it for his own purposes. Since Simon's
ideas on this topic have been quite influential, they deserve a
brief discussion.

Simon disliked concepts such as creativity and discovery,
which to his mind smelled of metaphysics. In his view they
should be replaced by the notion of problem solving and the
idea that you solve problems by following certain rules. "Discovery is plain, garden-variety of problem solving," as he famously
put it (Simon 1991b: 369).

Simon also thought that one could program machines to solve
problems and spent quite a bit of energy on this enterprise in the
1960s. Many others who were interested in artificial intelligence
around this time also worked along similar lines, before it was
realized that it was a dead end (for example, Dreyfus and Dreyfus
1986).

But even if the attempt to eliminate discovery and creativity
by devising special rules for problem solving turned out to be a

failure, you can learn quite a bit from Simon's way of approaching problems. There is also the fact that Simon, as it turned out, had one set of official rules for problem solving and another set for his personal use.

One of Simon's collaborators has outlined some of his personal rules (Langley 2004). One is to be bold and attack problems that others do not want to touch, because they are too large and difficult. Another is to find a "secret weapon" in the form of a metaphor or method that other social scientists do not know about. It is also important, according to Simon, to just push ahead and not be a perfectionist. "Anything worth doing is worth doing badly," as he used to say (Langley 2004: 5).

Polya's idea of developing a kind of manual for how to solve problems has also inspired some works in the social sciences. In sociology, there exist today two well-known books in this genre: Howard Becker's *Tricks of the Trade: How to Think about Your Research while You're Doing It* (1998), and Andrew Abbott's *Methods of Discovery: Heuristics for the Social Sciences* (2004).

The emphasis in Becker's book is on providing a number of practical tips ("tricks") that may help the student to conduct research and also to move on in the analysis when he or she gets stuck. The focus in Abbott's book is on encouraging students to realize that in order to say something new or worthwhile, they have to come up with a different approach to some problem (a "move," in Abbott's terminology). Both books are aimed at undergraduates, but can also be used in graduate courses.

Abbott's book is divided into two parts, one about social science in general and the other about heuristics. In the first part the reader is introduced to the different types of explanation that can be found in the social sciences, such as standard causal analysis, historical narration, and ethnography. This is followed by a chapter on the central debates in the social sciences, such as positivism versus interpretivism, individualism versus emer-gentism, behaviorism versus culturalism, and a few more.

According to Abbott, you should start your research with a puzzle and then try to solve it. A precondition for doing this in a creative way is that you have a broad knowledge of the main ar-guments in social science, including the main debates that are going on. This is what part 1 of his book takes care of.

In part 2 on heuristics Abbott presents a number of different types of heuristics, from what he calls "routine heuristics of nor-mal social science" to "fractal heuristics." In routine heuristics you just add a new variable or the like, along the lines of Kuhn's normal science. In fractal heuristics you make use of Mandel-brot's idea that certain patterns are repeated when you go from a smaller scale to a larger scale and vice versa.

Abbott illustrates the idea of fractal heuristics with examples from his chapter on major social science debates. When you take a close look at the advocates of say positivism, in the debate of positivism versus interpretivism, you will find that they also re-produce this opposition within themselves. Some positivists are "soft," while others are "hard."

In order to give the reader a sense for Abbott's take on heuris-tics, I have put together a list of the different types of methods of discovery that can be found in his book. Each of these suggests its own set of moves.

Abbott's book is very interesting and contains several memo-rable passages. Take for example his description of how he came up with an idea for a paper on boundaries he was working on:

> Boundaries and boundary crossing had become very fash-ionable, so I was bored with the idea. "Boundaries, bound-aries of things, of boundaries of things," I sang to myself in the shower one day. Suddenly the commas moved, and I had the phrase "things of boundaries." What could that

---

## Abbott's Heuristics for the Social Sciences

THE ROUTINE HEURISTICS OF NORMAL SCIENCE
   Adding a new variable or the like

SEARCH HEURISTICS
   Making an analogy
   Borrowing a method

ARGUMENT HEURISTICS
   Problematizing the obvious
   Making a reversal
   Making an assumption
   Reconceptualizing

DESCRIPTIVE HEURISTICS
   Changing context
   Changing levels
   Setting conditions: lumping and splitting

NARRATIVE HEURISTICS
   Stopping and putting in motion
   Taking and leaving contingency
   Analyzing latent functions
   Analyzing counterfactuals

FRACTAL HEURISTICS
   Repeating the structure

*Source*: Andrew Abbott, *Methods of Discovery: Heuristics for the Social Sciences* (2004).

---

mean? I puzzled over it (after I got out of the shower) and tried to give it a real sense. Maybe social things like professions (groups I have spent much of my life studying) are "created" out of boundaries. The edges come first, then the thing. (Abbott 2004: 128; for the paper on boundaries, see Abbott 1995)

Howard Becker's *Tricks of the Trade* is organized very differently from most books on heuristics. The author describes the sociological research process in general terms, and while doing so he also mentions various tricks that can be useful to know when you conduct your own research.

Becker was a student of Everett C. Hughes and deeply influenced by his approach to sociology. In some ways *Tricks of the Trade* can be seen as an attempt to present Hughes's way of doing sociology to a general public.

Hughes was very suspicious of abstract theory; and so is Becker. Theory is something you learn by conducting research, Becker says, and when you confront the problems that emerge in this process. A trick is what allows you to solve a problem in your research and to proceed.

As opposed to many works on heuristics Becker clearly wants to stay away from providing formal rules for how to conduct research, and his tricks are presented in a casual way. Many of the tricks come from Hughes, even if Becker has also come up with some tricks of his own.

Hughes, for example, used to give his students the following advice: "Doubt everything anyone in power tells you" (Becker 1998: 91). Another of his tricks was to see all social phenomena as essentially relational in nature.

An ethnic group, for example, is not just a collection of individuals who share some objective feature, such as being, say, of German or Italian origin. It is instead a number of people who view themselves as having something in common and who are also viewed by others in this way:

> An ethnic group is not one because of the degree of measurable or observable difference from other groups; it is an ethnic group, on the contrary, because the people in and the people out of it know that it is one; because both the

*ins* and the *outs* talk, feel, and act as it were a separate group. (Becker 1998: 2)

But an ethnic group is not only constituted by the people on the inside and on the outside. It is also defined through its relation to other groups:

> It takes more than one ethnic group to make ethnic relations. The relations can no more be understood by studying one or the other of the groups than can a chemical combination by the study of one element only, or a boxing bout by the observation of only one of the fighters. (Becker 1998: 2)

It is clear from the works by Abbott and Becker that one can take the idea of heuristics of the Polya type and use it in a fruitful way also in social science. Abbott's book illustrates that some thumb rules can be developed for social science research in general. Becker's book does something similar, but mainly for one type of social research—namely, fieldwork.

One weakness of both works, from the perspective of this book, is that neither fully addresses the issue of a heuristic for *theorizing*. A precondition for heuristics of this type, I argue, is that a separate and independent space is allotted for theorizing. You also need to focus squarely on theory and how to construct a theory. In Abbott's book the main focus is on getting ideas for your research ("moves"). Becker, as we soon shall see, is not very interested in theory at all.

Abbott's notion of getting an idea does have something in common with theorizing, but the two are not identical. While theorizing is a process that starts with observation and ends with an explanation, in *Methods of Discovery* Abbott is mainly concerned with how you come up with an idea. This does not allow the author to address the very special problems that theorizing poses.

But in a later conference speech, titled "Andrew Abbott's Short List of Rules for Theorizing," Abbott does precisely this and argues, for example, that when it comes to theorizing, observation is absolutely necessary:

> Most of them [the classics in sociology] were in fact data-heads, awash in facts and data. They tended to invent theory to make sense of the data in front of them. Moreover, they changed their theories as they went along and the data posed new questions. Bourdieu's perpetual rewriting of the habitus concept is a good example . . . ALL THEORY WORTH READING ARISES FROM REFLECTION ABOUT DATA. Write this phrase on your computer. Paste it on the bathroom mirror. Mention it softly while making love. "All theory worth reading arises from reflection about data." (Abbott 2011: 2, 7)

If we now turn to Becker, it is clear that *Tricks of the Trade* displays a certain ambivalence to theory. For one thing, theory has a tendency to be subsumed under research methods and is not assigned an independent place in the research process.

The reader also gets the impression that theory is something you just come up with when you do your field research, while studying theory and theorizing is pretty much a waste of time. In brief Becker's approach is close to what is known as *grounded theory* (Glaser and Strauss 1967; for a critique, see, for example, Tavory and Timmerman 2012).

When asked to participate in a conference on theorizing that the author organized in 2012, Becker answered that he unfortunately could not attend, and added:

You know that I would probably say something about "theory being a necessary evil" and all that. I've come increasingly, too, to think of theory and methods really being the same thing. In the sense that every theory implies the methods you would have to use to implement the theory in research. And every method implies the theory that underlies it. Hughes implemented this idea all the time, without perhaps writing much about it. (Becker 2011)

It should be made clear that Becker himself is a brilliant theoretician and that he has made a number of important contributions to social and sociological theory (for example, Becker 1973; 1982). The point here, to repeat, is a different one—namely, that Becker does not assign theory much of an independent place in the research process and also that he tends to conflate it with methods.

## Heuristics as Shortcuts

To complete this introduction to heuristics and its relevance for learning the art of theorizing in social science the time has now come to examine the work of Amos Tversky and Daniel Kahneman. The study of heuristics turned in yet another direction in the 1970s, as a result of their pioneering article "Judgments under Uncertainty: Heuristics and Biases."

While heuristics of the Polya type had dealt with solving problems and coming up with ideas, Tversky and Kahneman were primarily interested in a different topic: how decisions are made in situations of uncertainty. What they found was that people took mental shortcuts and tended to follow "heuristic rules" when they were in this type of situation (Tversky and Kahneman 1974: 1124).

If one of the two poles of heuristics is creativity and the other is simply moving ahead in the analysis, it is clear that the research of Tversky and Kahneman is very close to the latter. They were interested not in creativity but, to repeat, in the ways in which people make up their mind in situations when it is not clear how to proceed.

What especially fascinated Tversky and Kahneman, however, was not so much the mental shortcuts that people take as the mistakes that come with following certain rules for making decisions. In their article from 1974 they singled out three such heuristic rules, all of which have their own specific bias. They gave the rules the following names: *availability, anchoring*, and *representativeness*.

The weakness or possible bias of basing a decision on availability is that you rely on what most easily comes to mind. The weakness in basing it on anchoring is that different starting points lead to different decisions. And basing your decision on representativeness assumes that your cognitive stereotypes are correct.

The Tversky-Kahneman approach to heuristics soon became very popular and has led to an avalanche of studies as well as a Nobel Prize. When Kahneman recently summarized the findings of this type of work, in *Thinking, Fast and Slow* (2011), he also added some new heuristic rules and the errors that come with these.

Several of these new heuristic rules have to do with emotions. If you are positive or negative to something, this may influence your judgment and spill over to all of the aspects of the phenomenon you are dealing with. Another new rule is that people tend to generalize on the basis of very few observations. They also often find patterns and create stories where none exist.

In Kahneman's view, people tend to think in two modes: quickly and intuitively, on the one hand, and slowly and deliberately, on the other (system 1 and system 2). Intuitive thinking often leads to errors and needs to be corrected with the help of deliberate thinking. An exception of sorts is the kind of intuition that experts develop. The reason for this is that the intuition of experts has developed over time and also been tempered by experience (Kahneman 2011: 234–44).

Is the Tversky-Kahneman take on heuristics of value also for theorizing in social science? My answer is yes, but in a different way from the work by Polya and his followers. The work of Tversky and Kahneman does not help the social scientist to come up with good ideas, as Polya's work does, but it does help him or her to check for certain mistakes. As mentioned in chapter 5, this is important since theorizing during the stage of the prestudy is prone to errors.

It can be useful for someone who is theorizing to go down the list of typical errors that Kahneman discusses in *Thinking, Fast and Slow* and check each off. Have some facts been assigned a key place just because they first came to mind? Has the general attitude of the analyst to some phenomenon unduly influenced his or her analysis?

At this point the reader may want to look again at the sidebar in chapter 5, which contains a checklist for possible errors during the prestudy. Note that not only the factual material that has been collected in the prestudy needs to be confronted with the type of errors that Tversky and Kahneman have investigated, but also the theoretical approach that is being used. Concepts, typologies, theories—all of these are susceptible to errors of the availability type, the anchoring type, and so on.

While the Tversky-Kahneman approach to heuristics has resulted in a number of important and useful insights for theorizing, it is probably also true that the picture of thinking that can be found in Kahneman's recent book is wanting in some respects.

This is especially true for the idea that thinking is either fast and often wrong, or slow and mainly correct.

As already mentioned Kahneman says that the intuition of experts does not fit his general schedule of fast versus slow thinking. It is also a fact that while intuition is fast, once it occurs, to trigger it and make it possible in the first place, you typically need a long period of slow thinking and research (for example, Knorr Cetina 2014).

There is also some new and intriguing research in cognitive science that does not fit Kahneman's argument. According to a recent study, for example, people tend to be more creative when they are tired than when they are alert. The reason for this is that they cannot remember everything that they normally would (Wieth and Zachs 2011). In brief some complexity needs to be added to the notion of slow versus fast thinking.


### Develop Your Own Heuristic Rules!

The works by Abbott and Becker are very useful for a number of reasons, not least since they contain many interesting heuristic rules. By reading these works you also get a good sense for what a heuristic rule in social science looks like, something that makes it easier to develop your own.

This last point is important because what matters when you theorize is not so much to have access to a number of interesting heuristic rules that others have developed. These are often instructive, fun to read, and good to know. But what is much more important is to develop a set of heuristic rules of your own making, which help *you* to theorize (for example, Koedinger and Roll 2012: 791–93). Books in heuristics should in other words be used for inspiration, but what they advocate should not be copied.

By way of example of this do-it-yourself heuristics, I will mention my own rules. They have come into being over the years, and they help me to move forward when I try to theorize:

> *Do what others don't.* Many things in social theory are predictable, which means that others will figure them out too—so I try to pick another angle.
> *Use your subconscious.* To come up with something good I know that I somehow have to access what is deep down in my being.
> *Don't stop too early.* When I have a good idea, I don't stop. Instead I try to push ahead as much as possible—and eventually end up with many new ideas.
> *Don't get lost in language.* It is easy for me to get lost in formulations when I theorize, so I try to argue while skipping over troublesome words and concepts.

My heuristic rules are all quite general in nature, since I have found that when I try to use precise rules, they usually lead to a mechanical kind of thinking. While some of my rules are cognitive in nature, others are difficult to articulate and more instinctive. While both are necessary, the latter are ultimately more important in my view.

......................................................

## CHAPTER 7

# Practical Exercises

> Work on philosophy—like work in architecture in many
> respects—is really more work on oneself. On one's own
> conception. On how one sees things. (And what one
> expects of them.)
>
> —Ludwig Wittgenstein, *Culture and Value*[1]

Work on philosophy, according to Wittgenstein, is work on one-self. He also says that it is the same with work in architecture, and one is tempted to add work in theorizing. One reason for this is that you can theorize well in social science only if you acquire a new way of thinking, a new set of mental habits.

What Wittgenstein says is applicable not only to the situation when a person tries to learn how to theorize in social science but also when you try to teach others to theorize. The students have to be willing to "work on themselves"—and they have to be given an opportunity to do so.

The goal of exercises in theorizing is to help students to become skilled in theorizing and to acquire confidence in their skill. It is a skill that draws on a practical know-how of how to theorize, in combination with knowledge of social science. What this latter knowledge consists of will be discussed in the next chapter. For now the focus will be on the topic of exercises which can help to develop a practical know-how of theorizing.

The exercises that will be discussed in this chapter are of two types: those that the reader can do himself/herself, and those that can be used to teach theorizing to students. The two are linked to each other; it is also very important to start changing the way that students are taught theory in social science.

Currently, established exercises in theorizing do not exist, especially of the type that will be advocated in this book. What does exist, however, is a small number of suggestive exercises that have been developed by social scientists interested in their students doing creative work. I will begin by presenting some of these that have been developed by Charles Lave and James G. March in their book on the use of models in the social sciences. I will also say something about a different approach to theorizing that has been used by Diego Gambetta in his classes at Oxford.

## Some Existing Exercises

In *An Introduction to Models in the Social Sciences* (1975), which can be described as a sophisticated textbook, Lave and March set about to teach the reader how to construct theories and models in the social sciences. Their book, they say, should be seen as "a practical guide to speculation" (Lave and March 1993: 2). "We think that playing with ideas is fun. . . . We think that an interest in the quality of speculation both in the social sciences and in everyday life would be good" (Lave and March 1993: 3).

In separate chapters Lave and March introduce the reader of their book to a number of theories in social science, such as individual decision making, exchange, and diffusion. Throughout the book they also suggest ways for the reader to engage with these theories and learn to use them for his or her own purposes.

Concrete problems are provided in each chapter; and the reader is encouraged to stop reading when he or she comes across these and try to solve them. At these places in the text, there are statements of the following type, in big bold letters: STOP AND THINK.

To give a sense of the problems that Lave and March use, I will present one of their best-known examples. This is: why are football players in college considered dumb? The reader is encouraged to come up with possible reasons for this, and create models based on these.

The authors suggest, for example, that one reason why college athletes are considered dumb may be that they do not have much time to study, since they spend most of the day on their sports. Another reason could be that people who are successful in one area of life are less interested in excelling also in another one. Or maybe people are just jealous of those who are successful and therefore call them dumb. The reader is also encouraged to try to figure out how to discriminate between the various theories.

While the book by Lave and March is excellent in many respects, it is also clear that its approach to theorizing differs especially on one point from the perspective advocated here. This is that Lave and March do not emphasize that it is necessary for the students to do some empirical research on the topic they are interested in before they start to theorize it (cf. chapter 2).

Instead Lave and March suggest that the students start from the common notion that football players on campus are often regarded as dumb and then try to figure out why this is the case. The emphasis, in other words, is on training the students to come up with a number of hypotheses and how to discriminate between these.

This, however, means that the current view of some topic is taken for granted, something that is always dangerous and brings us back to Durkheim's preconceptions (*prénotions*). Let us stay with the example of the football players. Could the reason why these are considered dumb perhaps be that athletes tend to live together on campus and create a collective culture that devalues studying? Maybe there are other reasons as well? Perhaps yes, perhaps no—but how would we know, unless we study the phenomenon empirically?

Diego Gambetta has taken another approach to the teaching of theorizing than Lave and March. In the classes on sociological theory that he has been conducting at Oxford since the 1990s, he has let the students start out from a particularly striking empirical puzzle. The basic idea is that this will jolt them into trying to theorize and conduct interesting research.

A puzzle is defined by Gambetta as "a correlation, which defies the expectations of common sense or the predictions of some theory" (Gambetta no date: 1). Some, but by no means all, of the puzzles he uses in his classes are of social importance.

Many of the puzzles that Gambetta lists as having used in his class are definitely thought-provoking and interesting; and one can easily see how they can inspire students to do research and engage in creative theorizing. To let the reader enjoy Gambetta's inventiveness, I have included a short list of some of the topics he has used in his "puzzle class."

It is my impression that Gambetta's way of teaching his puzzle class has been quite successful. It has helped the students to realize that they should theorize themselves and that this activity should be linked to serious empirical work.

One additional point I would like to make, however, has to do with Gambetta's idea of presenting the students with puzzles. The fact that students have not invented or even discovered these puzzles themselves does not encourage independence. Nor are the students explicitly taught how to theorize and develop a skill in such specific tasks as naming, handling concepts, coming up with an explanation, and so on.

---

### Puzzles from Diego Gambetta's Class

Why is the suicide rate higher in Scotland than in England?
Why are women better investors than men?
Why do teenagers in Britain drink more than most other European teenagers?
Why do more people file for divorce after the holidays?
Why are wives of unemployed men more likely to be unemployed than wives of employed men?
Why do science students live longer than art students?
Why are theology books more frequently stolen from libraries than books on other subjects?

*Source*: Diego Gambetta, "Empirical Puzzles" (no date).

---

## Exercises in Theorizing for Small Classes of Students

As already mentioned there exists a definite need for exercises in theorizing, while little material of this type is currently available. We need answers to questions such as the following: Can you teach theorizing by lecturing or should you do it with the help of practical exercises? Should you teach theorizing together with social theory or should the two be taught separately? How do you teach theorizing to a small number of students of students versus a large number of students? What are the differences between teaching theorizing to graduate students and undergraduate students?

Hopefully many people will soon begin to teach classes in theorizing, and hopefully they will share their experiences. Because of the current lack of material, however, I will describe how I have taught theorizing myself and what exercises I have used. I will also describe an interesting experiment in teaching theorizing to undergraduates in sociology that has gone on since the 1990s.

Over the last few years I have taught graduate seminars in theorizing at Cornell University and two other universities with which I am affiliated. The number of students has typically been small, and each session has lasted for two to three hours.

During the first hour I have lectured on theorizing, leaving time for questions and discussion. This has been followed by a break and a session in which the students present the results of their exercises in theorizing. During the second hour I try to say very little, and if I say something it is mainly to encourage the students to speak up.

During the first hour I have tried to lecture on each of the stages of the theorizing cycle and on related topics. This means that I have talked about the need to begin the theorizing process by observing something in a broad but nonsystematic manner, to then name the phenomenon, and so on. Once this has been done I have talked about such topics as memory, imagination, and intuition and why knowing some cognitive science is useful for theorizing.

I have sometimes also mixed the teaching of theorizing with lecturing on theory during the first hour. In these cases I have started out the course by explaining what theorizing is all about and also argued that if you are interested in theorizing, you will want to read works in theory from a different perspective than what is usually done. What is said in the text is always of interest, but you also want to know how the author got to that point and what you can learn from this.

My general impression is that both of these approaches work fairly well. Which of them is preferable, I have also found, depends to some extent on how much sociological theory the students know. Many students take only one course in theory during their graduate education, and when this is the case, giving them some knowledge of theory and theorizing at the same time is necessary.

The second hour of the class, when I teach theorizing, is devoted to a discussion of practical exercises. I try to follow the principle that all students must get a chance to speak, and that all should get the same amount of time. The students typically use their allotted time to speak about their exercises—what they have come up with, and what happened when they tried to carry out the exercise.

I have experimented with two different types of exercises in theorizing. Both of them have been take-home exercises, with one for each meeting of the course. I have by now come to the conclusion that the first of my two types of exercises was not very good. I will nonetheless describe it, to give a sense of what I tried to accomplish.

The first type of exercise I experimented with had as its goal to teach the students how to carry out the full cycle of theorizing, all the way from selecting a topic to coming up with a tentative explanation. If the students were to do this repeatedly during the course, I thought, they would get the gist of it and soon be able to theorize on their own.

The first task when you theorize, I argued to myself, is to come up with a topic you are really interested in and for which you have some kind of affinity. But how can this be done in an exercise? My answer was the following. Why not let the students read an inspiring article and pick something that they think is really interesting. Once they have done this, they should try to explore this topic with the help of free association.

The purpose of making the students use the technique of free association was to make them develop their topics in new and creative directions. They should also feel free, I told them, to change their topic if they come across something more interesting in the process. In thinking about topic X, they might start thinking about Y—and end up with topic Z.

Once they had settled on a topic for good, the students were told that they should try to name it, develop some concepts, and so on. They should continue with this all the way until they had come up with a tentative explanation. I told the students that it is often hard to complete the full cycle of theorizing, and that they might not always be able to get to the stage of providing an explanation.

Another reason for having the students repeatedly engage in free association during the course was to make them aware that they can use certain ways of thinking that they normally would not associate with theory to become better at theorizing. It was also a way to make them focus squarely on themselves, and realize how creative they can be.

The texts I had chosen were social science texts that I thought were full of ideas and therefore would be inspiring. Some of the texts I used were the following: "Body Techniques," by Marcel Mauss; "Sociology of the Senses," by Georg Simmel; and "Lyrical Sociology," by Andrew Abbott.

Occasionally I would also let the students read texts by poets and philosophers, and the reason for this was that I wanted them to realize that work in these two genres can be very inspiring for social scientists. For philosophy I used Kant's "What Is Enlightenment?" For poetry I relied on the work of Emily Dickinson, and poems such as "Remembrance has a rear and front" and "The heart asks pleasure first."

After having taught theorizing in this way for a while, however, I began to realize that the idea of using an inspiring text to help the students select a topic to theorize from had one serious weakness. This was that it did not teach the students the importance of empirical observation. Related to this, there was not much for them to theorize about, except the text itself and what they already knew.

The idea of engaging in free association appealed to the students because it made them feel that they could be creative, and that they had a source of creativity within themselves that they could draw on. Still, it was no substitute for observation. I also noticed that the students tended to select topics that they already had some knowledge of; and this finally made me realize that it would be better if I somehow could include the stage of observation into the exercise.

As a result I have now changed the initial part of the exercise, and today I ask the students to select a topic they are interested in but have not already worked on. My reason for having them select a totally new topic is that several students have told me that they feel freer to theorize when they are not already familiar with a topic.

The students are also told to quickly research the topic they have chosen, and that they can use whatever source they think can teach them something about the topic. Since time is short, one way of doing the research is to use the Internet, with its many different types of material. Alternatively, a few interviews can be conducted, perhaps in combination with introspection or self-observation and a physical inspection of the research site.

After having done mini-observations of this type, the students will proceed, as in the first version of this exercise, to give a name to the phenomenon they have chosen, develop concepts related to it, and suggest an explanation. As they work their way through each of these stages, I tell them that they should use their concepts, types, and so on also for heuristic purposes, and that the technique of free association can be helpful in this.

Since I still think that it is important for the students to run through the full cycle of theorizing a few times, I assign the students three of these exercises during the course of a term. This means in practice that each cycle is allotted three weeks or three meetings (in a three-semester system).

During week one, a topic is chosen and observed. During week two, it is named, and concepts plus perhaps a typology are developed. During week three, an effort is made to come up with an explanation.

My experience from teaching classes according to this schedule is that this works pretty well. But people also sometimes get stuck at stage two or extend the stage of observation into stage two. My response to this is to emphasize that the initial effort should always be to go from observation over concept formation and the like to an explanation—but also that things may end up a bit differently.

In the most recent class that I taught at Cornell (spring 2013) some of the students felt strongly that it was too much to both come up with a topic and make observations at stage one. They preferred to come up with a topic at stage one. At stage two they would do a second, more focused empirical search plus share their ideas about concepts and the like with others in the class. I have not yet decided if I should make any changes in response to this.

During each meeting in class the students report on what they have done. In preparation for this, and also as a way to record their thoughts, they have been instructed to write down how they have proceeded, using one to two pages. I give no instructions for how these notes should be written, since I want the students to develop their own capacity to record what they consider important about their attempts to theorize and what these have led to.

The notes are not to be handed in or in some other way approved or disapproved by the teacher; they are exclusively for the use of the students. I do not want the students to feel that the teacher is standing behind them when they write their notes, whispering in their ear that this is excellent, this is not so great, and the like.

Besides these weekly tasks, the students also have to write a paper about their experience, which I describe to them as a kind of autoethnography in theorizing. In this paper the students are to record how they have tried to theorize during the course, what they think has been successful, and what they did not do so well. The papers, I say, should be ten to twenty pages long.

The students are told to comment on each of the exercises during the course in their papers. They are also told that they can include excerpts from their written notes, since it is important to be able to document how they went about things at the moment when they tried to theorize. This represents an attempt from my side to draw on Polya's suggestion that it is helpful to study how you went about solving a problem after it has been done.

The papers I have received in these courses are among the most interesting and alive student papers I have ever read. My general impression is also that the students really like that the focus of the course is squarely on them, on how each of them has as a task to develop their own capacity to theorize.

The positive response that I have had to these courses shows, in my view, that they answer to a deeply felt need among the students to learn theory in a new way, one that focuses on how to theorize in practice and not just on the content of various theories. In a few cases I have also been able to follow the work of the students after they have taken a course in theorizing; and it is my impression that the course has been helpful for them in their later work.

## Practical Exercises in Theorizing for Large Classes

I have never tried to teach theorizing to undergraduates, mainly because I have not been able to figure out a way to do this effectively. When I teach theorizing I feel that it is necessary to focus on every student and let every student speak, and the classes with undergraduates usually have far too many students for this approach.

How then would you go about teaching theorizing to a large class? For one thing it is clear that undergraduates are very interested in theories and conceptualizations. According to a recent survey by the American Sociological Association (ASA), for example, "interesting concepts" constitute the number one reason why students want to major in sociology (ASA 2013: 4). One way to make students interested in theorizing, in other words, might be to assign an important role to concepts in the teaching.

In thinking about the problem of how to teach theorizing to a large class of undergraduates, I have also come across one attempt to do this. It took place in the 1990s and was made by Jane Rinehart, who has described her experience in an article in *Teaching Sociology* (Rinehart 1999). Rinehart's approach has also been successfully used at another university several years later (McDuff 2012).

Rinehart works at Gonzaga University, which is a small private university. Her teaching philosophy is inspired by the theory of collective learning, and she describes her educational approach as a form of collaborative theorizing.

The way she taught collaborative theorizing in the 1990s is as follows. The students in her classes on classical sociological theory usually consisted of seniors and were about twenty to thirty in number. The students were divided into small groups, typically together with students they did not know very well.

For each class every student was given an individual task to prepare; these were then discussed in the group. The group later reported its conclusions to the whole class, where more discussion took place.

The course began with a class exercise called "Everyone Theorizes." Its theme was that "we are all theorists," and some exercises were conducted to make the students realize that they themselves "theorize" what is around them—but also that they have to become conscious of this and better at it. The examples in the exercises included such items as drug use, eating disorders, and business fraud.

This is also where the classics—Marx, Weber, and so on—come into the picture. According to Rinehart, it is important for the students not only to know the content of their works but also how these were produced. As she puts it,

> It is most important here to break the spell of the theory as a product, which masks its production. I want students to move away from treating major theories as static "things" and toward a sense that a theory is composed of moves—this way instead of that way—that each theorist makes and justifies. I want them to understand these moves, the reasons for them, and their consequences. Emphasizing choices transforms theories into actions. (Rinehart 1999: 222)

The way that the students were taught to lay bare the moves of Marx and others was as follows. They were told that you can get a better handle on the way that someone theorizes by studying his or her ideas with the help of a paradigm. For each of the classics the students were therefore told to produce a paradigm, which summed up the key ideas of Marx, Weber, and so on, as well as the ideas they opposed. By proceeding in this way, Rinehart explains, it would be easier for the students to draw on the classics when they analyzed some concrete topic.

As mentioned earlier, Rinehart's approach to teaching theorizing has also been used more recently, by Elaine McDuff at Truman State University (McDuff 2012). Again the result was positive. The students lost their initial fear of "theory," and felt at the end of the course that they were able to theorize a bit on their own.

Something worth mentioning also happened when McDuff wanted to link theorizing closer to verification. In one of her courses she tried not only to teach the students how to theorize but also to take the step from theorizing to the testing of hypotheses.

The result, however, was negative:

> I found that encouraging students to narrow their focus from general theorizing to hypothesis testing early in the semester reduced their interest in learning to think theoretically. Instead of seeing theorizing as an inherently valuable activity, they were learning that theory has value only in relation to a set of narrowly focused scientific goals. (McDuff 2012: 173)

As a result of the criticism by the students, McDuff removed the part with hypotheses testing from her course in theorizing. Remembering that students had earlier said that it would be great if they could be taught how to theorize everyday problems, she now also included some new reading of this type. The result, she says, was very positive, and the comments of the students suggested an "even greater confidence in their ability to 'think theoretically'" (McDuff 2012: 174).

In my view, Rinehart is correct in starting from the notion that students, like people in common, engage in "theorizing" in their everyday lives. I also think that the attempt to teach the classics in a new way and to confront the fear of "theory" is excellent.

Perhaps it would also be helpful to teach the students something about the parts that make up a theory. Knowing what constitutes a concept, an explanation, and so on is essential if you want to understand what a theory is and how you go about constructing one.

You could also ask the students to deconstruct a theory into its different parts. This could be done with texts by Marx, Weber, and so on, and by proceeding in this way the students would also get a sense for what it takes to create a full theory.

I would also try to have some exercises that would be aimed at the individual student rather than the group. Just like you cannot learn how to swim or bike as a group, you need to learn how to theorize yourself. This is not a task that someone else can do for you.

## The Need for New Exercises in Theorizing

More generally it seems to me that we also need to experiment with different kinds of exercises that can help students to learn how to theorize in social science. This goes for exercises aimed at graduate students as well as undergraduates.

Besides the exercises that have been described in this chapter, one can easily imagine a number of other ones. Some of these would aim at having students produce full theories, in the spirit of do-it-yourself theory and that you do not have to be Max Weber to create a theory.

It should also be possible to develop exercises for each of the elements in the cycle of theorizing. This would mean exercises for how to become better at observation, create concepts, make comparisons, come up with an explanation, and so on.

By way of illustration, let me suggest two simple exercises that have as their aim to teach students to become better at developing social forms and using metaphors. In order to learn how to create a social form, one can present students with a set of, say, three phenomena, and ask them to try to come up with a social form based on these.

Here are three such sets, two from existing research and one that has been made up for this occasion:

boarding schools—ships—prisons
playing soccer—praying—giving away money
bishop—osteopath—salesclerk in a clothing store[2]

As to developing a skill in using metaphors, I have often found it useful myself to proceed in the following way. Take some topic you are interested in and then choose something else to compare it with. Assume you are interested in firms. Take the notion of a firm and compare it to, say, a house, a tree, and a song. See where this takes you.

What you find when you engage in this type of exercises is that you will come up with a lot of strange ideas, some of which are useful and others not. You will surprise yourself.

You will also find that even if the exercise is about finding a good metaphor or a social form, you may get ideas on a host of other topics that can be very useful. You may, for example, get some inspiration for how to produce a new concept, a new typology, a new explanation, and so on. Theorizing is often a kind of spill-over activity.

It should also be possible to use so-called think-aloud protocols (TAPs) in theorizing exercises. This type of method was developed by Herbert Simon and a colleague as a way of using subjective data in a more objective way (for example, Ericsson and Simon 1993). According to Simon, these protocols are very helpful and can be used for a number of purposes. For one thing, they inspired Simon himself to develop his theory of problem solving (Simon 1991b: 384–85).

In TAPs the subjects usually describe what they are thinking as they perform an assigned task. They may, for example, have been given a problem to solve. What they think, as they go about the task, is then recorded and studied (for an example, see Nersessian 2008: 61–90).

It seems to me that this procedure can also be used for theorizing. You can, for example, speak aloud as you carry out some exercise on the suggestion of a teacher or when you try to theorize some data of your own. What you say can, for example, be recorded on your smartphone and then transcribed and studied.

This also represents a way to get a better handle on what you are actually doing when you are theorizing. It encourages a better knowledge of yourself, even if it is heavily dependent on quickly and accurately verbalizing what is going through your mind. It should also be made clear that it is not possible to tap into the tacit knowledge that is part of the theorizing process.

An exercise that I have found useful for making students learn social theory in a meaningful way is to encourage them to create their own dictionary in sociology or whatever social science they are studying. When they read *The Wealth of Nations* by Adam Smith, *Suicide* by Durkheim, and so on, the students can be told to create entries for what they see as essential in these works.

The advantage of proceeding in this way is that concepts and the like are decoupled from the person who came up with them. Instead of learning to think in terms of "what Weber or Durkheim or Marx says," and trying to figure out what the author "really" means, the students get to focus on the concepts and arguments themselves. They also get to think about how to best define a term, how to rephrase it in a way that will be helpful for them in the future, and related issues.

Another advantage with this type of exercise is that students can also add to the dictionary once the course is over. A dictionary represents a good way of storing and accessing information and thoughts.

A last topic to be addressed in this section is whether it would be possible to teach theorizing with the help of the case method. Many years ago there was a shift to the case method in American law schools and business schools, on the grounds that students first of all need to learn a practical skill. Since theorizing is a practical skill, one might argue that the case method should also be used in classes on theorizing, especially when you have a large number of students in the class.

It would be interesting to have a discussion about the pros and cons of using the case method when you teach theorizing. Personally I feel a certain skepticism, and the reason is the following. In law schools the point is to teach the students how to apply existing law to a concrete case in a correct way, and in business schools the point is to teach the students to make the right decision when confronted with a specific problem.

In theorizing, however, the situation is somewhat different. First, the factual situation needs to be explored by the student himself/herself. To present the case as something given does not encourage good theorizing. Also the idea of there being one correct answer does not go well with the project of theorizing.

Still, the focus on developing a practical rather than a theoretical skill, and to do so by solving empirical problems, is a positive quality of the case method. If one could somehow bypass the limitations I have just mentioned, the case method could perhaps be used also for teaching theorizing in a large class.

## The Role of the Teacher

It is reasonable to assume that just as exercises in theorizing will differ from the kind of quizzes and paper topics that are traditionally used in theory courses, so will the role of the professor who teaches theorizing rather than theory.

In teaching theory, the goal is primarily to transmit to the student a certain amount of important knowledge. In teaching theorizing, in contrast, the goal is to teach the students to develop a skill of their own. In the former case the teacher may want to act as an enlightened guide; in the latter, more as a coach. In many sports the coach is someone who is too old to be an active participant in the game itself but who knows some things that can help the young and agile players to perform better.

Polya was very interested in how to teach mathematics to students in an effective way. He insisted that the teacher must never just tell the students the solution but should teach them how to solve a problem step by step themselves. If a student is unable to solve the problem, the teacher should try to hint at how to proceed, suggest some analogous problem, or in some other way try to get the student going.

After several decades of trying to translate his ideas on how to solve problems into effective classroom practices, Polya formulated his view of pedagogy in a short text titled "Ten Commandments for the Teacher." When you read these through, it is hard not to think that many of them could also be useful for teachers of theorizing. This is for example, the case with the following commandment: "Realize that the best way to learn anything is to discover it by yourself" (Polya 1959: 525).

The idea that you learn something more effectively by discovering how to do it yourself sums up Polya's approach to teaching mathematics. According to Polya his philosophy especially suited the mentality of the Americans, since they have a very practical approach to things and also like to fix things themselves.

In Europe, in contrast, the attitude was very different:

> *How to Solve It* was really written twice. I wrote something, a draft, in German while I was still in Zurich. Then I came to America and in this respect, my coming to America was, I think, useful, because here, in this country, there is more interest in the "How to" books. And, by the way, Hardy [one of Polya's collaborators] predicted it to me. When I

---

### Ten Commandments for Teachers (from Polya)

1. Be interested in your subject.
2. Know your subject.
3. Try to read the faces of your students; try to see their expectations and difficulties; put yourself in their place.
4. Realize that the best way to learn anything is to discover it by yourself.
5. Give your students not only information, but know-how, mental attitudes, the habit of methodical work.
6. Let them learn guessing.
7. Let them learn proving.
8. Look out for such features of the problem at hand as may be useful in solving the problems to come—try to disclose the general pattern that lies behind the present concrete situation.
9. Do not give away your whole secret at once—let the students guess before you tell it—let them find out by themselves as much as it is feasible.
10. Suggest it; do not force it down their throats.

*Source*: George Polya, "Ten Commandments for Teachers" (1959: 525–26).

---

told him about the "How to" book, he said, "Oh, you must go to America." (Polya 1979: 19)

For Polya, the key point in teaching was not to supply the students with information, but to somehow make them develop the know-how for how to solve mathematical problems themselves. As part of this, they should also be taught how to guess. "Let them learn guessing," to cite Polya's sixth commandment for the teacher (Polya 1959: 525).

The philosophy of teaching that has inspired Jane Reinhart is, as earlier mentioned, the theory of collaborative learning (for example, Bruffee 1993). Like Polya, she does not want to assume the role of the old-fashioned theory teacher, who just lectures for the students and explains to them what some theorist has said.

According to the approach of collaborative learning, the

students must share the responsibility with the teacher for what is going on in the classroom. The teacher engages in conversations with the students, and must be willing to experiment with different approaches to teaching and learning. Rinehart has recently described the way in which she teaches as "teaching with the mouth shut" (Rinehart 2012).

According to Rinehart, the ideas of collaborative learning go well with the teaching of theorizing:

> When instructors employ collaborative learning methods in the sociological theory course, student passivity and fears about *theory* (as a set of difficult concepts students have to learn for the tests) are transformed into an engaging practice of *theorizing* (an activity learned by performing it with each other in the classroom and beyond). Such practice is not without conflicts and failures, but it is a powerful form of resistance to lethargy and routine. (Rinehart 1999: 216)

Finally, in relation to the students I would agree with Polya and Rinehart in their attempts to deemphasize the role of the teacher and instead focus on the individual student. You do not learn theory by listening to lectures on "how to do it," and especially not to lectures on how super-talented people have done it. The key to learning how to theorize in social science is the same as learning how to use methods: by doing it yourself.

To elaborate a bit on how you go about setting the student at the center, you can also draw inspiration from the example of Socrates. By bringing up Socrates in this context I am not so much thinking of the Socratic method in its modern version, according to which the teacher calls on students in class and asks questions to which they intuitively know the answer (*anamnesis*). In my view, asking questions in this way often paralyzes the students and installs fear in them, instead of setting them free.

But despite the fact that Socrates lived more than two thousand years ago, and despite the fact that the modern classroom has little in common with the marketplace in Athens where Socrates practiced his philosophy, he is still a very inspiring figure. There is much to learn from him also today.

What I am in particular thinking of are the three ways in which a philosopher should behave, according to Socrates. All of these are also inspiring for the teacher of theorizing, I would argue. The philosopher, Socrates says, should act as a midwife, a stingray, and a gadfly.

The midwife does not give birth to a child herself. Instead she assists in the birth of somebody else's child. The kicking and screaming child has been created by the student, not by the teacher. The teacher should intervene only if something is about to go wrong.

This nicely captures the way that theorizing should be taught, in my view. The student should be made to understand that he or she can give birth to something very precious and alive, and that the child is exclusively his or her creation. The teacher is there to assist with the birth, which is very important. But it is secondary to giving birth.

As the student talks about his or her research, the teacher's task is to show which ideas of the student have the potential of growth and life. This can be done by giving the student's ideas back to him or her and saying: see what you can do; take what you have accomplished seriously. It is alive; now feed it and make it grow.

There is also the fact that you can give birth to something new and interesting only if you decide to seek the truth and break with the existing view of things, according to Socrates. Theorizing demands that all preconceptions about a phenomenon are removed and replaced by true knowledge. You do not want a false pregnancy, Socrates says. There has to be a real child there.

The teacher must also show the students that conventional

wisdom and preconceptions cannot be trusted. When these types of ideas are bandied about, the teacher should quickly step in and show that they are false. This is where you need to be a bit like a stingray, which in an instant can paralyze its victim.

And maybe the teacher should also be able to act a bit like a gadfly and encourage the student to do the same. This little insect, according to Socrates, stings the horse, but the horse hardly notices the gadfly and just keeps swinging its tail, easily brushing it off.

But despite the fact that this happens over and over again, the gadfly does not go away. It is a tenacious little insect. Similarly, Socrates says, the true philosopher-teacher will try to arouse and provoke the community of citizens over and over again, even if the community tends to be sluggish and ignore the philosopher and his or her love for seeking the Truth.

## CHAPTER 8

## The Role of Theory

> The whole aim of science is to find out the facts and to
> work out a satisfactory theory of them. Still, a theory does
> not necessarily lose its utility by not being altogether true.
>
> —Charles S. Peirce and Christine Ladd-Franklin, "Theory"[1]

So far heuristics and practical exercises have been suggested as ways of preparing yourself and students for theorizing. But much remains to be said on this topic. Most importantly what is at issue is not theorizing in general but theorizing in social science. Just as one may speak of, say, a legal mind or the capacity to look at things from a legal perspective, one can also speak of the capacity to look at reality from a social perspective. My argument is that for successful social theorizing, you need to have this capacity.

What does it mean to look at things from a social perspective? And how do you develop this capacity? These are two issues of obvious interest, not just for those who want to theorize creatively, but for anyone who is seriously interested in social science.

But to be a skillful theorizer in social science you also need to know some social theory and be able to handle it well. You may, for example, need to take a concept from one theory and combine it with a concept from another theory. You may want to eliminate some part of a theory and replace it with a new idea of your own, and so on.

Lacking this type of knowledge of theory, and focusing mainly on developing your very own theory, concepts, and the like, you run the risk of becoming the type of dilettante that Weber speaks of in "Science as a Vocation." You will not be able to make full use of your idea; and the reason is the following:

> Normally . . . an idea grows out of hard work alone, though this is certainly not always the case. In science, a dilettante may have an idea of exactly the same or greater significance than an expert. We owe many of our best ideas of approaching a problem and many of our best perceptions to dilettantes. A dilettante differs from an expert—as Helmholtz has said about Robert Mayer—only in that he lacks complete certainty in his working methods. He is thus normally not in a position to control, gauge, or carry through his idea in all its significance. An idea does not replace work. On the other hand, work cannot replace or force out an idea, just as little as enthusiasm can. Both work and enthusiasm— above all, both *together*—can entice an idea out. (Weber 2004: 271)

## What to Know of Social Theory

Knowing theory, in order to be good at theorizing in social science, is not the same as having a knowledge of the history of social theory. It is true that it is helpful to have some of the skills of an intellectual historian when you try to figure out what a concept means, why a theory looks the way it does today, and similar issues. But this is not the kind of knowledge that you basically need to have in order to be good at theorizing.

What type of knowledge do you then need? This is a difficult question to answer, and it would be helpful with a discussion in which a number of people who are interested in this issue could take part. In the meantime, and in the absence of such a discussion, I suggest that it is important to have two kinds of knowledge. First, you need to have a deep knowledge of what makes something social; and second, you need to be familiar with a number of different concepts, mechanisms, and theories.

The first kind of knowledge is about the foundations of social science. This means knowledge of such items as the following. What is the social? What causes the social and what are its effects? And how does the social change?

This type of knowledge has to be truly *appropriated* by the individual. By the term *appropriated* I mean that it must have sunk deeply into your mind and be thoroughly absorbed. A subjective sign that this is the case is that you perceive the knowledge as coming from your inside rather than from the outside. You do not need to call it up when you theorize; it is part of your thinking.

When you have really appropriated some knowledge, you have not only absorbed the knowledge in question. You are now also in a position to use it and transform it for your own particular purposes, as you proceed in your research.

As it so happens, the term *appropriation* also has another meaning besides that of absorption, which is suggestive in this context. In the art world, the term appropriation means making somebody else's work your own. The so-called ready-mades by artists such as Marcel Duchamp and Elaine Sturtevant are examples of this type of appropriation. Similarly, you want to make the ideas of the best social scientists truly your own.

The type of deep knowledge of what constitutes the social comes close to what Everett C. Hughes has tried to capture with his expression "the sociological eye" (Hughes 1984b). It refers to the kind of vision that allows you to eliminate what is irrelevant and zoom in on what is social about some phenomenon. Only when this way of looking at things has become nearly instinctual is it possible to theorize well.

To focus in on the social in this manner represents a distinct skill that is not easily acquired. Neither is it clear exactly how you go about acquiring it, even if reading social science in bulk, doing social science research in bulk, and hanging out with good social scientists are all very helpful.

In discussing what constitutes the social, it may be helpful to refer to the French sociological term *break* (*rupture*). In order to be able to see the social aspects of something, according to Pierre Bourdieu, it is necessary to decisively break with the traditional way of looking at things (Bourdieu et al. 1991: 13–31).

This comes close to what Durkheim means with the term *preconceptions* (*prénotions*). Because we live in society we all have preconceived notions of what is going on, and these notions have to be pushed to the side if we want to see the social facts.

In my view, there are four questions in particular that need to be addressed in order to theorize well in social science. They are

*What is the social?*
*What are the causes and the effects of the social?*
*How does the social change?*
*What makes your topic important?*

Many social scientists spend a lot of time thinking about these four questions, not only because they are basic but also because they are very difficult to answer. There do not exist any definitive answers to them, only more or less sophisticated attempts to explore them.

As to the first question—*What is the social?*—it is clear that the point of departure for social science is the fact that human beings spend their lives in groups and societies. In doing this, the social is somehow constituted. There is also the difficult question of the role of human biology in this.

The second question—*What are the causes and the effects of the social?*—is as central to social science as the first one. One basic answer is that social scientists try to explain the effects of the social by referring to the social, just as they try to determine the causes of the social by referring to the social. This is done either by focusing on the individual level or an emergent level, such as the group. Again, exactly how this is done is hard to explain.

And again, what is the role of the biological? Current research suggests that different people, depending on their genetic makeup, are influenced by their environment in different ways. Exactly how the interaction between biology and the social operates is not known, but it is clearly of crucial importance for understanding the role of the social.

The third question is *How does the social change?* It is true that human beings live and function in groups and societies. But so do many species of animals. The level of change that human beings can effect in the social, however, decisively sets them off from other social animals. How and why this is the case are hard questions.

It is more difficult to state exactly why the fourth and last question has been included in a discussion of what is needed to theorize well in social science: *What makes your topic important?* A quick answer would be that unless you select a good topic to analyze, the result will be trivial; and there will be little room for interesting social theorizing (for example, Klein 2014). The sociological eye allows you to see some things clearly and others less clearly.

In this sense *What makes your topic important?* is a crucial question—and it has the potential of making or unmaking not only the attempt to theorize the social, but the whole research project. One suggested answer is that unless your topic is ultimately of some existential or social importance, there is little point in researching it and theorizing it.

It may be true that it is easier to say what is meant when we say that something is of existential importance than that it is of social importance. The only point that I want to make at this stage, however, is simply that the topic you choose should have some special quality to it—and that many topics lack this quality. You need a good topic to theorize well.

I will return to this question later and instead turn to another topic. In concrete terms, how do you teach yourself to look at things from a social perspective? As mentioned earlier, there probably exist many different ways to do this. In my own case I have found the classics in sociology to be very helpful. By the classics I mean the best works that were produced by the generation of academic sociologists during 1890–1920.

One reason why the classics are so useful is that they had to be extra clear about the new perspective they were trying to establish. The need to break with other types of knowledge, and to differentiate sociology from these, was urgent in their day. Add to this that the classics also had an exceptionally good sense for choosing great topics, from the "big" topics of someone like Weber to the "small" topics of someone like Simmel.

There exist two texts in sociology that to my mind are unsurpassed, in their lucidity as well as through the comprehensive way in which they outline the social vision. These are *The Rules of Sociological Method* by Durkheim and the opening chapter in *Economy and Society* by Weber (chapter 1, "Basic Sociological Terms"). Both of these works cover in detail what the term *social* means. They also spell out very carefully what a sociological explanation looks like.

These two texts define the social in quite different ways, however, reminding us that what constitutes the social is by no means agreed upon in social science. This was as true a hundred years ago as it is today.

For Weber, the exact meaning of the term *social* is the following. An action is social if it is *oriented to the behavior of other actors*. He also argues that a sociological explanation must take into account *the meaning* with which the actors invest their actions. Without this meaning, there is by definition no action and no social action.

For Durkheim, social means something else—namely, an activity that is related to *the group* (*société*). The group exists at a different level than the individual. So-called emergence is involved when you go from the level of the individual to that of the group or society. What sets human beings apart from other animals who live in groups, according to Durkheim, is that they can pass on information about institutions to the next generation and also change institutions in fundamental ways.

To explain the effects of the social, according to Weber, you first have to focus on the social actions of individuals, and then follow the ways in which these evolve and what their consequences are. In Durkheim's succinct formulation, a social fact can only be explained by another social fact. He importantly adds that you want to establish not only the cause of some social facts but also their function.

Finally, what do Weber and Durkheim have to say in response to the fourth question, *What makes your topic important?* Durkheim has a very straightforward answer: an analysis that does not address the question of why human societies are holding together or falling apart is neither of much scientific value nor of moral value. For Durkheim, in other words, what is social and what is moral come close to being one and the same thing.

Weber is much more cautious than Durkheim when he discusses what topics a social scientist should choose. In his view, social analysis should deal with the major cultural values of the time and the questions that these raise. These values, however, tend to change as society moves on, something that means that what one generation finds important, another may not.

The point, once more, is not so much whether Weber's or Durkheim's answers to the basic questions of social science are correct or not. What is crucial is that the social scientist should be able to nearly automatically look at reality in terms of the social, its causes and effects, and how it changes; and that Weber and Durkheim take us straight to these questions and make us think about them.

The second type of knowledge that is needed for creative theorizing, I suggest, is of a very different kind from the type of knowledge that has just been discussed. It does not so much have to do with your general capacity to see something in social terms as with your capacity to carry out a social analysis in a competent manner. What is needed for this is especially knowledge of a number of concepts, mechanisms, and theories in social science.

It is useful to know a number of concepts, mechanisms and theories so that you have plenty to choose from when you try to theorize some phenomenon. In fact when you try to figure out some social phenomenon, the more of these that you have at your disposal the better. In chapter 3 I mentioned some authors whose works are especially rich in concepts, such as Weber, Simmel, and Merton. To be more concrete I here refer the reader to the sidebar, which contains what Weber viewed as the basic concepts of sociology and how he defined these.

It is similarly useful to have some knowledge of as many social mechanisms as possible. By reading the works of authors such as

## The Basic Concepts of Sociology according to Max Weber in *Economy and Society*

### 1. SOCIOLOGY AND SOCIAL ACTION

Sociology is a science that attempts to give a causal account of the course and consequences of social action through an interpretive understanding of this type of action. Social action is behavior invested with meaning that is oriented to other people.

### 2. TYPES OF SOCIAL ACTION (INSTRUMENTALLY RATIONAL, VALUE RATIONAL, AFFECTUAL, AND TRADITIONAL)

The orientation to social action may differ, according to the actor's rationally calculated ends (instrumentally rational action), the values that guide the action independently of success (value-rational action), the emotional state of the actor (affectual action), and ingrained habits (traditional action).

### 3. SOCIAL RELATIONSHIP

A social relationship consists of two or more actors who orient their behavior to one another. If the actors invest their actions with different meaning, there is an asymmetric relationship.

### 4. TYPES OF ACTION ORIENTATION (USAGE, CUSTOM, AND SELF-INTEREST)

Empirical uniformities are called usage when their existence is based on the regular occurrence of some action; custom when they are based on actions of long-standing use; and determined by self-interest if the actions are oriented to certain expectations, based on instrumental rationality.

### 5. LEGITIMATE ORDER

An order consists of ways of doing things with a certain meaning ("maxims"), to which actions can be oriented. If actors orient their actions to a belief in such orders, these orders can be called legitimate or valid.

### 6. CONVENTION AND LAW

A convention ("norm") is a legitimate order when deviations from the prescribed actions are enforced through disapproval. An order is a law when these deviations are enforced through physical or psychical coercion by a staff of people.

## 7. BASES OF LEGITIMACY

The legitimacy of an order can be based on tradition, faith, and law.

## 8. CONFLICT, COMPETITION, AND SELECTION

Conflict is a social relationship in which action is intentionally carried out against the will of the other actor(s). Competition is a peaceful type of conflict over advantages or utilities. Selection comes about through conflict and competition, and means the ascendance of those who have what it takes to succeed in these.

## 9. COMMUNAL AND ASSOCIATIVE RELATIONSHIPS

Communal social relationships are those relationships that are based on the actors' feeling of belonging together. Associative relationships are instead based on rational motives for the relationship. The family and the nation are examples of the former; the market and the firm are examples of the latter.

## 10. OPEN AND CLOSED RELATIONSHIPS

A social relationship is open if someone who wishes to join it can do so, and it is closed when this is not the case. Property is an example of a specific kind of a closed social relationship.

## 11. REPRESENTATION AND MUTUAL RESPONSIBILITY

Representation comes about when the actions of certain members (the representatives) is attributed to others (the represented). Mutual responsibility comes about when the action of one actor in a social relationship is attributed to all of the other actors.

## 12. ORGANIZATION

An organization exists when the order of a closed or a limited social relationship is carried out by a staff or a person in authority.

## 13. CONSENSUAL AND IMPOSED ORDER IN ORGANIZATIONS

The order of an organization may be imposed or voluntarily agreed upon.

## 14. ADMINISTRATIVE AND REGULATIVE ORDER

Rules that govern the actions of an organization are called administrative unless the benefits of the members are involved, in which case they are called regulative.

### 15. ENTERPRISE, FORMAL ORGANIZATION, AND VOLUNTARY AND COMPULSORY ASSOCIATION

A rational organization is called an enterprise. When its staff is rational, it is called a formal organization. Depending on the authority it has over its members, the organization will be voluntary or compulsory.

### 16. POWER AND DOMINATION

Power exists when an actor can enforce his or her will in a social relationship despite resistance. When a group obeys a command, there is domination. Discipline exists when domination has become a habit.

### 17. POLITICAL AND HIEROCRATIC ORGANIZATIONS

A ruling political organization is one where the order in a territory is enforced through physical coercion. A hierocratic organization is one where the order is enforced through psychological coercion, via access to religious benefits or a denial of these. A state is a compulsive ruling political organization whose staff has a monopoly on legitimate physical violence. A church is a compulsive hierocratic organization whose staff claims a monopoly on the legitimate use of hierocratic coercion. A sect is a voluntary religious organization that demands a certain religious qualification of those who join.

*Comment*: These concepts can be found in chapter 1 of Weber's *Economy and Society*, titled "Basic Sociological Terms" ("Soziologische Grundbegriffe"; Weber 1978: 3–62). When it comes to organizations the terminology is especially difficult to capture in English and in a few sentences. I have used the standard translation by Talcott Parsons (as revised by Roth and Wittich), but an alternative translation by Keith Tribe exists (Weber 2004: 311–58).

Thomas Schelling, Albert O. Hirschman, and Alexis de Tocqueville you can quickly get to know a number of mechanisms that are very useful to have at the back of your head when you try to theorize. Someone should put together a catalogue of the most important social mechanisms, but until that has been done, reading people like Schelling, Hirschman, and Tocqueville is very helpful.

When you build up your storage of concepts, mechanisms, and theories it is also important to pick out imaginative social scientists and avoid dull ones. There are plenty of creative authors to choose from, such as Hayek, Simmel, Schumpeter, Freud, Goffman, and so on. There also exist a number of excellent studies by little-known authors.

No one can read everything, so it is good to select a small number of works that contain plenty of concepts and theories. Browsing and casual reading is also recommended in this effort, as opposed to the kind of focused and slow reading that you need to do when you try to learn what is meant by the social.

In my view, it is also helpful to live with many books and theories, a bit like Keynes suggested in a radio talk that he gave in 1936. He had the general reader in mind, but what he says applies perhaps also to the theorizer. Where Keynes says "books," think of "theories":

> May I conclude with a little general advice from one who can claim to be an experienced reader to those who have learnt to read but have not yet gained experience? A reader should acquire a wide general acquaintance with books *as such*, so to speak. He should approach them with all his senses; he should know their touch and their smell. He should learn how to take them in his hands, rustle their pages and reach in a few seconds a first intuitive impression of what they contain. He should, in the course of time, have touched many thousands, at least ten times as many as he really reads. He should cast an eye over books as a shepherd over sheep, and judge them with the rapid, searching glance with which a cattle-dealer eyes cattle. He should live with more books than he reads, with a penumbra of unread pages, of which he knows the general character and content, fluttering around him. (Keynes 2010: 172)

## Presuppositions, Postulations, and Hinges

In the scheme for how to theorize in this book the role of observation has been emphasized. No good theorizing in social science can take place without observation, it has been said over and over. But there also exists an important form of theorizing that is not empirical in nature, and the time has now come to say something about it.

If the type of theorizing that has been presented in part 1 can be called *observation-based theorizing*, this other type may be called *fundamental theorizing*. It is not based on observation, or if so only in an indirect manner, meaning by this that its relationship to empirical observation is faint or several steps away.

Fundamental theorizing covers questions that are all prior to observation, such as: What is a fact? What is a concept? What is meant by causality? I have formulated these examples as questions, for the simple reason that they have to be addressed by everyone who aspires to be good at theorizing.

It is of course true that coming up with new theories that address this type of questions represents an important task as well. Since they are of a very basic nature, however, it is also extra difficult to come up with new answers to them. Talented theorizers of this type are rare.

While it is very hard to innovate when it comes to the fundamentals or presuppositions of social science, it is nevertheless important to give careful consideration to them. One important reason for this is that they in many ways make social science possible.

One of the terms that John Dewey and Arthur Bentley introduced in the 1940s, in one of their articles on epistemology, may be helpful in this context. It is the term *postulation*. The authors explain why they chose this word as follows:

The dictionaries allot to the word "postulate" two types of application. One represents something "taken for granted as the true basis for reasoning or belief"; the other, "a condition required for further operations." Our approach is manifestly of the second type. We shall mark this by speaking of postulations rather than of postulates, so far as our own procedures are concerned. This phrasing is more reliable, even though at times it will seem a bit clumsy. (Dewey and Bentley 1945: 646)

The idea that there exists a basic type of theory that enables the social scientist to proceed with the analysis, can also be found in Wittgenstein's idea of hinges. There exist certain concepts and ideas, Wittgenstein says, that make it possible for you to proceed in an argument. It is these that he calls "hinges."

Wittgenstein also makes the point that we do not need to raise this type of very basic questions. This is important to keep in mind, since some social theorists insist that there is something lacking with an analysis does not explicitly address what kind of social ontology it is based on.

Wittgenstein disposes of this argument in the following way. "The *questions* that we raise and our *doubts* depend on the fact that some propositions are exempt from doubt, are as it were the hinges on which those turn" (Wittgenstein 1972: 341).

The reason why they are exempt is the following:

We just *can't* investigate everything. And for that reason we are forced to rest content with assumption. If I want the door to turn, the hinges must stay put. (Wittgenstein 1972: 343)

Wittgenstein also suggests that the ultimate foundation upon which our arguments rest is a way of acting rather than an idea.

"The end is not an ungrounded presupposition: it is an ungrounded way of acting" (Wittgenstein 1972: 110).

## More on How to Learn Theory

Earlier in this chapter I suggested that the two types of social theory that are needed in order to theorize well are knowledge of the basics of social theory and knowledge of a number of concepts, mechanisms, and theories. It was also said that the former should be a deep kind of knowledge, while the latter can be relatively superficial.

Much more, however, needs to be said about these two kinds of knowledge and how to acquire them. In what follows I shall therefore return to the issue of how you can develop a sociological eye, and then say something about the way in which you can get to know a large number of concepts, mechanisms, and theories.

Having a deep kind of knowledge comes close to what Daniel Kahneman views as the intuitive thinking of experts (Kahneman 2011: 240–41). While Kahneman has little to say about the ways in which experts develop their intuition, philosopher Hubert Dreyfus and his brother Stuart Dreyfus have developed an interesting theory of how you turn knowledge into a skill and an intuition (for example, Dreyfus and Dreyfus 1986). Their ideas on this score also fit the way you develop a deep knowledge of theory as well as several other skills that are needed for theorizing.

The Dreyfus brothers envision the process of developing a skill as taking place in five steps. This starts with a number of rules that have to be followed by the actor, who will then gradually learn to deal with increasingly complex situations. As you become used to following the rules, you also become ready to take the context into account. At the very end of this process,

---

### How to Learn a Skill according to Hubert and Stuart Dreyfus

Step 1. You start by trying to learn some basic knowledge, while ignoring the surroundings or the context.

Step 2. You increase your basic knowledge, and also begin to take the surroundings or the context into account.

Step 3. You are now competent and begin to make independent decisions.

Step 4. You repeatedly make independent decisions in concrete situations.

Step 5. You have by now developed a skill; and since your knowledge is intuitive, you can concentrate on handling concrete situations in all their complexity.

*Source*: Hubert Dreyfus and Stuart Dreyfus, *Mind over Machine: The Power of Human Intuition and Expertise in the Era of the Computer* (1986: 50).

---

you will have internalized the rules to the point where you do not even think about them. You are now free to concentrate on what is new in a situation. In brief, you have developed a skill.

As an example of how you transition from being a beginner to becoming an expert, the authors use the example of learning to drive a car. In order to get started you may first want to drive around slowly in a parking lot. After some time of doing this you may venture out onto a street without too much traffic. The next stage might be to drive in city traffic or on a busy highway.

This may also be the way in which you learn the basics of social theory. As earlier mentioned, there exist a few good candidates for teaching this type of knowledge, such as *The Rules of Sociological Method* by Durkheim and chapter 1 in *Economy and Society* by Weber.

But even if this is the case, how *exactly* how do you go about learning the basics of social theory so that they really sink deep down into your mind? Is it through practical exercises? If so does one start by keeping close to what (in this example) Durkheim and Weber say, and then gradually try to take increasingly complex data into account?

Or should you rather try to think through the relevant issues on your own, using Weber and Durkheim more as guides? And after having done this for some time, do you just stop thinking about the basic ideas and start applying them intuitively?

There are no easy answers to these questions. Nonetheless, it seems to me that it is important to never stop thinking about the foundations of social science, partly because there is no consensus on these foundations, and partly because they are not particularly stable. Take the ideas of Durkheim and Weber as an example. Both insisted that sociology and biology should be kept apart in a way that is neither necessary nor desirable today. Both also created their theories long before there were sciences such as cognitive psychology and neuroscience.

Also, how is the type of basic knowledge about the social related to actual research and practical exercises? Would it help for students to study theory while they conduct a number of small research projects? Or is it better to use practical exercises. and if so, what should these look like?

While these are difficult and important questions, it should also be made clear that the activity of thinking through the basics of social theory in a slow and careful manner is very useful and should not be dismissed as "mere thinking" (for example, Heidegger 1976). There is also a real need for representatives from the different social sciences to weigh in and express their opinion on this type of issues. If this is done, knowledge of how to theorize in social science can truly become a collective good, accessible to all.

In contrast to how you develop a sociological eye, it would seem much more easy to figure out what you need to do in order to acquire a good store of concepts, mechanisms, and theories. Beyond what has already been said about reading works that contain many concepts and theories, it is also useful to make forays into the neighboring social sciences and occasionally also into philosophy and the natural sciences. In this way you can pick up new and interesting ideas that can often be turned into social science ideas in a relatively simple way.

## The Tradition of Theory, the Tradition of Theorizing

While it is true that quite a bit of information exists in today's social science on what to read on the topic of theory, it is less clear that this literature is also useful for those who are interested in learning how to theorize. In many of today's courses in social theory, a number of disparate books and articles are often used. Some of these are classics, while others are contemporary studies. Some deal explicitly with theory, while others summarize long strands of social theory and can be described as works in intellectual history, history of ideas, and the like.

Some rethinking of what to include in the tradition of social theory would therefore seem appropriate when the reader is someone who is mainly interested in learning how to theorize. It may also be useful to approach theory itself in a different spirit from what is often done today. Just as it is important to learn some theory, it is also useful to know something about the way in which the author went about producing the theory (for example, Heilbron 2011).

A kind of reverse engineering may be instructive. It may also be useful to read not only the final version of some article or book but also earlier versions. This type of material may exist in the form of notes, letters, or studies of how some work came into existence. We know, for example, quite a bit about the coming into being of *Democracy in America* (for example, Schleifer 1980). Tocqueville described his research in letters to family members; he filled notebooks with observations; and he made a number of changes in the final text.

In order to learn how to theorize effectively, it is critical that there exists a strong tradition of theorizing, something that is not the case today. While it is correct to say that theorizing and theory belong together, and also that they complement each other, theorizing has been sorely neglected in modern social science and is in great need of being developed. While the literatures on theory and theorizing overlap, they are by no means identical.

In this book I have stated a number of times what I consider to be the main topics to be covered in the art of creative theorizing. I have highlighted such topics as observation, concept formation, how to use analogies, how to come up with an explanation, and so on.

But one can also approach theorizing from another angle and enumerate the books and articles that make up what may be called the *theorizing tradition*. At the current stage it may be premature to provide such a list since the literature is very small. For those who nonetheless want one, I have put together a short list in the references section at the end of this book. Once theorizing gets going in social science, the literature will hopefully grow very quickly.

.............................................................................................

## CHAPTER 9

# Imagination and Art

> The Possible's slow fuse is lit
> By the Imagination!
>
> —Emily Dickinson[1]

While it is impossible to theorize well without a good knowledge of theory, the way in which this knowledge is handled is just as important. A discussion of how theory should be used needs to be complemented with a discussion how theory should *not* be used.

It is important, for example, not to squeeze the results into some existing theory. This will not only eliminate any potential originality of the research findings in a Procrustean fashion, it is also hard to accomplish ("it works in practice but not in theory").

It is similarly a mistake to just put a label on some phenomena and believe that this constitutes *theory*. It is not theory because a full theory is much more than a name; it has a body of concepts, suggests an explanation, and the like.

Some concepts are best used for heuristic purposes, but become obstacles if they are not discarded once they have fulfilled this function. Also, a heuristic theory is not a proven theory; it is supposed to get you going, not to be the final theory.

There exist a number of other common errors in dealing with theory, and many of these result from theory being taught in a

## Some Common Errors in Handling Theory

1. FOCUS ALL YOUR ATTENTION ON METHODS; THEORY IS THE EASY PART AND CAN ALWAYS BE FIXED LATER.

Since methods and gathering data take much time; concentrate on these. The theory part can be quickly dispensed with.

2. THERE IS NO NEED TO THEORIZE; KNOWING A BIT OF THEORY IS ENOUGH.

Theory will pop up into your head intuitively. There is no special need to work on it, nor to know much theory to be good at it.

3. START THINKING ABOUT THEORY AFTER THE EMPIRICAL RE-SEARCH HAS BEEN DONE.

Once the research has been done, and the whole thing has turned out somewhat disappointing, it is time to bring in some theory to spice the whole thing up. (The journals also want there to be some theory, especially at the beginning and the end of an article.)

4. ONCE THE RESULTS ARE IN, JUST STICK A LABEL ON THEM OR INTRODUCE SOME CLASSIFICATION.

Stick a label on your research results or classify them in some way. This represents a full analysis and there is no need for an explanation.

5. SQUEEZE YOUR FINDINGS INTO SOME EXISTING THEORY.

Once the research has been done, just look around for a theory that explains the findings. Keep in mind that old theories are considered boring and new ones interesting. Whatever the theory doesn't explain of your findings, just eliminate in a Procrustean fashion.

6. CONDUCT RESEARCH TO CONFIRM A THEORY YOU REALLY LIKE.

Liking a theory is a sign that it is correct. It is therefore a good idea to do research to prove that it is correct.

7. ADMIRE GREAT THEORETICIANS AND CONDUCT RESEARCH TO CONFIRM THEIR IDEAS.

Some theoreticians are very sexy and charismatic but provide no empirical evidence. Make it your task to prove that they are right.

> ### 8. USE HEURISTIC CONCEPTS AND THEORIES AS IF THEY WERE CONFIRMED RESEARCH FINDINGS.
> Insist that all heuristic theories and concepts should be tested empirically, and that they should be discarded if they do not hold up. By proceeding in this way with, for example, the classics you can show that you are smarter than they are.
>
> ### 9. STRING TOGETHER PIECES OF THEORY WITHOUT PROVIDING ANY LINKS TO EMPIRICAL REALITY.
> Theory is a conceptual and scholastic game, played by trying to piece together the theoretical ideas of a number of thinkers in some ingenious fashion.
>
> ### 10. SOME THEORISTS ARE GREAT—JUST REPEAT WHAT THEY SAY.
> There is no need to theorize, nor to do research—just repeat and rephrase what earlier great sociologists have said. And since they are considered great, you will be too.

mechanical and/or traditional fashion, and without an understanding of its role at the stage of theorizing. I have included a list of some typical errors, but no doubt others exist as well.

How then to proceed? In earlier chapters some rules or steps for how to go about theorizing have been suggested, and practical exercises as well as heuristic tips have been discussed. In this chapter another topic will be in focus, and that is imagination. However deep your basic knowledge of social theory is, and however many concepts, mechanisms, and theories you know, unless this knowledge is used in an imaginative way, the result will be dull and noncreative.

Besides imagination, I will also say something about the relationship of social theory to art. There are a number of reasons for this, including the fact that in modern society art is perceived as the height of imagination and creativity. Another reason, to cite the fine formulation of Hans Zetterberg, is that "art should be part of everything" (Zetterberg 2010). This, I would argue, also includes theorizing.

## What Is Imagination?

When one tries to understand the various aspects of theorizing it is usually helpful to see what cognitive science has to say. This, for example, is the case with such topics as concepts, memory, and analogy. Unfortunately, there exists much less research by cognitive scientists on imagination.

One can discuss why this is the case. One reason is probably that there exists no strong tradition in psychology of studying imagination, something that has to do with behavioral psychology and its lack of interest in purely mental phenomena.

When it comes to modern cognitive psychology, in contrast, it would seem that there exists so little research on imagination for the simple reason that it has not been seen as a particularly important topic to study. And when it has been studied, the approach has been somewhat mechanical.

In cognitive psychology imagination is often seen as a form of simulation. The term that is often used is *mental simulation*, and the key idea is that when you imagine something, it is as if you were running a simulation model in your mind (for example, Kahneman and Tversky 1982; Markman et al. 2009).

From the perspective of theorizing in social science this is not very helpful, and a more suggestive approach to imagination is needed. Such an approach can in my view be found in the philosophical literature. Imagination was, for example, a key concept in Kant's philosophy; and it represents according to some commentators one of his most important contributions to the theory of the mind (for example, Arendt 1992: 80).

It is not easy to summarize Kant's view of imagination. One way to approach it is to say that imagination is necessary, not only to art but also to knowledge. It essentially provides unity to the multitude of impressions that our senses present us with. It does this through an act that both synthesizes and schematizes. From the perspective of theorizing Kant's idea that imagination is a necessary and organic part of the production of knowledge is perhaps the most suggestive.

There also exist more recent theories of imagination in philosophy, such as those of John Dewey and Jean-Paul Sartre. While Dewey never developed a full theory of imagination, many interesting and suggestive ideas can be found in his work (for example, Dewey 1934a, 1934b; see, for example, Chambliss 1991).

According to one of these ideas, imagination is neither a distinct faculty nor something that only artists have. It is instead the general capacity of every human being to see things in turns of possibilities. Being a pragmatist, Dewey emphasized that these possibilities have to be realistic. There exists a clear difference between reverie and dreams, on the one hand, and imagination, on the other. While the former belong exclusively to your inner experience, imagination links the inner and the outer experience in a form of interaction.

Jean-Paul Sartre was from early on very interested in imagination and also presented an original theory of his own, in a book titled *The Imaginary* (1940). His approach is very suggestive and can be used not only for philosophical purposes but also to some extent for social science purposes.

One of Sartre's ambitions was to break with the strong tradition in philosophy to view imagination in terms of perceptual images. He wanted to develop a much broader theory and, as part of this, introduced the term *analogon*. An analogon is an object that stimulates imagination—say, in the way that a photograph of someone makes you think of that person.

This idea resonates with the topic of theorizing in several ways. A good research topic should among other things operate as an analogon—that is, it should be able to set off the theoretical imagination of the social scientist. And when a social scientist writes, he or she may want to write in such a way that the reader's theoretical imagination is stirred.

While the notion of analogon is interesting, Sartre also presents a full theory of imagination in *The Imaginary* that is bold and original. His ideas on this topic grew out of his reading at the time of *Being and Time* by Heidegger. While Heidegger had argued that everything can be reduced to the category of being, Sartre disagreed. And the reason was precisely because this argument disregarded the role of imagination.

Imagination—and this constitutes Sartre's contribution—is what allows human beings to step outside the being of which they are part and imagine another kind of being, one that does *not* exist. "If it were possible to conceive for a moment a consciousness that does not imagine, it would be necessary to conceive it as totally bogged down in the existent and without the possibility of grasping anything other than the existent" (Sartre 2004: 187).

This means that because human beings are endowed with imagination, they also have a way of questioning existing reality. They can judge what exists by contrasting it to what does not exist. The link between Sartre's work on imagination and his later philosophy of existentialism in *Being and Nothingness* is clear. "It is because we are transcendentally free that we can imagine" (Sartre 2004: 186).

In his later existential work Sartre went on to argue that human beings are condemned to freedom and responsible for their lack of freedom. He would later back off from this position and argue that people are not responsible for their situation. According to Sartre's later writings, there is more to freedom and the lack of freedom than the existential state of man.

From what has just been said about freedom and existentialism it is clear that Sartre's concept of imagination needs to be reigned in, properly qualified, and so on, in order to become useful. Still, it is based on a very powerful idea that is much more suggestive than the ideas of mental imaging and mental simulation. We can also see how imagination, along the lines that Kant and Sartre suggest, can be conceptualized as the mental force behind such notions as counterfactuals, utopias, and even the notion of theory itself.

Another interesting idea from the philosophical and literary tradition is the distinction between imagination and fancy. In its best-known formulation, which is that of Coleridge, *imagination* refers to what the mind combines in an inventive and organic manner, while *fancy* stands for a mechanical, nonoriginal combination (Coleridge 1967; cf. Engell 1981).

One social scientist who has picked up on the notion of fancy versus imagination is Karl Weick. One example of fancy, he says, would be the idea of Pegasus, which is the result of a mechanical combination of a horse and a set of wings (Weick 2003). Contrast this, one could add, to the monsters that can be found in the paintings by Hieronymus Bosch.

Applied to the use of social theory Weick's line of argument seems suggestive, even if not as clear as one might wish. What you want to avoid, he seems to be saying, is the mechanical addition of a concept or a theory to that of another concept or theory. Neither do you want to add theory to empirical material in an artificial fashion. Truly imaginative theorizing comes into existence when a concept or a theory, on the one hand, and the subject matter, on the other, are merged together in an organic and creative fashion—as in the hellish figures of Hieronymus Bosch.

## How to Train Your Imagination

On the assumption that the theorizer needs not only to know social theory but also to be able to use it in an imaginative way, how can this capacity be trained? This may seem like a difficult question to answer, but a few social scientists have tried to do so, and it is to their answers we now shall turn.

The foremost pioneer in this context is C. Wright Mills, and his views can be found in *The Sociological Imagination*. While this book is often and ritualistically praised, it has led to very little research on its main topic, which is the role of imagination in social science and how it can be strengthened.

C. Wright Mills defines imagination as the capacity to make an unexpected combination, an argument that is reminiscent of Schumpeter's definition of an innovation as a new combination of already existing materials. Imagination, Mills says, is used to put things together. "Its essence is the combination of ideas that no one expected were combinable—say, a mess of ideas from German philosophy and British economics" (Mills 1959: 211).

Mills also provides the reader with some practical tips for how social scientists can become more imaginative. He argues that you cannot "train" yourself to be more imaginative, and the reason for this is that you can train yourself only in "what is already known" (Mills 1959: 212). What you can do, however, is to "cultivate" your imagination, and you do this by being playful and ready to entertain what at first may seem "loose and even sloppy" (Mills 1959: 212).

In the famous appendix on intellectual craftsmanship, the reader of Mills's book is presented with a list of practical tips for how to cultivate his or her sociological imagination. "There are," Mills writes, "definite ways, I believe, of stimulating the sociological imagination" (Mills 1959: 212).

The ways that Mills mention are the following:

- Scramble and mix up your notes
- Be playful with words
- Construct new classifications and typologies
- Look at the opposite of what you are studying
- Invert your sense of proportion
- Look for comparable cases
- Write and think in terms of themes

(Mills 1959: 212–17)

Each of these seven tips in *The Sociological Imagination* is explicated in the text and well worth studying closely. Some of Mills's advice is in the tradition of playful anarchy, such as his suggestion that you rearrange your files in the following way: "You simply dump out heretofore disconnected folders, mixing up their contents, and then re-sort them" (Mills 1959: 212).

Some of Mills's other pieces of advice are equally playful, such as the idea of inversing the proportions: "If something is very minute, imagine it to be simply enormous, and ask yourself: What difference would that make? And vice versa for gigantic phenomena" (Mills 1959: 215).

Can society be organized as a firm? Can a firm be organized as a society? Do you speak in the same way to a single person as you do to a giant audience? Questions of this type can be asked for each of Mills's seven ways in which you can train your imagination. They also lend themselves to practical exercises, which may be worth developing.

Attempts to reflect on what constitutes the sociological imagination have also been made by a few other social scientists other than Mills. One of these is Everett C. Hughes, who argued that the essence of the sociological imagination consists of free association. Hughes often used the technique of free association himself, both in his teaching and when he theorized.

When Hughes used free association in his teaching, the result was a subtle form of lecturing, in which anecdotes were mixed with references to research findings and theories (for example, Weiss 1996: 543). Lewis Coser, who was one of his colleagues, has recounted how he first reacted to Hughes's style of lecturing:

> He moved from large events to seemingly small matters and back again—all in a very few minutes. One's ear had to be closely attuned to his peculiar type of delivery. When I heard him [lecture] for the first time in Chicago in 1948 I reported home that the man was utterly confused and confusing. When I heard him a second time, I reported that he was a sociological genius. (Coser 1994: 8)

Hughes himself has described the way in which he used free association in his research. The following statement comes from the preface to *The Sociological Eye*:

> In my work I have relied a great deal on free association, sometimes on a freedom of association that could seem outrageous to the defenders of some established interest or cherished sentiment. Wright Mills must be given credit for the phrase *the sociological imagination*. The essence of the social imagination is free association, guided but not hampered by a frame of reference internalized not quite into the unconscious. It must work even in one's dreams but be where it can be called up at will. When people say of my work, as they often do, that it shows insight, I cannot think what they could mean other than whatever quality

may have been produced by intensity of observation and the turning of the wheels to find a new combination of the old concepts, or even a new concept. I think I even do my reading by free association: "Didn't Simmel, or Durkheim, Weber, Mead, Marshall, or someone say something on that point?" I do a good deal of my reading by starting with the index. (Hughes 1984b: xvi)

Since the use of free association in social science is a topic that is rarely discussed, something more should be said about it. Another reason for exploring this topic is that free association represents a useful technique when you try to theorize.

While it may not have been Freud who invented the technique of free association, he definitely popularized it. He used it not only when he analyzed his own dreams; Freud also encouraged his patients to use free association as a way of getting to the core of their problems.

Freud's view of free association is more complex than he is often given credit for. What his translator for example rendered as *free association* is in reality two terms, with somewhat different meanings: *freie Assoziation* and *Einfall*. While the former refers to two or more things that are loosely linked together in one's mind, the latter means roughly a sudden and spontaneous thought.

It is also clear that Freud did not view free association as a kind of mental game in which you say everything that comes to mind, when you think of a special word. He basically regarded it as a technique that allows you to engage in "self-observation," and it does so by providing you with a way in which you can bypass your "critical faculty" (Freud 1998: 132–33).

In order to lead the patient to the source of his or her pain, it is necessary according to Freud to bring about "two changes":

"an increase in the attention he pays to his own psychical perceptions and the elimination of the criticism by which he normally sifts the thoughts that occur to him" (Freud 1998: 133). In other words, you have to focus your attention on yourself, and you have to be nonjudgmental if you are to understand what is going on inside yourself.

Freud liked to cite a quote by Friedrich Schiller on the topic of free association. By removing your critical faculty, the German poet and philosopher said, you will not only gain access to certain thoughts that you otherwise would have been unaware of. You will also become more creative.

The quote by Schiller that Freud referred to can be found in a letter that he wrote to a friend, who had complained about being uncreative: "The ground for your complaint seems to me to lie in the constraint imposed by your reason upon your imagination. . . . On the other hand, where there is a creative mind, Reason—so it seems to me—relaxes its watch upon the gates, and the ideas rush in pell-mell, and only then does it look them through and examine them in a mass" (Freud 1998: 135).

How does modern psychology look at free association? Just as it has rejected most of Freud's ideas, it has also rejected his theory of free association as a privileged way to gain access to people's innermost emotions.

In its approach to free association modern psychology emphasizes its cognitive rather than its emotional uses. According to the so-called Remote Association Test, for example, free association works extremely fast, and the reason for this is that it does not draw on people's reasoning capacity.

But there also exist some findings on free associations in modern psychology that are suggestive for theorizers. Daniel Kahneman, for example, has described how surprised he was when he found out that according to some recent research, people are much better at free association when they are happy (Kahneman 2011: 67–70). The modern theorizer, in brief, can perhaps learn both from Freud and cognitive science.

## Reverie

A related way of accessing and exercising your imagination is that of *reverie*, sometimes referred to as *daydreaming* and *mindwalking*. According to cognitive psychologists, daydreaming is a common activity and may even constitute a kind of default mode of the human brain (for example, Klinger 2009).

An early and deliberate example of the use of reverie in social science can be found in the work of Rousseau, who was keenly interested in anything that could spark his imagination. One way for him to get his ideas flowing was to take a walk. Rousseau writes in his autobiography: "I can only meditate when I am walking. When I stop, I cease to think; my mind only works with my legs" (Rousseau 1953: 382).

Rousseau also loved to lose himself in various ways, especially in nature. One of his favorite pastimes was to lie on his back at the bottom of a boat that was slowly drifting downstream . . .

In *The Reveries of the Solitary Walker* Rousseau says that one of his happiest times was in the fall of 1765, when he often engaged in this type of activity:

> I would slip away and go throw myself alone in a boat that I rowed to the middle of the lake when the water was calm; and there, stretching myself out full-length in the boat, my eyes turned to heaven, I let myself slowly drift back and forth with the water, sometimes for several hours, plunged in a thousand confused, but delightful, reveries. (Rousseau 1992: 66)

Another social scientist who has been deeply interested in reverie is Gaston Bachelard, whose main expertise was the history of science. After having produced a number of brilliant studies in his academic specialty in the 1920s and 1930s, Bachelard surprised his academic colleagues by publishing a number of books on reverie and poetry. These had titles such as the following: *Water and Dreams*, *The Flame of a Candle*, and *The Poetics of Space*.

According to Bachelard, both poetry and science have their roots in reverie and dreaming, but the creative impulse is worked out in different ways. One important reason for the scientist to become aware of what reverie is, besides courting its creative powers, is that unless reverie is checked, it will lead the scientist wrong.

In his argument about the dangers of reverie, Bachelard echoes the views of a number of thinkers. Both Kant and Weber, for example, praised imagination, but also felt that it needed to be disciplined by the conscious mind. Things tend to flow together in reverie, and especially concepts are missing.

Some modern social scientists have taken a similar stance as Kant and Weber (for example, Weick 1989). In my own view, all of these people are somewhat harsh on reverie, which has an important role to play in theorizing. It is by drifting away from established meanings that new meanings are sometimes discovered. Discipline has a limited role to play in the early stage of theorizing; while it is important at a later stage.

## Art and Theorizing

Art is often seen as an area where imagination can be exercised much more freely than anywhere else in modern society. To the extent that this is true, it is obviously the result of a special institutional arrangement, and this brings me to my first observation about social science and its relationship to art. This is that science and art are seen as two separate cultures in modern society but that this is by no means inevitable nor somehow inherent in their nature.

The same can be said about the view that art is the area par excellence in society where you can express yourself freely and experience things subjectively. For objectivity and analytical thought, in contrast, you have to go elsewhere—namely, to science.

Closely linked to the notion of two separate cultures is the idea that bringing art and science together is basically a utopian enterprise. It was perhaps possible to do so during the Renaissance, as exemplified by the work of such geniuses as Brunelleschi and Leonardo da Vinci. But this historical moment is long gone and will not come back.

The two ideas of art as a separate sphere of its own and of art as the incarnation of creativity and subjectivity block the interaction between social science and art. In my view the relationship between art and social science needs to be looked at from a different perspective and redefined in such a way that social scientists can begin to learn from art.

This idea of learning from art resonates strongly with Wittgenstein's critical remark on how art was seen in his time:

> People nowadays think that scientists exist to instruct them, poets, musicians, etc. to give them pleasure. The idea *that these have something to teach them*—that does not occur to them. (Wittgenstein 1980: 36e)

The attempt to change the institutional relationship between art and social science can take many expressions. Social science departments may, for example, decide to have artists on their faculty, and students in social science can be required to take art classes. When social scientists look for a place to live, they may want to pick an area with many artists, and so on.

It is often said that you cannot teach creativity. But there is also the fact that art schools have been trying to do precisely that for a very long time. Maybe there is something that can be learned from this experience and used to redesign the way that social science is currently being taught.

James G. March has suggested some other ways of using art to make social scientists more imaginative, or "making artists out of pedants" as he puts it (March 1970). One of his proposals is that an attempt should be made to attract a different type of students to the social sciences than those who have traditionally gravitated toward these.

The type of students that March would like to take courses in social science should, among other things, be very interested in analytical and abstract thinking. But this is not enough; they must also be interested in developing an artistic stance to what they do. The reason for this, according to March, is closely linked to the type of thinking that is needed to produce creative social science:

I think I can summarize the major emphasis here quite simply: It is to develop the *artistry* of thinking analytically about social science. The focus on analysis as an art form is not empty. It is intended to communicate the importance of aesthetic excitement, creative imagination, and unanticipated discovery to be found in creating models in social science. (March 1970: 65)

To what March says, it can be added that it is also possible to make use of art in practical exercises that have as their aim to increase the skill of theorizing. The main purpose of these exercises would be to make students of social science realize that they have much to learn from art. There currently exists a huge difference in the skills with which social scientists, on the one hand, and artists, on the other, observe reality and express it. Practical exercises may be one way of narrowing this gap.

## The Style of Writing

A few social scientists have singled out one particular form of art as potentially being of much use for rejuvenating sociology. This is literature, and the argument is that social scientists have much to learn when it comes to language from poets and novelists.

Several sociologists have, for example, argued for a sociological poetry in one form or another. The way that social scientists write, it has been noted, is often dull to the point of being expressionless.

---

### Some Exercises in Art and Social Science

1. State what you can express through some art form—such as painting, photography, dance, music, and so on—that you *cannot* express through social science.
2. Do the same thing for social science, but this time focus on its advantages in relation to the art form.
3. Suggest some way in which you can make social science express what some art form does better.
4. Do the same thing, but now for the art form: how can you change it so that it expresses some of what social science does better?
5. Repeat all of this, but this time you should also execute a piece of art in the genre that is discussed.
6. Discuss the statement by Neil Jenney that "art is a social science."

*Note*: For providing inspiration for these exercises, I thank Andreas Glaser and Susan Ossman.

---

According to Andrew Abbott, in an article advocating "lyrical sociology," social scientists need to become much better at expressing emotions in their writings (Abbott 2007). There exist many other critiques of the bloodless type of language that social scientists often use, accompanied by calls for "poetic metaphors of sociology," "a poetic for sociology," and so on (for example, Stein 1963; Nisbet 1976; Brown 1977).

Quite a bit of this type of argument can be understood as a reaction against the attempt of some social scientists to develop a type of language that is strictly objective and scientific in nature. The impulse to be scientific has always been strong in social science, and it has taken many expressions, from calls to root out all subjectivity to, say, walking around in white labcoats, as Fernando Henrique Cardoso and other sociology students did in São Paulo in the 1950s (Cardoso 2006: 47).

This type of attitude, to repeat, has also colored the language of sociologists. During the nineteenth century, in contrast, the border between social science and literature was fairly open. Social scientists wanted to express themselves well in their writings, and many literary authors consciously mixed social science with literature in their writings.

Balzac, for example, originally wanted to use *Etudes Sociales* as the title for what became *Comédie Humaine*. Zola described his novels as a form of "sociologie pratique" (Lepenies 1988: 4–7). Some authors went even further and produced what today would be considered social science: August Strindberg in his study of rural life in *Among French Peasants* (1889); Anton Chekhov in his study of prisoners in *Sakhalin Island* (1894); and Jack London in his account of the London poor in *The People of the Abyss* (1903).

But parallel to these tendencies there was also the hardcore scientific impulse. Auguste Comte, the father of sociology, detested the tendency to mix literature with social science and worked hard to develop a scientific, nonornamental style of writing. Order and objectivity were his two main objectives, in writing as in everything else.

Toward the end of his life Comte tried to formulate some of the rules that should be followed when you write on sociological topics. A chapter should have three parts; each part, seven sections; each section, twenty-two sentences, and so on. To repeat: order and objectivity.

This way of proceeding clearly makes it easier to write, and most of today's social scientists seem to have little trouble writing. They sit down and they write. In candid accounts of research projects, for example, you rarely find a social scientist who complains about writing blocks. The exception is graduate students, and the reason for this may well be that they have not yet caught on how to write in an objective and voiceless manner.

The reason why social scientists proceed more or less like Comte when they write is that they are usually not very interested in exploring the possibilities of language, nor are they especially drawn to ambiguous and hard-to-capture phenomena. As opposed to literary authors and poets, social scientists also do not believe in cultivating their creativity. I have never, for example, heard of a social scientist who experimented with drugs or alcohol (or was looking for a muse) in order to be more creative.

About a century after Comte, several American sociologists advanced similar arguments as their positivist ancestor about the need for an objective and scientific way of writing. In an article titled "Scientific Writing" from 1947, for example, William Ogburn states that sociologists should write like photographers and not like impressionist painters. They should use short sentences (not more than twenty words) and stay away from "useless words," especially emotional words and words with many associations (Ogburn 1947: 384–85). Sociologists should also remember that "the use of personal pronouns is not considered good form in scientific writing" (Ogburn 1947: 388).

Modern sociology is deeply influenced by what happened at Columbia University during the decades after World War II, and this makes Robert K. Merton's advocacy of a scientific style of writing, as opposed to an artistic style of writing, quite important. In his article on middle-range sociology, which is still widely read, Merton argues that sociologists must break with the tradition of writing well. Instead they should learn to write objectively.

Social scientists, Merton says, should not write "vividly and intensely" and in other ways try to convey "the rich fullness of the human scene" (Merton 1967: 69). This "handsome but alien heritage" of literature must be "disavowed." Instead they should write in such a way that they can capture "generalizable, objective concepts and relationships."

C. Wright Mills, who was also at Columbia University after World War II, was very skeptical of Merton's attempt to create an objective style for social scientists. In his own view you either write like a person, and that means with a "voice," or you write like a "machine" (Mills 1959: 220–21; cf. Espeland 2012).

In his own books and articles, Mills showed that it is possible to be both a good social scientist and a good stylist. His advice to social scientists for how to become a good writer is still worth thinking about: "To overcome the academic *prose* you first have to overcome the academic *pose*" (Mills 1959: 219).

A last question to be discussed is the following: should the way in which you write when you theorize be different from the way you write when you present your research? My own view is that there should be a difference. Theorizing is by nature experimental; it tries to capture and follow associations; and it thrives on what is fragmentary and suggestive. The notes that you take when your ideas fly tend to be short and telegraphic, similar to the way in which, say, Wittgenstein wrote.

An argument can also be made for using texts with this type of writing when one teaches theorizing. Fragments, incomplete statements, and the like can be very stimulating to read, and they tend to set off ideas in the mind of the reader. They may also teach the students how to take notes when they theorize.

But when the final results of a research project are to be presented, the situation is different. At this stage the task is to present a project that has been carefully and methodically carried out, and it is natural that this way of proceeding should also be reflected in the style of the writing. Virtues at the stage of theorizing can become vices when one presents the research results, and vice versa.

Still, it is also clear that the style of writing that Comte-Ogburn-Merton advocate is deadening in many ways and discourages a creative approach to social science. Writers of nonfiction have recently developed a genre called *creative nonfiction*, which is defined as "factual prose that is also *literary*— infused with the stylistic devises, tropes, rhetorical flourishes of the best fiction and the most lyrical of narrative poetry" (Forché and Gerard 2001: 1). Maybe we need a genre called *creative social science* as well. And maybe social scientists also have something to learn from nonfiction writers, especially when it comes to communicating with the reader (see, for example, Wallace and Garner 2013).

Note also that some of the advocates of the objective-scientific style in sociology did not themselves always follow the advice that they gave to others, a little bit like Herbert Simon did not always use his own approach to problem solving. Merton, for example, was an excellent stylist and always cherished finding the right word. In fact, Merton's favorite novel, which he read and reread over the years, was *Tristram Shandy*, best known for its wonderfully whimsical style.

I once asked Merton whom he considered to be the best stylist among social scientists. At the time I was reading a lot of Schumpeter and hoped he would say the author of *Capitalism, Socialism, and Democracy*. Instead he answered with the name of another economist: John Maynard Keynes. And it is true that Keynes was not only a superb social scientist but also a superb writer. Some of his friends, as we know, were members of the Bloomsbury Group.

In my own view the style to strive for, when one presents one's findings, is one that is logical, clear, and analytical. But once the general argument has been made, and the empirical proof presented, it is often important to suggest ways in which the research can be carried forward, and for this a suggestive style of writing may be appropriate.

There also exist a few other places in an article or a book where you can use a more artistic style. You may, for example, want to give the reader a sense for the actual way in which the research was conducted.

There is finally also a distinctly artistic quality to the prose that can be found in many of the key passages in the works of great scholars such as Marx, Weber, Keynes, and C. Wright Mills. At some point in an interesting argument it would seem that what is artistic and what is scientific often come close together.

.............................................................................

## CHAPTER 10

# Summary and More

Ideas are necessary.

—William Whewell, *On the Philosophy of Discovery* [1]

This chapter is mainly devoted to a summary of the argument so far. First, in order to do good social science, you need three things: solid empirical data, a skillful handling of methods, and some good theorizing. Today's social scientists are usually well trained to handle the two first of these requirements—but not the third. This book represents an attempt to remedy this situation, primarily through its focus on how to theorize in practical terms.

Having said this, it should immediately be added that there exist different types of theorizing, and that it is important to be clear about the way in which the term is being used. I have argued for a special approach to theorizing in social science, and I will try to show what is conventional as well as what is new about it.

Some other issues will be also discussed, which have as their goal to complete the argument in this book. What, for example, is the relationship of theorizing to politics? Does theorizing have a normative dimension? Is the type of theorizing that is suggested in this book overly individualistic, and related to this, what exactly is the role of the community in theorizing?

I will also argue that we know very little empirically about theorizing, and that research on this topic is needed. It is important to know more about the way that social scientists actually theorize—when, where, and how? This knowledge is crucial so we will be better able to diagnose the current situation and improve it.

There is also the problem of how to link up the stage of the prestudy to the main study. So far I have mainly discussed how to come up with new research ideas and theories that precede the drawing up and execution of the research design. But how exactly do the prestudy and the main study fit together? What is the role of theorizing during the main study? And does not the introduction of a theorizing stage before the main study influence the way in which the latter is carried out?

## Summing Up the Approach of Creative Theorizing

It is clear that different ways of theorizing exist, in the natural sciences as well as in the social sciences. The appendix to this book contains, for example, a presentation of an approach to theorizing that in my view deserves to be much better known—namely, that of Charles S. Peirce. His model contains a number of original and thought-provoking features. It is also universal in the sense that it is supposed to apply to the natural sciences as well as to the social sciences.

The approach that has been presented in this book is in contrast only applicable to the social sciences. Some of its features are not original, in the sense that they can also be found in other approaches to theorizing. But it also contains some elements that are relatively new. And the overall combination that makes up the approach is, to my knowledge, not to be found elsewhere.

In my mind I refer to my approach as *creative theorizing*, a term that I owe to Frank Dobbin. What first and foremost characterizes it is the argument that *a distinct space must be assigned to theorizing in the research process.* This goes for the prestudy as well as the main study. Theory is often just squeezed in somewhere in the process of inquiry, and given much less attention than the methods part. It lacks its own distinct space.

Theorizing, I argue, must be provided with a space that is large enough not only for some early observation to take place but also for the steps or procedures that I call *building out the theory.* This latter part consists of naming; constructing concepts, typologies, and the like; plus coming up with an explanation.

A second distinctive feature of my approach is that it represents *a deliberate attempt to shift the main focus from theory to theorizing.* The social sciences currently speak a lot about theory but less so about theorizing. While the two obviously belong together, my stance is to prioritize theorizing over theory. The reason for this is simple: theorizing is where theory is produced.

My definition of theorizing also follows from this, in the sense that I define theory in terms of theorizing rather than the other way around. Theory is the end product of theorizing. And theorizing is what precedes the final formulation of a theory, before it is set in print, once and for all, and presented to other people. Theorizing is what gives birth and life to theory.

A third distinctive feature of my approach is that *theorizing draws on a number of different types of thinking, feeling, and going about things that are currently mainly studied in cognitive science.* While reasoning of the traditional type is central to theorizing well, there is also guessing, hoping, speculating, using free associations, engaging in reverie, being intuitive and imaginative, and quite a bit more. Related to this, *it is important to try to somehow access your subconscious.*

Another distinctive feature of my approach is that *theorizing is a practical activity*. This idea is quite common, but less so the realization that the kind of knowledge we need to theorize well is also of a practical nature. What we most of all need are *practical tips for how to theorize well*, less so social science studies of theorizing. We also very much need to learn how to teach theorizing and what kind of practical exercises to use.

This emphasis on the need for practical knowledge is one reason why the title of this book refers to the art of theory. *Art* is to be understood in its old-fashioned meaning of practical skill in doing something.

The next feature of the kind of theorizing that I advocate has to do with the fact that it is a form of *social theorizing*. You first need to develop a sociological eye, I suggest, to theorize well. This represents a kind of *deep knowledge*. Second, you need to have an arsenal of concepts, mechanisms, and theories at your disposal. These do not need to be as deeply absorbed as the capacity to see things from a social perspective. It is enough that you can access them with more or less ease, as you need them. What is involved here is not deep knowledge but *familiarity*.

Another defining feature of the approach to theorizing in this book is that theorizing should take place not only during the main study but also—and creatively so—during the stage that I call *the prestudy*. This stage is currently not part of the research process, but I suggest that it should be.

I also advocate very strongly that *the tools that are needed for theorizing* (such as concepts, types, and so on) *should also be used for heuristic purposes*. This is particularly the case during the prestudy. The processes of trying to figure out a name for the phenomenon you study, turning the name into a concept, and the like can all also be used to discover something new about the topic that is studied. This constitutes an important part of my argument about theorizing.

I suggest as well that *theorizing during the prestudy and the main study must be carried out in close connection with the study of empirical facts.* This is what the slogan "you cannot theorize without facts" refers to. It is also why I argue that *observation represents an integral part of theorizing.* You should typically begin by studying some phenomenon; and your tentative theory represents an attempt to explain this phenomenon.

The type of theorizing that takes place during the prestudy can be called *early theorizing.* But there also exist two other kinds of theorizing in social science. One of these I call *fundamental theorizing,* and it deals with presuppositions and other nonempirical parts of theory such as what constitutes a fact, a concept, causality, and so on. The other type of theorizing occurs when the research design is drawn up and as it is executed, and it can be called *theorizing during the main study.* This type of theorizing is in many respects similar to that of early theorizing but is less exploratory and typically based on data that has been gathered in a methodical way.

There is also the issue of the kind of topic that the social scientist should work on. I have earlier said that *you need a good topic to theorize well.* What is meant by a good topic, however, is not so clear, beyond the general notion that it should be socially or existentially important.

Finally, the stage of early or creative theorizing should in principle be followed by the main study. If the result of the prestudy is promising—if you are on to something promising and interesting—you will want to proceed to the next stage, which is to draw up a research design and then execute it. But if the prestudy is not successful, it is probably best to abandon the topic or at least set it aside for now and proceed to something else.

# The Art of Creative Theorizing in Social Science

1. Theorizing means a preference for developing your own ideas, as opposed to using other people's theory.
2. Theorizing is a practical activity and something you learn by doing.
3. In theorizing you draw on many ways of thinking such as using metaphors and analogies, intuitive as well as logical thinking, speculation, free association, guessing, reverie, and more.
4. To theorize well you somehow need to access your subconscious.
5. Theorizing needs its own distinct space in the research process.
6. An important part of theorizing takes place during the first stage of the research process, well before its second stage, during which the research design is drawn up and a full study is carried out in accordance with accepted methods (the *prestudy* precedes the *main study*).
7. There are several parts, or steps, to theorizing: observation, building out the theory, and coming up with an explanation. These steps also take place during the main study.
8. Building out the theory, or giving it structure, consists of activities such as naming, constructing concepts, perhaps coming up with a typology, and using metaphors and analogies. In the prestudy building out the theory is preceded by observation and followed by an explanation.
9. Carrying out the different tasks of theorizing eventually turns into a skill, at which point these tasks will be handled in a more intuitive manner.
10. Concepts, types, and the other elements of theorizing should be used not only to construct a preliminary theory but also for heuristic purposes.
11. In addition to *early theorizing* during the prestudy, theorizing takes place when the research design is drawn up and executed (*theorizing during the main study*). Also a nonempirical kind of theorizing exists that deals with the presuppositions for empirical research and similar issues (*fundamental theorizing*).
12. You need a good topic to theorize well.
13. If the result of the early theorizing phase is positive, in the sense that you have come up with something promising and interesting, you should proceed to the main study. If not, you may want to switch to another topic.

*Comment*: These points summarize the approach to theorizing that is advocated in this book. I refer to it as the *art of creative theorizing* in social science. By *creative* I mean that just as knowledge of methods creates a competence in dealing with data, a knowledge of theorizing makes it possible to be creative in dealing with theory. The word *art* refers to the practical nature of theorizing.

## Again: Theorizing Can Be Learned

I have several times argued that theorizing is not something that can be done only by exceptionally gifted individuals, but something that anyone can learn how to do ("anyone can theorize"). In making this argument I have referred to the learning model of the Dreyfus brothers, according to which you start out by following certain rules, and then, at a later stage, let go of these rules. If you do not let go of them at this point, they will block your capacity to advance to the final stage, at which point your skill is intuitive.

But there also exists another model of learning that I think fits the theorizing process quite well and that highlights some issues that the Dreyfus brothers do not address. It has been developed by Howard Becker, as part of his well-known account in *Outsiders* of how people learn to become marijuana smokers.

There are especially two aspects to Becker's theory of learning that also fit the example of learning how to theorize. First, what Becker discusses is how you learn to do something that represents a bit of a mystery before you have tried it and know what it is like. And second, Becker discusses an activity that you may eventually come to really enjoy.

According to Becker, learning to enjoy marijuana is an activity that is social; it also proceeds in stages. "Vague impulses and desires—in this case, probably most frequently a curiosity about the kind of experience the drug will produce—are transformed into definite patterns of action through the social interpretation of a physical experience which is in itself ambiguous" (Becker 1973: 42).

In order to become a marijuana smoker you first have to learn to inhale in a special way. You do not, for example, inhale in the same way as when you smoke a cigarette. There is a special technique that you have to learn. You also have to learn to identify the effects of marijuana and try to reproduce these.

And finally, you have to interpret the effects of smoking marijuana as enjoyable:

> The user feels dizzy, thirsty; his scalp tingles; he misjudges time and distances. Are these things pleasurable? He isn't sure. If he is to continue marijuana use, he must decide that they are. (Becker 1973: 53)

Becker claims a certain generality for the way that this learning process operates, and in my view it is perhaps not so different from when you learn how to theorize. Also in the latter case you basically start out with a vague desire and little knowledge of what the end result will be. You similarly have to learn the technique of theorizing from others. And you have to study yourself as you engage in theorizing, and see what its effects are on your way of thinking.

There is finally also the enjoyment and sense of satisfaction that comes at the end. There is a very special joy that comes with theorizing, in seeing how your mind interacts with empirical reality and how you can come up with ideas. It is also very enjoyable to work out these ideas into a full theory, all the way from observation to explanation. You have created something yourself and this is deeply satisfying.

## Empirical Research on Theorizing

It is clear that we need to know more about theorizing than we currently do in order to get a better handle on it. This is especially true since theorizing of the type advocated here has not only a practical side but also an educational one. We need to know not only how to theorize ourselves but also how to teach theorizing to others.

It may be helpful to start out by distinguishing between two different topics to study. The first is how theorizing is currently being conducted. How, when, and where? Many different means can be used to study this topic, such as surveys, interviews, diaries, participant observation, time studies, and the like (see, for example, Latour and Woolgar 1986).

The same tools can also be used to study the second and more important topic—namely, how to theorize in a more creative way. Some new tools might be needed for this, since creative theorizing draws on some forms of thinking that are currently not very much discussed among social scientists. Theorizing-aloud protocols might be one of these tools. Other tools—say, to probe some of the tacit knowledge of successful theorizers—may have to be invented.

If we now turn from the problem of teaching yourself how to theorize to that of teaching others, a number of new issues emerge. These too need to be much better understood and discussed.

First, it would seem desirable that teachers of theorizing have learned how to theorize themselves, so that they are aware of the process involved. The point is not to have a small number of charismatic teachers who lecture on theory or theorizing, but to develop practical ways in which the average professor can learn how to teach the basic skills of theorizing to the average student.

The more we learn about teaching theorizing, and the more communication there is between those who teach classes in this topic, the easier it will be to reach the goal of developing a general approach to this topic that is both effective and can easily be reproduced.

Still, there are many traps to avoid for those who teach theorizing. One study of instructor pilots in the US Air Force, for example, found that the way in which the instructors told the students to carry out a task differed from the way in which they demonstrated how this should be done in the classroom. They told the students to scan the instruments in a special way, while they did so in a different way themselves (Dreyfus and Dreyfus 1986: 152–53).

It may well be the case that the example of the instructor pilots has some generality to it. Some of us may be blind when we describe how we ourselves theorize. We may also teach students how to do something in one way, while we proceed in a different way when we do it ourselves.

One way to counter this tendency is to be observant of yourself and closely study how you actually go about doing things. Keeping a diary when you teach theorizing might be useful; occasionally taping and filming the classes could also be useful.

This example also reminds us that there is an ethical side to theorizing. In medicine one of the ethical maxims says that you should act in such a way that no harm is done ("first, do no harm"). Some similar maxim is perhaps also needed when theorizing is being taught.

## Theorizing and Research Design

Despite repeated statements to the contrary some readers may think that theorizing of the type advocated in this book is seen as a goal in itself, and for this reason undermines empirical research. This, however, is not a correct reading of the argument I have made in this book.

This argument is instead that it would be helpful to have a stage of theorizing *before* the research design has been drawn up and executed, and that this stage is currently being neglected or rushed through much too quickly. The research question that results from the way of doing things today has a good chance of not being creative. This book wants, among other things, to draw attention to this fact, and also suggest a way to remedy it.

The goal is not to challenge the methods that are currently being used in the social sciences. Nor do I argue that no theorizing takes place when you draw up the research design or when it is executed. In fact, there are a number of works on what should be done with theory *after* the prestudy, and it is imperative for the theorizer to know this literature. Without adequate knowledge on this point, the study cannot be completed.

The various steps that make up theorizing during the prestudy also take place during the main study. They do not necessarily do so in the same form or in the same order, but they nonetheless have to be present during the main study. The purpose of the prestudy and the main study is also the same: to come up with an explanation of an empirical (social) phenomenon.

Still, having said all of this, it would also seem that the idea of adding a stage of theorizing to the research process, without changing this process in some way, is probably illusory. A more realistic stance would be that some changes may have to be made to the way in which we currently view the research design and how it should be executed.

It has already been mentioned that research projects that fail at the early theorizing stage should probably not be carried out. It is also likely that the projects that do make it to the stage of the research design will be better conceptualized and understood than they currently are.

This argument also works the other way around. The skill and experience that a researcher has in executing a research design will also be reflected in his or her skill at the early theorizing stage, once a decision has been made to include a prestudy. The dividing line between the early theorizing stage and the traditional research process will in other words be somewhat eroded.

It is probably also true that by adding a full stage of theorizing to the research process, there will be somewhat less theorizing during the main study. Unless, of course, it turns out that the initial theory was wrong, in which case you have to redo all or some of the parts of the theorizing during the main study (name the phenomenon, create concepts, and so on).

Having more and better data may similarly make it necessary to engage in retheorizing. Some problems can be solved only far into the main research process. Having sound data does not translate into immediate understanding but often to long bouts of iterative behavior before the final explanation has been produced.

There also exist some theory-related tasks that in principle belong only to the stage of the main study. These include straightening out and adjusting your tentative theory, giving it a logical form, and going over it repeatedly.

Another of these tasks is the formulation of hypotheses (or their equivalents). A creative and tentative theory hopefully exists at this point, as a result of the prestudy, but it is now imperative to translate this theory into testable hypotheses. This kind of activity demands its own distinct skill and creativity (for example, Goertz 2006).

The important tasks of carefully embedding the theory in the existing literature, and of linking it up to some strand of current theory, also take place during the main study. The embedding of the proposed theory in a broader strand of theory is crucial in order to show that what is being researched represents a problem that has not already been solved and that there exists some good reason for the research.

By linking the tentative theory to some existing strand of theory, you also show how it fits the tradition of your discipline, and how this tradition can be enriched by the new research. If this is not done the new theory, however insightful it might be, risks being forgotten and turning into a dead end. This is incidentally also where the problem of theorizing meets the important problem of cumulativity of knowledge in social science (for example, Abbott 2006).

Beyond general statements of this type about theorizing during the prestudy and the main study, it should be added that the literature on theorizing and the literature on research design currently constitute two separate literatures with little overlap. They need in my view to be moved much closer to one another. At a minimum each should start referring to the other in a systematic manner.

At a practical level it would also seem that each of these literatures would benefit from more contact with the other. It is dangerous, for example, to engage in theorizing without having a good knowledge of what to do once you come to the research design, and vice versa.

To this can be added that the literature on research design, and how you carry out your research plans, includes much material that is of help to the theorizer. Again I refer as an example to the literature in political science on comparative analysis and how to construct and operationalize concepts.

There also exist some ideas in the literature on theorizing that may improve the literature on research design. Take, for example, the idea of using concepts, metaphors, and so on in a heuristic manner. This approach may also be used for research designs.

C. Wright Mills makes precisely this point in *The Sociological Imagination*. Just by drawing up a research design, he says, you may come up with some interesting and unexpected ideas:

Although you will never be able to get the money with which to do many of the empirical studies you design, it is necessary that you continue designing them. For once you lay out an empirical study, even if you do not follow it through, it leads you to a new search for data, which often turns out to have unsuspected relevance to your problems. (Mills 1959: 205)

## Theorizing and Its Political-Ethical Presuppositions

One can argue that all social theories, including those that deal with theorizing, have a political-ethical dimension, in the sense that they take certain features of society and human nature for granted. This type of political-ethical notions can sometimes come close to the presuppositions that were discussed in chapter 8.

If I take myself as an example, I know that I hold a number of political-ethical opinions that are probably related to many of the ideas I have advocated in this book. In the rest of this section I will try to present these, in an effort to make my own thinking more transparent and also to draw attention to this type of issue.

Many readers will not be interested in my political-ethical ideas, and they may want to skip the next few paragraphs and proceed to the next section. This section deals with a related but different topic—that is, should there be a normative dimension to theorizing and, if so, what should this normative dimension be like?

Human beings, as I see things, are all unique and equal. Each person is endowed with a capacity to think, and thinking freely is invaluable to the individual. A society in which these values are respected, encouraged, and seen as a collective good represents a good society to me.

To a large extent these ideas come from Immanuel Kant, and the type of theorizing that I advocate goes well with several aspects of his philosophy. I am also influenced by the work of some of Kant's followers, especially that of Hannah Arendt (1978).

Thinking for oneself (*Selbstdenken*), and treating each person as a goal and not as a mean, are two central themes in the Kantian tradition. Two others that I find inspiring are that each individual represents a new beginning (*natalism*) and that you should always try to incorporate the viewpoint of others when you think (*sensus communis*). There is also the idea that your thoughts and actions should in principle be able to stand up to the Court of Reason in your mind.

One text by Kant that has inspired me when I have thought about theorizing is "What Is Enlightenment?" Kant here argues that every person has the capacity to think for himself or herself—but also that there exist forces that try to prevent this. Some of these forces can be found outside the individual and others inside the individual.

For questions of conscience, Kant says, we tend to go to a priest. Or we read a book to avoid making up our mind ourselves. Dogmas and formulas have the same effect.

There are also certain people who like to think for other people, whom Kant calls guardians. They are always ready to think for us, and they encourage us to rely on them, instead of thinking ourselves.

But we should not listen to the guardians, Kant says. It may well be true that the first few times that we try to think for ourselves, we will fail and fall flat on our face. But we can learn from this experience, and after a few failures we will succeed.

Like many other philosophers Kant is of the opinion that thinking is a solitary business. But even if it is true that Kant did not develop a theory of thinking centered around a vision of a community of thinkers, he also says that "company is indispensable for *the thinker*" (Arendt 1992: 10).

Humans are sociable beings and our mode of living and thinking is with other people, Kant says. The thinker should not only seek the company of others, he or she should also try to develop a capacity to look at things from the perspective of other people. *Sensus communis* is a sense just like the other senses, such as hearing, seeing, and so on. It operates mainly through imagination, and it is linked to ethics as well as art.

## The Normative Dimension

So much for the philosophical and ethical roots of my ideas. But what is the situation like if we turn to a different but related topic: should theorizing have an explicit and openly normative dimension? One person who thought so was C. Wright Mills, and since he was deeply concerned with this issue as well as with theorizing, his argument deserves a hearing.

Based on the research that he was conducting on the social structure of the United States, Mills felt that work was increasingly becoming meaningless in modern society. In *White Collar* he outlines what an alternative kind of work would look like. He called this "the craft model of work" (Mills 1953: 220–28).

Modern people, according to Mills, are typically not allowed to decide themselves what to do at work, nor how to execute their tasks. As a result, they tend not to develop their selves when they work, and they basically work to get paid. They also separate play from work, and invest their leisure activities with the creativity that would have gone into their work, if it had been organized as a craft.

But there do exist a small number of jobs in the modern world, according to Mills, where craftsmanship and "the craft ethic" are still possible (for example, Mills 1953: 220, 224). This is especially true for the activities of privileged professionals and intellectuals. It is important to note that Mills is speaking about an *ethic* in connection with craftmanship, since it is precisely this quality that makes his view normative in nature, including what he has to say about theorizing.

In *The Sociological Imagination* Mills sharply criticizes the attempt to mechanize social science, and he opposes this trend to an alternative view of what social science could be like. This is where we find his well-known statement that the social scientist should regard his or her job as a craft. He spells out his view in the following way:

> Be a good craftsman: Avoid any rigid set of procedures. Above all, seek to develop and to use the sociological imagination. Avoid any fetishism of method and technique. Urge the rehabilitation of the unpretentious intellectual craftsman, and try to become such a craftsman yourself. Let every man be his own methodologist; let every man be his own theorist; let theory and method again become part of the practice of a craft. Stand for the primacy of the individual scholar; stand opposed to the ascendency of research teams of technicians. (Mills 1959: 224)

But Mills not only urges the social scientist to be a good craftsman and says what this entails in terms of work habits and attitudes. He also tries to outline the kind of topics that the social scientist should work on.

Mills refers to his ideas on this subject as "the classic tradition" (see also Mills 1960). But the works in the classic tradition are not defined by Mills in the conventional way—say, as works of exceptional quality and lasting value. Instead he defines the classic tradition as social science works that contain deeply original attempts to answer the following three questions: *What does the structure of some particular society look like? What is its place in history? What kinds of people prevail in it?*

The classic tradition, Mills says, provides the average social scientist with *general models* for how to address these questions. In fact one of the strengths of these classical models (as we may call them) is precisely that they have the capacity to inspire social scientists to create new theories by drawing on their general insights.

Another strength is that the rejection of a theory that has been created in this way does not necessarily invalidate the general model. The reason for this seems to be that this type of model, in Mills's view, is of a very broad and elastic kind, and therefore difficult to prove wrong.

The normative dimension of the classic tradition is quite visible in Mills's own production, from his early work on American workers to his later work on the threat of World War III. It is also implicit in his argument that a good social scientist should have the capacity to link up individual biography to history. Private troubles are public issues, and public issues can be solved through politics.

At this point it should be clear that there exists a definite connection between Mills's normative stance and the kind of topics he chose to study. It should also be clear that Mills's approach to sociological theory differs on several key points from, say, Merton's idea of middle-range theory. For one thing, Mills did not reject general theory or general models, to use his terminology. He also argued that social scientists who are deeply immersed in the major problems of their time stand a better chance of coming up with interesting topics to theorize than those who are not.

## The Role of Community

Throughout this book I have argued that it is possible for the individual student of social science to learn how to theorize and how this may lead to a more creative social science. Theorizing, I have also suggested, is something you learn by doing, and you have to do it yourself.

In an earlier article I used the term *personalism* for my approach to theorizing, in an attempt to make clear that I was not advocating a form of individualism but nonetheless thought it was crucial to focus on the individual (Swedberg 2012). The main point of theorizing, according to this view, is to develop your own ideas and not use other people's theory.

Some colleagues and friends who know my viewpoint, and who agree that a new approach to theorizing should be encouraged, differ when it comes to my emphasis on the individual. They feel that my stance is too individualistic and that community should be at the center of theorizing (for example, Reed and Zald 2014).

Their argument is that the individual scholar is a product of the community and that no real progress in theorizing can take place till this basic fact is properly realized. To stress the role of the individual, along the lines that I do, is to fall into the trap of individualism and ignore the organic link that exists between theorizing and the community.

My response to this criticism is that it is indeed true that the individual scholar is a product of society and that all major social changes are collective in nature. Where I differ is that I find references to the powerful impact of the community on the capacity to theorize somewhat frustrating. The reason for this is that it is difficult to translate this type of insight into practical directives for the individual. They invite instead a kind of sociology of knowledge analysis that is correct—but also not very helpful when it comes to providing practical guidelines for how to theorize.

At a more general level, my argument has been well expressed by Wittgenstein in one of his aphoristic statements:

> If life becomes hard to bear we think of a change in our circumstances. But the most important and effective change, a change in our own attitude, hardly even occurs to us, and the resolution to take such a step is very hard for us. (Wittgenstein 1980: 53e)

Beyond this viewpoint, I would also argue the following. It may be possible already today to create something of *a culture of creative theorizing in social science*. Such a culture would not only mean that students would be able to find courses in theorizing and that these would provide them with as much competence in dealing with theory as today's courses in methods provide them with a competence in handling facts. It would also mean that the students, once they begin their studies in social science, would become members of a community of sorts in which creative and autonomous theorizing is highly valued, not only as an indispensable skill that you need to have in order to produce good social science but also as an intrinsic value in itself.

# How to Theorize according to Charles S. Peirce

> Suppose, for example, that I have an idea that interests me. It is my creation. It is my creature; . . . it is a little person. I love it; and I will sink myself in perfecting it. It is not by dealing out cold justice to the circle of my ideas that I can make them grow, but by cherishing and tending them as I would flowers in my garden.
>
> —Charles S. Peirce, "Evolutionary Love"[1]

Some approaches to theorizing are of extra interest to those who want to learn how to theorize in a creative way. One of the most suggestive can to my mind be found in the work of Charles S. Peirce. There are many references to his work in this book, especially in the introduction and in chapter 5 on explanation. Peirce's approach, however, is so rich that it deserves a full account of its own. Ending as well as beginning this book with Peirce also constitutes an appropriate tribute to his work.

I will mainly focus on two topics in this appendix. The first is abduction, but not so much abduction in general as the practical tips that Peirce developed for how to become good at making abductions (see, for example, Paavola 2006 for a review of the literature on abduction). In doing so I will add substantially to what has been said earlier.

I will also outline Peirce's view of the whole research process, not only the role of abduction, as is often done. While Peirce liked to point out that discoveries are made through abduction, he always emphasized that abduction was just one part of the research process. By way of concluding, I will also discuss the differences between Peirce's approach to theorizing and the one I am advocating in this book.

## A Difficult Life

First, however, a brief account of Peirce's life is in order since it deeply affected his ideas and the way that his work has been received (see especially Brent 1993). Charles Sanders Peirce (1839–1914) was born into the sophisticated middle-class society that existed in Cambridge, Massachusetts, during the mid-nineteenth century. His father was a professor of astronomy and mathematics at Harvard University and regarded by many as the foremost mathematician of his generation. His mother was the daughter of a senator.

Peirce went to Harvard, where he earned a B.A. in 1859 and an M.A. in 1862. But he was also educated at home by his father. Realizing the talents of his son, Peirce Sr. early set out to teach him the basic skills of a scientist, a bit like James Mill tutored John Stuart Mill. In this way Peirce especially learned mathematics and chemistry.

At the age of twelve Peirce discovered logic, which from now on would be his first and foremost intellectual love. He also read widely in philosophy and science on his own. He attended the Lawrence Scientific School, from which he graduated with a B.Sc. in 1863.

In these different ways the foundations were laid for a life in science that would make Peirce not only a polymath, but one of the few individuals who can compete with Aristotle in terms of breadth of knowledge and originality.

Peirce helped to found pragmatism and semiotics. He was the first experimental psychologist in the United States. He pioneered several forms of symbolic logic. To this can be added that he had a professional knowledge of many sciences, such as astronomy, metrology, geodesy, physics, mathematics, philosophy, and the history of science.

But there was also a dark side to Peirce. His father pushed him to the point of breakdown. The two also shared an extremely painful illness that was known at the time as facial neuralgia and today as trigeminal neuralgia. Peirce used various drugs to fight the pain, such as opium and morphine, to which he became addicted.

Peirce was also very willful, indifferent to social conventions, and totally focused on his goal of creating a new kind of logic. He had little sense of money and lost most of what he had through various get-rich schemes. There was a violent streak to his nature, to which especially his wives and his servants were exposed.

Peirce's career as well as his life falls into two distinct phases. In the first he was gainfully employed and part of the comfortable middle-class society in which he grew up. In 1861 he began to work for the Coast and Geodetic Survey, an activity that provided him with an income as well as an opportunity to work on some scientific tasks that interested him.

His main desire, however, was to work full-time on logic and have an academic career. In 1879 he seemed to be well under way to reach this goal, when he was hired at Johns Hopkins University as a lecturer in logic, with the promise of tenure.

Peirce soon showed his skill as a scientist at the Coast and Geodetic Survey and made several important contributions to geodesy. His work at Johns Hopkins University flourished as well. Johns Hopkins was the first research university in the United States, founded in 1876, and Peirce was one of the people who helped to make it a place where original scientific work was carried out.

Peirce also trained a number of exceptionally talented students at Johns Hopkins, many of whom went on to prominent careers. Joseph Jastrow was one of these, and he has described how Peirce interacted with his students in the following way:

> The terms of equality upon which he met us were not in the way of flattery, for they were too spontaneous and sincere. We were members of his "scientific" fraternity; greetings were brief, and we proceeded to the business that brought us together, in which he and we found more pleasure than in anything else. This type of cooperation and delegation of responsibility came as near to a pedagogical device as any method that he used. (Jastrow 1916: 725)

The second and very difficult period of Peirce's life began in the early 1880s. He was first denied tenure at Johns Hopkins. He was then vilified in a congressional inquiry into the Coast and Geodetic Survey, and he was finally forced to leave his position there. From the mid-1890s till his death in 1914, Peirce lived in great poverty and well outside the type of society in which he had grown up.

There are several reasons for the abrupt end to Peirce's official career. He was willful and eccentric. He lacked tact when he commented on fellow scientists' work. He was also seen as immoral by high-standing citizens because of his unconventional ideas about Christianity, and even more so since he had begun to live with a woman before his divorce from his first wife came through.

Unbeknownst to Peirce, he had also made a bitter enemy of a fellow scientist, who repeatedly blocked his ever more desperate attempts to get back into academia or at least get a research grant. His name was Simon Newcomb, an astronomer and a mathematician who is today remembered only as Peirce's nemesis. Peirce never knew of Newcomb's enmity but thought that people conspired against him.

After the mid-1880s Peirce was sometimes homeless and often starved. In 1897 he wrote to his friend William James,

> I have learned a great deal about philosophy in the last few years, because they have been very miserable and unsuccessful years,—terrible beyond anything that the man of ordinary circumstances can possibly understand or conceive . . . a new world of which I knew nothing, and of which I cannot find that anybody who has written has really known much, has been disclosed to me, the world of misery. (Brent 1993: 258–59)

During the second period of his life Peirce mainly lived with his second wife, Juliette Pourtalai, in Milford, Pennsylvania, in a house he called Arisbe. Most winters they could not afford to heat the house and there was little to eat. As a result, Peirce and his wife soon suffered from malnourishment and various illnesses.

Throughout his years of extreme hardship Peirce tried to complete the tasks he had set for himself as a young man, especially to work out a new type of logic. He could not afford to keep up with the scientific literature, and he often had to write on the back of old manuscripts.

Despite these adversities Peirce doggedly kept thinking and writing. After his dismissal from Johns Hopkins he produced some 80,000 pages of manuscript. Most of this material, and most of his books, were donated to Harvard University after his death in 1914. His wife kept the rest of his writings and books, which were either lost or burned by the new owner of Arisbe, after her death in 1934.

## Peirce's View of the Research Process

It is hard to quickly summarize Peirce's position on any topic, and this is as true for the way he viewed the research process as the kind of exercises he prescribed for those who wanted to learn how to theorize. For those who are interested in these two topics I especially recommend the following writings: "Training in Reasoning" (a lecture from 1898); "How to Theorize" (a lecture from 1903); and "Guessing" (a manuscript from circa 1907) (Peirce 1929; 1935b; 1992b).

Peirce's view of the research process has mainly two origins: his own work in science and his interest in logic. Through his scientific training Peirce knew how to carry out experiments; and through his work in logic he became very interested in finding out the most efficient way of thinking. In his later work his view of logic expanded into a broad philosophy that also came to encompass the research process.

Peirce viewed the research process in terms of stages, each of which demanded its own form of thinking. He believed that the scientist could be trained in these ways of thinking and also train himself or herself. Following Aristotle, Peirce called these stages *abduction*, *deduction*, and *induction*.

What to Aristotle was applicable to logic, Peirce extended to the way that scientific research in general should be conducted.

He also invested each of Aristotle's three terms—abduction, deduction, and induction—with a distinct meaning of his own.

Peirce especially thought that abduction, or the process of coming up with a new scientific idea, was commonly confused with induction:

> Nothing has so much contributed to present chaotic or erroneous ideas of the logic of science as failure to distinguish the essentially different characters of different elements of scientific reasoning; and one of the worst of these confusions, as well as one of the commonest, consists in regarding abduction and induction taken together (often mixed also with deduction) as a simple argument. (Peirce 1958a: 218)

According to Peirce, in order to become a good scientist it is essential to realize that the research process must draw on three different types of thinking, and that each of these should be used for a different task. You begin by trying to come up with a new idea (*abduction*). You then proceed to developing hypotheses from this idea (*deduction*). The final stage of the research process is centered around the testing of the hypotheses (*induction*).

You can improve your skill in induction and deduction through practical exercises. Abduction, in contrast, is not something you can easily train yourself in. You basically have to hope that you will come up with a new idea and somehow see to it that you do.

Peirce developed a complex system of thought over the years, in which each of these three types of thinking was related to his system of signs as well as to his theory of cosmology. Since this part of Peirce's thought has little consequence for the practical aspects of his view of the research process, I will set it aside here.

## Step 1 in the Inquiry: Abduction

The centerpiece of Peirce's view of the research process is his notion of abduction. Throughout his life Peirce tried to understand how scientific discoveries are made from the perspective of the scientist, and many of his ideas on this topic became part of his notion of abduction.

Toward the end of his life Peirce decided to write "a small book" in which he would present "the real nature" of abduction. Like so many of the projects that he tried to carry out during his years of poverty, it was never completed (Fann 1970: 60).

The research process, according to Peirce, starts with abduction, or the attempt to come up with an idea for how to explain something. As is clear from the lecture "How to Theorize" (1903), by the term *abduction* Peirce roughly meant the same as theorizing.

One can get a good sense for how Peirce viewed the role of abduction in the research process by studying the following two quotes. Both make clear that getting an idea is more of a process than just having a sudden flash of insight.

The first quote, where *A* stands for the abduction, is exemplary in its brevity:

> The surprising fact, C, is observed;
> But if A were true, C would be a matter of course;
> Hence, there is reason to suspect that A is true.
> (Peirce 1934a: 189)

The second quote illuminates the nature of abduction in a phenomenological rather than logical manner:

A mass of facts is before us. We go through them. We examine them. We find them a confused snarl, an impen-
etrable jungle. We are unable to hold them in our minds.
We endeavor to set them down upon paper; but they seem
so multiplex intricate that we can neither satisfy ourselves
that what we have set down represents the facts, nor can we
get any clear idea of what it is that we have set down. But
suddenly, while we are poring over our digest of the facts
and are endeavoring to set them into order, it occurs to us
that if we were to assume something to be true that we do
not know to be true, these facts would arrange themselves
luminously. That is *abduction*. (Peirce 1997: 282)

Each of the different elements that make up the process of abduction deserves a brief comment. According to Peirce, you start
out by working on some problem. You continue with this till you
find something surprising, and this is what you want to explain.

You now intensify your observation and hope that you will be
able to come up with an explanation. To do so you have to guess.
Or more precisely you have to guess in order to come up with a
suggestion for an explanation, since it is not possible to know
the value of an explanation until it has been tested against the
facts.

Surprise plays a key role in Peirce's version of inquiry. You
study something until you encounter some surprising phenomenon, and it is this phenomenon that needs to be explained. The
phenomenon is surprising, because based on your knowledge
you would expect something else to happen.

Peirce writes,

The whole operation begins with *Abduction*, which is now
to be described. Its occasion is a *surprise*. That is, some be-

lief, active or passive, formulated or unformulated, has just been broken. (Peirce 1998a: 287)

Once you are surprised you will continue and also intensify the observation. You zoom in on what has surprised you in order to come up with an explanation for it. You do this in the hope that you will be able to figure out an explanation for what is going on. You hope two things: that an explanation exists, and that you will find it.

There can be any number of possible explanations, Peirce says, and the problem is to come up with the right one. He writes,

> We are . . . bound to hope that, although the possible explanations of our facts may be strictly innumerable, yet our mind will be able, in some finite number of guesses, to guess the sole true explanation of them. *That* we are bound to assume, independently of any evidence that it is true. Animated by that hope, we are to proceed to the construction of a hypothesis. (Peirce 1958a: 219)

The way that the scientist goes about finding the right explanation is through guessing. As human beings we are born with a capacity to somehow guess right, or at least more correctly than if we just guessed at random.

Ultimately this talent for guessing has to do with the mysterious powers of the human mind, and that we are an organic part of the very universe that we are studying:

> I infer in the first place that man divines something of the secret principles of the universe because his mind has developed as a part of the universe and under the influence of these same secret principles; and secondly, that we often derive from

observation strong intimations of truth, without being able to specify what were the circumstances we had observed which conveyed those intimations. (Peirce 1929: 281–82)

This quote comes from Peirce's article "Guessing," in which he also discusses the role that our expertise as scientists plays in guessing. While it is necessary to have a good knowledge of what science says, in order to be surprised by something that is unknown, this knowledge does little for our capacity to guess right:

We may be aided by previous knowledge in forming our hypotheses. In that case they will not be pure guesses but will be compounds of deductions from general rules we already know, applied to the facts under observation, for one ingredient, and pure guess, for the other ingredient. (Peirce 1929: 268)

Through guessing we come up with a tentative explanation. While this activity means that we have done something new and creative, most guesses are wrong. Whether a guess is right or wrong is something we cannot know before we have tested the suggested explanation. For this reason an abduction can never represent the end of the inquiry.

## Steps 2 and 3 in the Inquiry: Deduction and Induction

Abduction, to repeat, must be followed by deduction and induction for the inquiry to be complete and for a scientific contribution to be possible. Both deduction and induction represent different ways of thinking as well as stages to go through once an abduction has been made.

Deduction is a kind of *"necessary reasoning,"* in that it has to proceed exclusively according to logic and has nothing to do with facts (for example, Peirce 1958a: 207). You deduct what is implicit in the abduction.

Two different tasks have to be carried out during the stage of deduction (Peirce 1935: 470–72). First, the suggested explanation or abduction has to be put in shape—that is, it has to be sharpened and made as clear as possible. Second, testable hypotheses have to be derived from the suggested theory.

Once testable hypotheses have been formulated, they must be confronted with facts, and this is done during the stage of induction. You essentially want to find out whether the abduction is true or not. Peirce calls the kind of testing that is characteristic of induction "experimental research" (for example, Peirce 1958b: 209).

Depending on the situation, induction will take different forms. If the empirical material can be quantified, you want to proceed in one way; if not, in another. The theory of probability is typically involved at this stage.

Economic concerns come into the picture at the stage of induction as well. The scientist has a limited amount of time,

---

### How to Carry Out an Inquiry according to Charles S. Peirce

1. Start your research and continue until you are surprised by something (abduction, part 1).
2. Observe intensely what surprises you (abduction, part 2).
3. Hope that there exists an explanation for the surprising facts and guess what this might be (abduction, part 3).
4. Explicate the tentative explanation and turn it into clear and testable hypotheses (deduction).
5. For reasons of economy of research, select one hypothesis to work on (induction, part 1).
6. Test the hypothesis against data (induction, part 2).

energy, and money. As Peirce explains in his writings on "The Economy of Research," these resources have to be carefully taken into account, when the scientist decides which hypotheses to pursue (Peirce 1958a: 139–61, 206).

## Peirce's Pedagogy and Practical Tips for How to Become Good at Abduction

While Peirce never developed a doctrine of pedagogy, he occasionally referred to his ideas on this topic (for example, Liszka 2011; Beauchamp 2012). His general attitude to education was also practical rather than abstract and theoretical. This can be exemplified by his lifelong concern with how to teach students to train themselves in reasoning.

A good example of this can be found in the lecture on "Training in Reasoning" that Peirce gave in Cambridge, Massachusetts, in 1898. He began the lecture by stating that he opposed the ruling view of pedagogy in the United States and instead believed in "liberal education" (Peirce 1992b: 398). In liberal education, according to Peirce, you teach students "the art of thinking," rather than some specific piece of knowledge (Peirce 1992b: 398).

The argument in this lecture fits well with Peirce's view of the task of the modern university. In a modern university teachers and students should learn together. Teaching has no place in a university, which is exclusively an institution of learning (for example, Fisch 1986: 35–36).

In "Training in Reasoning" Peirce outlines three different processes, which together make up the art of reasoning, as this should be taught to students. These are: *observation*, *experimentation*, and *habituation*. These three forms are not the same as abduction, deduction, and induction. They do, however, help the student to think effectively, and they are also useful if he or she later wants to engage in research.

Peirce's focus in "Training in Reasoning" is on the art of thinking, and is practical through and through. For those readers who are interested in developing their own capacity for abduction, this is a key text.

To be good at *observation* you have to develop a kind of thinking that is essentially passive, according to Peirce. By this he meant that you must learn not to interfere with what is going on. You must yield to it.

In observation you have to draw both on your capacity for "subconscious induction" and on your "upper consciousness" (Peirce 1992b: 397, 400). The former is linked to your "associational potency," and in order to benefit from it, you have to be relaxed and try to take in as much as possible of what you are studying.

Once this has been done, the turn comes to the upper consciousness. With its help, you try to understand the structure of whatever you are studying. There is always the temptation to let the upper consciousness take over and push the subconscious part of your mind to the side. This must absolutely not be allowed to happen, according to Peirce, or you risk not understanding the phenomenon at all.

The way to become good at observation, he also says, is to engage in various exercises to increase your capacity for discrimination. Peirce distinguishes between observing objects, emotions, and mental states, but he does not specify which exercises are good for each of these. Nonetheless, by engaging in exercises that sharpen your sense of discrimination for just one month, he says, it is possible to make huge progress.

The second element in the art of reasoning is *experimentation*. It is very different from observation, in that it appeals to your sense of activity rather than passivity. What matters here are energy, perseverance, and willpower. A good way to train your capacity for experimentation, Peirce says, is to lift weights.

An important part of learning how to experiment is to keep records. "Everything worth notice is worth recording" (Peirce 1992b: 408). If you take careful notes and save these, after a few years you will have a valuable collection that helps you to be a very effective thinker.

A key point to remember, when you keep track of knowledge in this way, is that you should keep your notes in such a way that you can quickly access them. You should also be able to easily "*rearrange*" them (Peirce 1992b: 408; italics in the original).

The third type of reasoning that is crucial to the art of thinking is *habituation*, by which Peirce means the capacity to form new mental habits and rid yourself of old ones. A mental habit is described as an "association of ideas" (Peirce 1992b: 411).

Children have a plasticity of mind that adults lack, according to Peirce, and it is important to try to re-create this capacity in yourself. "To be a philosopher, or a scientific man, you must be as a little child, with all the sincerity and simple-mindedness of the child's vision, with all the plasticity of the child's mental habits" (Peirce 1992b: 412).

A good way of developing your capacity for habituation is to read interesting books; another is to have conversations with interesting people. For these types of activity to have a positive effect, however, you have to deeply enter into the perspective of the author or the conversation partner. While entering into the perspective of others is not particularly hard, according to Peirce, good books and interesting people are difficult to find.

There also exist some other exercises that can be used to strengthen your power of habituation. One is to train yourself in how to divide a topic and classify it. Others have as their goal to teach you how to construct definitions and analyze ideas. To express theories and arguments in as few words, and in as concise manner as possible, is also helpful.

In Peirce's writings you can find several other practical tips for how to develop your thought. Some of these have to do with an activity to which Peirce attached a special importance ever since his early years. This is the capacity for playful reverie, or what Peirce calls "the Play of Musement" (Peirce 1935: 452–65).

Playful reverie belongs to the same family as the subconscious induction that Peirce refers to in "Training in Reasoning." It can be used to refresh your mind and also when you have a problem that seems "utterly insoluble" (Peirce 1935: 460).

The best way to engage in reverie or musement is to take a walk at dawn or at dusk. Peirce recommends spending 5 to 6 percent of your waking time in this way, which means something like one hour per day. During this magic time, you should just let go:

> Enter your skiff of Musement, push off into the lake of thought, and leave the breath of heaven to swell your sail. With your eyes open, awake to what is about or within you, and open conversation with yourself; for such is all meditation. (Peirce 1935: 461)

Before leaving Peirce and his practical tips for how to engage in reverie, it should be pointed out once more that he did not see his attempts to cultivate the subconscious as unscientific. While he worked at Johns Hopkins in the 1880s he carried out an experiment on the subconscious and how you can improve your access to it (Peirce and Jastrow 1885; see also Peirce 1868).

One reason why the resulting article, titled "On Small Differences," is still held in high regard has to do with its sophisticated research design, which includes an early use of randomization (for example, Hacking 1988). Another reason is the clever way in which the authors investigated the subconscious or, more precisely, the way in which people can somehow draw on what is going on in their subconscious.

Peirce and Jastrow took their point of departure in Fechner's famous finding that people have a threshold, below which they are unable to perceive small differences in sensations. Their key finding was that Fechner was wrong, and that people do perceive these small differences—but without being aware of it.

Generalizing from this finding, the authors conclude the article as follows:

> We gather what is passing in one another's minds in large measure from sensations so faint that we are not fairly aware of having them, and can give no account of how we reach our conclusions in such matters. The insight of females as well as certain "telepathic" phenomena may be explained in this way. *Such faint sensations ought to be fully studied by the psychologist and assiduously cultivated by every man.* (Peirce and Jastrow 1885: 83; emphasis added)

## Concluding Remarks

If you compare the version of theorizing that has been presented in this book to that of Peirce, you will find similarities as well as differences. As to the similarities, what I have called *creative theorizing* is close to some of Peirce's ideas on *abduction*, even if I mainly focus on very modest discoveries. Like Peirce, I have also tried to argue that theorizing is part of the research process as a whole, in which the testing of the theory against facts is seen as a necessary part.

But there exist some differences as well. While Peirce divides the research process into abduction, deduction, and induction, I divide it into the prestudy and the main study. Theorizing takes place in both of these but in somewhat different ways.

Another issue that deserves mention is that Peirce's research process is closely modeled on the natural sciences. My argument about theorizing, in contrast, only deals with the social sciences. There exists to my mind no compelling reason why you should want to draw a sharp line between the natural sciences and the social sciences. Still, it would seem that in dealing with the social sciences you have to pay more attention, and perhaps also a different kind of attention, to such phenomena as language, meaning, and subjectivity.

To Peirce, discoveries seem to be driven mainly by surprises, but in my view there may exist other causes as well. You can simply be interested in something, intrigued by something, or driven by various nonscientific motives to study something, including politics and religion. Arguing that discovery can take place only as a reaction to a surprise does not seem very useful.

It may also be the case that Peirce sometimes describes the research process in a too schematic manner, especially when he refers to the three stages of abduction, deduction, and induction. The message that the reader gets is that proceeding in this order constitutes the best way to make a discovery.

This view of things, however, may not capture the complexity of what is going on when a discovery is made, and therefore risks giving the researcher the wrong kind of advice. What may also be involved is an attempt from Peirce's side to model the research process closely after logic.

In the end, of course, these are minor points compared to the truly seminal ideas of Peirce. Creating a new and alive idea is for Peirce like giving birth to a child. It is also the case that his writings constitute a nearly inexhaustible source of richness for anyone interested in theorizing. On practically every topic in the process of theorizing that I have discussed in this book—such as observation, naming, explanation, and so on—the work of Peirce has been a great source of inspiration. It is my belief that other students of social science who are interested in theorizing will also find Peirce's work extremely rewarding.

# Acknowledgments

My main debt goes to Mabel Berezin, to whom the book is dedicated. I also owe a very special thank you to Eric Schwartz at Princeton University Press, whose advice and support have been very helpful. For fine assistance from the Press, I also thank Jennifer Harris and Ryan Mulligan.

Two anonymous reviewers gave a number of positive and constructive suggestions for changes. Many other people have helped as well, in some cases directly but more often inadvertently, often by something they said or how they reacted to some argument I made.

The list of helpful and inspiring people is very long. My thanks go especially to: Andy Abbott, Ola Agevall, Jeff Alexander, Patrik Aspers, Margareta Bertilsson, Richard Biernacki, Mikael Carleheden, Bruce Carruthers, Frank Dobbin, Alicia Eads, Nicolas Eilbaum, Laura Ford, Peter Gilgen, Andreas Glaser, Mark Granovetter, Mikael Holmqvist, Dan Klein, Karin Knorr Cetina, Thorbjørn Knudsen, Paul Lichterman, Michael Lynch, James G. March, Andrea Maurer, Elaine McDuff, Juan Diez Medrano, Hiro Miyazaki, Susan Ossman, Roland Paulsen, Trevor Pinch, Isaac Reed, Lambros Roumbanis, Erik Schneiderhan, Peter Sohlberg, Lyn Spillman, Iddo Tavory, Stephen Turner, Lars Udehn, Diane Vaughan, Karl Weick, Jeff Weintraub, and Hans and Karin Zetterberg.

I have also learned a lot from the students who have taken my courses in theorizing at Cornell University, Stockholm University, and Copenhagen University. Among those who have taught me a lot, I would especially like to thank the following: Angie Boyce, Christoffer Carlsson, Emily Goldman, Therese Heltberg, Emily Hoagland, Zhu Jinjing, Hernan Mondani, and the 2012 cohort of graduate students at Cornell.

Stockholm and Ithaca
*November 2013*

# Notes

## Chapter 1

1. Coleridge 1812: 132.
2. According to Jennifer Platt, little is currently known about pilot studies (Platt 2011; cf., for example, van Teijlingen and Hundley 2001). Pilot studies can be described as unofficial trial runs. One wants, for example, to see whether some part of a questionnaire will work. An exploratory study, in contrast, is usually conducted when one knows very little about a topic, but does not want to undertake a full study. "An exploratory paper," according to Robert K. Merton and Harriet Zuckerman, "can take us to a problematics of our subject: the formulation of principal questions that should be investigated with the rationale for considering these as questions worth investigating" (Merton and Zuckerman 1973: 497–98, 559). A prestudy differs from both a pilot study and an exploratory study in that it is intended as an organic part of a full study. Its purpose is also primarily theoretical.

## Chapter 2

1. Doyle 1892: 7.

## Chapter 3

1. Whitehead 1929: 4; cf. Parisi 2012: 232.

## Chapter 4

1. Bacon 1902: 72.

## Chapter 5

1. Peirce 1902: 427.

## Chapter 6

1. Polya 1954: 68.

## Chapter 7

1. Wittgenstein 1980: 24e.
2. The first line: total institutions (Goffman 1961); the last line: laying of hands (Hughes 1984b: 570–71). The second line is an invented example.

## Chapter 8

1. Peirce and Ladd-Franklin 1902: 693.

## Chapter 9

1. Dickinson 1914: 29.

## Chapter 10

1. Whewell 1860: 134.

## Appendix

1. Peirce 1893: 178.

# References

Currently not many books and articles exist that address the issue of how to theorize in a practical and creative way in social science. Why this is the case I discuss in a preliminary version of my argument, "Theorizing in Sociology and Social Science: Turning to the Context of Discovery" (Swedberg 2012). A huge number of books and articles, however, do contain brief sections and passages that are of much interest. Some of these have been included in the following list of references.

The two authors who in my view have developed the most instructive and helpful approach to theorizing are Charles S. Peirce and Max Weber. A drawback with both of them is that what they have to say on this topic is scattered throughout their writings and not easily located. While their writings are very exciting, they are also difficult and time-consuming.

Peirce is more explicit about what goes into theorizing than Weber. On the other hand, he is primarily interested in the natural sciences. Weber, in contrast, is mainly interested in the social sciences, and especially attempts to address ways of including meaning into the analysis.

Three important and fairly easy texts by Peirce that I have found very useful are "Guessing" (1929), "How to Theorize" (1934b), and "Training in Reasoning" (1992b). Several anthologies of Peirce's key writings exist, the most useful of which is a two-volume set titled *The Essential Peirce* (1992a).

As for Weber, his essays on the philosophy of science are especially relevant, and these are today available in a new translation under the title *Collected Methodological Writings* (2012). "Science as a Vocation" (1946) and the first paragraph in chapter 1 (in part 1) of *Economy and Society* (1978) also contain much relevant material.

After Peirce and Weber I would recommend the following three books, which not only discuss theorizing in general but also outline some of the steps to follow: *An Introduction to Models in the Social Sciences* by John Lave and James G. March (1993); *Constructing Social Theories* by Arthur Stinchcombe (1968); and *The Sociological Imagination* by C. Wright Mills (1959).

In the book by Lave and March, special attention should be paid to chapter 2, where the authors present their "model of the model-building process" (Lave and March 1993: 19–20, 40–42). In the work by Stinchcombe some of the best material can be found in the first two chapters. Mills's most useful statement about theorizing can be found in the appendix to *The Sociological Imagination*, called "On Intellectual Craftmanship."

A very accessible and general article on theorizing is "Theory Construction as Disciplined Imagination" by Karl Weick (1989; see also Weick 1995, 2014). Another useful article, written by another major figure in social science, is Robert K. Merton's "Three Fragments from a Sociologist's Notebooks" (1987). The subtitle to Merton's article indicates its three major themes: "Establishing the Phenomenon, Specified Ignorance, and Strategic Research Materials."

Many of the authors who have contributed to the anthology *Theorizing in Social Science: The Context of Discovery* (Swedberg 2014) have been interested in theorizing for a long time. They include Karin Knorr Cetina, James G. March, Stephen Turner, Diane Vaughan, and Karl Weick. Many suggestive ideas can also be found in the chapters by the other authors.

Some interesting material on theorizing can be found in the following two books, even if theorizing is not their main focus:

*Methods of Discovery* by Andrew Abbot (2004); and *Tricks of the Trade* by Howard S. Becker (1998).

I also recommend *Social Science Concepts* by Gary Goertz (2006), for the topic of concept formation; *Creating Scientific Concepts* by Nancy Nersessian (2008), for analogies; and *Models and Metaphors* by Max Black (1962), for the role of metaphors.

Explanation and causality are rarely discussed from the perspective of theorizing but are usually seen as part of methods and the philosophy of science. Two general texts on this topic that I have found useful are *A Tale of Two Cultures: Qualitative and Quantitative Research in the Social Sciences* by Gary Goertz and James Mahoney (2012); and *The Oxford Handbook of Political Methodology*, edited by Janet M. Box-Steffensmeier, Henry Brady, and David Collier (2008).

It is also important to have some knowledge of cognitive science and especially cognitive psychology in order to understand the theorizing process. One way to acquire this is to read an introductory textbook in cognitive science and/or in cognitive psychology. There also exist a number of useful handbooks on these two topics, with chapters on concepts, memory, emotions, and so on (see, for example, *The Cambridge Handbook of Cognitive Science*, edited by Keith Frankish and William Ramsey [2012]; and *The Oxford Handbook of Cognitive Psychology*, edited by Daniel Reisberg [2013]). For useful information on how people reason and explain things, including how they use deduction, abduction, similarity, and so on, see *The Oxford Handbook of Thinking and Reasoning*, edited by Keith Holyoak and Robert Morrison (2012).

For heuristics, I recommend George Polya's *How to Solve It* (1954); and Daniel Kahneman's *Thinking, Fast and Slow* (2011). For the role of imagination, there is (again) *The Sociological Imagination* by C. Wright Mills (1959). For the origin of the words *theory* and *theorizing* in ancient Greece, see especially *Spectacles of*

*Truth in Classical Greek Philosophy:* Theoria *in Its Cultural Context* by Andrea Wilson Nightingale (2009). Last but not least, *Philosophical Investigations* by Ludwig Wittgenstein (1953) is a prerequisite for anyone who aspires to be a modern theorizer.

Abbott, Andrew. 1995. "Things of Boundaries," *Social Research* 62, no. 4 (Winter): 857–82.

———. 1997. "Seven Types of Ambiguity," *Theory and Society* 26, no. 2–3 (April–June): 357–91.

———. 2001. *Time Matters: On Theory and Method.* Chicago: University of Chicago Press.

———. 2004. *Methods of Discovery: Heuristics for the Social Sciences.* New York: W. W. Norton.

———. 2006. "Reconceptualizing Knowledge Accumulation in Sociology," *The American Sociologist* 37, no. 2: 57–66.

———. 2007. "Against Narrative: A Preface to Lyrical Sociology," *Sociological Theory* 25, no. 1: 67–99.

———. 2011. "Andrew Abbott's Short List of Rules for Theorizing." Comments presented at the Junior Theorists' Seminar, American Sociological Association, Las Vegas, August 19.

Abend, Gabriel. 2008. "The Meaning of 'Theory,'" *Sociological Theory* 26, no. 2 (June): 173–99.

Adler, Franz. 1947. "Operational Defintions in Sociology," *American Journal of Sociology* 52, no. 5: 438–44.

Agevall, Ola. 2008. *The Career of Mobbing: Emergence, Transformation, and Utilization of a New Concept.* Växjö: Department of Social Science, Växjö University.

Alexander, Jeffrey. 2006. *The Civil Sphere.* New York: Oxford University Press.

American Sociological Association (ASA). 2012. *Social Capital, Organizational Capital, and the Job Market for New Sociology Graduates.* Washington, DC: ASA.

———. 2013. "Recruitment and Retention of Sociology Majors," *ASA Footnotes* 41, no. 1 (January): 1, 4.

Anderson, Chris. 2008. "The End of Theory: The Data Deluge Makes the Scientific Theory Obsolete," *Wired Magazine*, June 23. Available at http://www.wired.com/science/discoveries/magazine/16-07/pb_theory (accessed November 8, 2013).

Arendt, Hannah. 1978. *The Life of the Mind*. New York: Harcourt.

———. 1992. *Lectures on Kant's Political Philosophy*. Chicago: University of Chicago Press.

Aristotle. 1984. *The Complete Works of Aristotle*. Ed. Jonathan Barnes. Rev. Oxford trans., 2 vols. Princeton, NJ: Princeton University Press.

———. 1991. *The Art of Rhetoric*. Trans. H. C. Lawson-Tancred. London: Penguin Books.

———. 2001. *The Basic Works of Aristotle*. Ed. Richard McKeon. New York: Modern Library.

Bachelard, Gaston. 1984. *The New Scientific Spirit*. Boston: Beacon Press.

Bacon, Francis, 1902. *Novum Organum*. Ed. Joseph Devey. New York: P. F. Collier and Son.

Bailey, Kenneth. 1973. "Constructing Monothetic and Polythetic Typologies by the Heuristic Method," *Sociological Inquiry* 14 (Summer): 291–308.

Beach, Derek, and Rasmus Brun Pedersen. 2013. *Process-Tracing Methods: Foundations and Guidelines*. Ann Arbor: University of Michigan Press.

Beauchamp, Richard. 2012. "Peirce, Thirdness, and Pedagogy: Reforming the Paideia." Available at http://www.bu.edu/wcp/Papers/Amer/AmerBeau.htm (accessed November 25, 2012).

Becker, Gary. 1976. *The Economic Approach to Human Behavior*. Chicago: University of Chicago Press.

Becker, Howard S. 1973. *Outsiders: Studies in the Sociology of Deviance*. New York: Free Press.

———. 1982. *Art Worlds*. Berkeley: University of California Press.

———. 1998. *Tricks of the Trade: How to Think about Your Research while You're Doing It*. Chicago: University of Chicago Press.

———. 2011. E-mail message to Richard Swedberg, April 27.

———. 2012. "Learning to Observe in Chicago." Available at http://home.earthlink.net/~hsbecker/articles/observe.html (accessed July 24,

2012). First published as "Learning to Observe in Chicago," in *La goût de l'observation*, ed. Jean Peneff, pp. 60–61, 76–77, and 126–27. Paris: La Découverte (in French).

Berezin, Mabel. 2009. "Exploring Emotions and the Economy," *Theory and Society* 35: 335–46.

Biello, David. 2006. "Fact or Fiction?: Archimedes Coined the Term 'Eureka!' in the Bath," *Scientific American* (December 8). Available at http://www.scientificamerican.com/article.cfm?id=fact-or-fiction -archimede (accessed January 8, 2013).

Biernacki, Richard. 2012. *Reinventing Evidence in Social Inquiry*. New York: Palgrave Macmillan.

Black, Max. 1962. *Models and Metaphors: Studies in Language and Philosophy*. Ithaca, NY: Cornell University Press.

Bloch, Marc. 1964. *The Historian's Craft*. New York: Vintage Books.

Blumer, Herbert. 1954. "What Is Wrong with Social Theory?" *American Sociological Review* 19: 4–10.

Boudon, Raymond. 1995. "Massimo Borlandi Interviews Raymond Boudon," *Schweizerische Zeitschrift für Soziologie* 21, no. 3: 559–73.

Bourdieu, Pierre. 1988. "Vive la Crise! For Heterodoxy in Social Science," *Theory and Society* 17: 773–87.

Bourdieu, Pierre, Jean-Claude Chamboredon, and Jean-Claude Passeron. 1991. *Sociology as a Craft: Epistemological Preliminaries*. New York: Walter de Gruyter.

Box-Steffensmeier, Janet M., Henry Brady, and David Collier (eds.). 2008. *The Oxford Handbook of Political Methodology*. New York: Oxford University Press.

Brady, Henry. 2008. "Causation and Explanation in Social Science." In *The Oxford Handbook of Political Methodology*, ed. Janet M. Box-Steffensmeier, Henry Brady, and David Collier, pp. 217–70. New York: Oxford University Press.

Brent, Joseph. 1993. *Charles Sanders Peirce: A Life*. Bloomington: Indiana University Press.

Brown, Richard. 1977. *Poetic for Sociology: Toward a Logic of Discovery for the Human Sciences*. Cambridge, UK: Cambridge University Press.

Bruffee, Kenneth. 1993. *Collaborative Learning: Higher Education, Inter-*

*dependence, and the Authority of Knowledge*. Baltimore: Johns Hopkins University Press.

Bruun, Hans Henrik. 2007. *Science, Values and Politics in Max Weber's Methodology*. Expanded ed. Aldershot, UK: Ashgate.

Bulmer, Martin. 1984. *The Chicago School of Sociology: Institutionalization, Diversity, and the Rise of Sociological Research*. Chicago: University of Chicago Press.

Camic, Charles, and Neil Gross. 1998. "Contemporary Developments in Sociological Theory: Current Projects and Conditions of Possibility," *Annual Review of Sociology* 24: 453–76.

Cardoso, Fernando Henrique. 2006. *The Accidental President of Brazil: A Memoir*. New York: Public Affairs.

Carrère, Sybil, and John Gottman. 1999. "Predicting Divorce among Newlyweds from the First Three Minutes," *Family Process* 38, no. 3: 293–301.

Cartwright, Nancy. 2011. "A Philosopher's View of the Long Road from RCTs to Effectiveness," *The Lancet* 77, no. 9775: 1400–1401.

Chambliss, J. J. 1991. "John Dewey's Idea of Imagination," *Journal of Aesthetic Education* 25, no. 4: 43–49.

Chomsky, Noam. 1991. "Linguistics and Cognitive Science: Problems and Mysteries." In *The Chomskyan Turn*, ed. Asa Kasher, pp. 26–55. Cambridge, UK: Blackwell.

———. 2004. "The Creative Experience." In *Language and Politics*, ed. C.-P. Otero, pp. 89–102. Oakland, CA: AK Press.

Coleman, James. 1964. *Introduction to Mathematical Sociology*. New York: Free Press.

Coleridge, Samuel Taylor. 1812. *The Friend: A Series of Essays*. London: Gale and Curtis.

———. 1967. *Biographia Literaria*. Oxford, UK: Oxford University Press.

Collier, David, and John Gerring (eds.). 2009. *Concepts and Method in Social Science: The Tradition of Giovanni Sartori*. New York: Routledge.

Collier, David, Jody Laporte, and Jason Seewright. 2008. "Typologies: Forming Concepts and Creating Categorical Variables." In *The Oxford*

*Handbook of Political Methodology*, ed. Janet M. Box-Steffensmeier, Henry Brady, and David Collier, pp. 152–73. New York: Oxford University Press.

Collier, David, and James Mahon Jr. 1993. "Conceptual 'Stretching' Revisited: Adapting Categories in Comparative Analysis," *American Political Science Review* 87, no. 4 (December): 845–55.

Conté, Rosaria, et al. 2012. "Manifesto of Computational Social Science," *European Physical Journal Special Topics* 214: 325–46.

Coser, Lewis. 1994. "Introduction." In *On Work, Race, and the Sociological Imagination*, ed. Everett C. Hughes, pp. 1–17. Chicago: University of Chicago Press.

Damasio, Antonio. 2003. *Looking for Spinoza: Joy, Sorrow, and the Feeling Brain*. New York: Mariner Books.

Davis, Murray. 1971. "That's Interesting! Towards a Phenomenology of Sociology and a Sociology of Phenomenology," *Philosophy of the Social Sciences* 1: 309–44.

Dewey, John. 1934a. *Art as Experience*. New York: Minton, Balch & Company.

———. 1934b. *A Common Faith*. New Haven, CT: Yale University Press.

———. 1938. *Logic: The Theory of Inquiry*. New York: Henry Holt.

Dewey, John, and Arthur Bentley. 1945. "A Terminology for Knowing and Naming," *Journal of Philosophy* 42, no. 9 (April): 225–47.

Dickinson, Emily. 1914. *The Single Hound: Poems of a Lifetime*. Boston: Little, Brown, and Company.

Dobbin, Frank. 2009. "How Durkheim's Theory of Meaning-Making Influenced Organizational Studies." In *The Oxford Handbook of Sociology and Organization Studies: Classical Foundations*, ed. Paul Adler, pp. 200–222. New York: Oxford University Press.

Doyle, Conan. 1892. *Adventures of Sherlock Holmes*, vol. 2. New York: Harper & Brothers.

Dreyfus, Hubert. 2009. *On the Internet*. London: Routledge.

Dreyfus, Hubert, and Stuart Dreyfus. 1986. *Mind over Machine: The Power of Human Intuition and Expertise in the Era of the Computer*. New York: Free Press.

Dunbar, Kevin and David Klahr. 2012. "Scientific Thinking and Reasoning." In *The Oxford Handbook of Thinking and Reasoning*, ed. Keith Holyoak and Robert Morrison, pp. 701–18. New York: Oxford University Press.

Durkheim, Emile. 1964. *The Rules of Sociological Method*. Trans. S. Solvay and J. Mueller. New York: Free Press.

———. 1974. "Individual and Collective Representations." In Emile Durkheim, *Sociology and Philosophy*, ed. Talcott Parsons, pp. 1–34. New York: Free Press.

———. 1978. "Course in Sociology: Opening Lecture." In Emile Durkheim, *On Institutional Analysis*, ed. Mark Traugott, pp. 43–70. Chicago: University of Chicago Press.

———. 1982. "The Method of Sociology." In Emile Durkheim, *The Rules of Sociological Method*, trans. W. D. Halls, pp. 245–47. New York: Free Press.

Engell, James. 1981. *The Creative Imagination: Enlightenment to Romanticism*. Cambridge, MA: Harvard University Press.

Ericsson, K. Anders, and Herbert Simon. 1980. "Verbal Reports as Data," *Psychological Review* 87, no. 3: 215–51.

Espeland, Wendy Nelson. 2012. "Theorizing Is a Verb," *Perspectives: Newsletter of the ASA Theory Section* 34, no. 2 (December): 1–3.

Fann, K. T. 1970. *Peirce's Theory of Abduction*. The Hague: Martinus Nijhoff.

Firebaugh, Glenn. 2008. *Seven Rules for Social Research*. Princeton, NJ: Princeton University Press.

Fisch, Max. 1986. *Peirce, Semiotic, and Pragmatism: Essays by Max H. Fisch*. Bloomington: Indiana University Press.

Forché, Carolyn, and Philip Gerard (eds.). 2001. *Writing Creative Nonfiction*. Cincinatti: Story Press.

Frankish, Keith, and William Ramsey (eds.). 2012. *The Cambridge Handbook of Cognitive Science*. Cambridge, UK: Cambridge University Press.

Freud, Sigmund. 1998. *The Interpretation of Dreams*. Trans. James Strachey. New York: Avon Books.

Gambetta, Diego. No date. "Empirical Puzzles." The webpage of Diego Gambetta, Nuffield College, Oxford University. Available at http://

www.nuffield.ox.ac.uk/People/sites/Gambetta/Other%20Papers
/Empirical%20puzzles%20for%20teaching%20and%20research.pdf
(accessed December 15, 2012).

Gardner, Howard. 1987. *The Mind's New Science: A History of the Cognitive Revolution.* New York: Basic Books.

Geertz, Clifford. 2000. "Thick Description: Towards an Interpretive Theory of Culture." In *The Interpretation of Cultures*, pp. 3–30. New York: Basic Books.

Gentner, Dedre. 1982. "Are Scientific Analogies Metaphors?" In *Metaphor: Problems and Perspectives*, ed. David Miall, pp. 106–32. Sussex: Harvester Press.

———. 2003. "Analogical Reasoning, Psychology of." In *Encyclopedia of Cognitive Science,* ed. Lynn Nadel, vol. 1, pp. 106–12. London: Nature Publishing Company.

Gentner, Dedre, and Linsey Smith. 2013. "Analogical Learning and Reasoning." In *The Oxford Handbook of Cognitive Psychology*, ed. Daniel Reisberg, pp. 668–81. New York: Oxford University Press.

Gert, Heather. 1997. "Wittgenstein on Description," *Philosophical Studies* 88: 221–43.

Glaser, Barney, and Anselm Strauss. 1967. *The Discovery of Grounded Theory: Strategies for Qualitative Research.* Chicago: Aldine Publishing Company.

Goertz, Gary. 2006. *Social Science Concepts: A User's Guide.* Princeton, NJ: Princeton University Press.

Goertz, Gary, and James Mahoney. 2012. *A Tale of Two Cultures: Qualitative and Quantitative Research in the Social Sciences.* Princeton, NJ: Princeton University Press.

Goffman, Erving. 1961. *Asylums: Essays on the Social Situations of Mental Patients and Other Inmates.* New York: Anchor Books.

Goldthorpe, John. 2001. "Causation, Statistics, and Sociology," *European Sociological Review* 17, no. 1: 1–20.

Groopman, Jerome. 2007. *How Doctors Think.* Boston: Houghton Mifflin.

Hacking, Ian. 1983. *Representing and Intervening: Introductory Topics in the Philosophy of Natural Science.* Cambridge, UK: Cambridge University Press.

———. 1988. "Telepathy: Origins of Randomization in Experimental Design," *Isis* 79, no. 3 (Special Issue): 427–51.

Hart, H.L.A., and A. M. Honoré. 1958. *Causation in the Law*. New York: Oxford University Press.

Hedström, Peter, and Richard Swedberg (eds.). 1998. *Social Mechanisms: An Analytical Approach to Social Theory*. Cambridge, UK: Cambridge University Press.

Heidegger, Martin. 1976. *What Is Called Thinking?* Trans. J. Glenn Gray. New York: Harper.

———. 1977. "Science and Reflection." In Martin Heidegger, *The Question Concerning Technology and Other Essays*, pp. 154–82. New York: Harper.

Heilbron, Johan. 2011. "Practical Foundations of Theorizing in Sociology: The Case of Pierre Bourdieu." In *Social Knowledge Making*, ed. Charles Camic, Neil Gross, and Michèle Lamont, pp. 181–205. Chicago: Chicago University Press.

Heltberg, Therese. 2011. "What Is—Really—in a Dataset?," *Nordic Studies on Alcohol and Drugs* 28: 501–19.

Holyoak, Keith and Robert Morrison (eds.). 2012. *The Oxford Handbook of Thinking and Reasoning*. New York: Oxford University Press.

Hughes, Everett C. 1984a. "The Place of Field Work in Social Science." In *The Sociological Eye: Selected Papers*, pp. 496–506. New Brunswick, NJ: Transaction Press.

———. 1984b. *The Sociological Eye*. New Brunswick, NJ: Transaction Press.

Hughes, Everett C., and Helen MacGill Hughes. 1952. "What's in a Name?" In *When Peoples Meet*, ed. Everett C. Hughes and Helen MacGill Hughes, pp. 130–44. New York: Free Press.

Iggers, Georg G., Edward Wang, and Supriya Mukherje. 2008. *A Global History of Modern Historiography*. Harlow, UK: Longman.

Ionnadis, John P. 2005. "Why Most Published Research Findings Are False," *PLoS Medicine* 2, no. 8: e124. Available at http://www.plosmedicine.org/article/info:doi/10.1371/journal.pmed.0020124 (accessed February 23, 2013).

Jackson, Michelle, and D. R. Cox. 2013. "The Principles of Experimental Design and Their Application in Sociology," *Annual Review of Sociology* 39: 27–49.

Jastrow, Joseph. 1916. "Charles S. Peirce as a Teacher," *Journal of Philosophy* 13, no. 26 (December 21): 723–26.

Jefferies, Janis. 2012. "Pattern, Patterning." In *Inventive Methods: The Happening of the Social*, ed. Celia Lury and Nina Wakeford, pp. 125–35. London: Routledge.

Kahneman, Daniel. 2011. *Thinking, Fast and Slow*. New York: Farrar, Straus, and Giroux.

Kahneman, Daniel, and Amos Tversky. 1982. "The Simulation Heuristic." In *Judgment under Uncertainty: Heuristics and Biases*, ed. Daniel Kahneman, Paul Slovic, and Amos Tversky, pp. 201–8. Cambridge, UK: Cambridge University Press.

Kang, Min Jeong, et al. 2009. "The Wick in the Candle of Learning: Epistemic Curiosity Activates Circuitry and Enhances Memory," *Psychological Science* 20, no. 8: 963–73.

Kant, Immanuel. 1970. "An Answer to the Question 'What Is Enlightenment?'" In Immanuel Kant, *Kant's Political Writings*, ed. Hans Reiss, pp. 54–63. Cambridge, UK: Cambridge University Press.

———. 1998. *Critique of Pure Reason*. Trans. Paul Gruyer and Allen Wood. Cambridge, UK: Cambridge University Press.

Kaplan, Abraham. 1964. *The Conduct of Inquiry: Methodology for Behavioral Science*. San Francisco: Chandler Publishing.

Ketner, Kenneth Laine. 1981. "Peirce's Ethics of Terminology," *Transactions of the Charles S. Peirce Society* 17, no. 4 (Fall): 327–47.

Keynes, John Maynard. 2010. "On Reading Books." In John Maynard Keynes, *Keynes on the Wireless*, ed. Donald Moggridge, pp. 164–73. New York: Palgrave Macmillan.

Kincaid, Harold (ed.). 2012. *The Oxford Handbook of Social Science*. New York: Oxford University Press.

King, Gary, Robert Keohane, and Sidney Verba. 1994. *Designing Social Inquiry: Scientific Inference in Qualitative Research*. Princeton, NJ: Princeton University Press.

Klamer, Arjo, and Thomas Leonard. 2004. "So What's an Economic Metaphor?" In *Natural Images in Economic Thought: "Markets Read in Tooth and Claw,"* ed. Philip Mirowski, pp. 20–51. New York: Cambridge University Press.

Klein, Daniel. 2014. "Three Frank Questions to Discipline Your Theorizing." In *Theorizing in Social Science,* ed. Richard Swedberg, pp. 106–30. Stanford, CA: Stanford University Press.

Klinger, Eric. 2009. "Daydreaming and Fantasizing: Thought Flow and Motivation." In *Handbook of Imagination and Mental Simulation,* ed. Keith Markman, William Klein, and Julie Suhr, pp. 225–39. New York: Psychology Press.

Knorr Cetina, Karin. 2014. "Intuitionist Theorizing." In *Theorizing in Social Science,* ed. Richard Swedberg, pp. 29–60. Stanford, CA: Stanford University Press.

Koedinger, Kenneth, and Ido Roll. 2012. "Learning to Think: Cognitive Mechanisms and Knowledge Transfer." In *The Oxford Handbook of Thinking and Reasoning,* ed. Keith Holyoak and Robert Morrison, pp. 789–806. New York: Oxford University Press.

Kuhn, Thomas. 1970. *The Structure of Scientific Revolutions.* 2nd enlarged ed. Chicago: University of Chicago Press.

Lakatos, Imre. 1974. "The Role of Crucial Experiments in Science," *Studies in History and Philosophy of Science* 4, no. 4: 309–25.

Langley, Pat. 2004. "Heuristics for Scientific Discovery: The Legacy of Herbert Simon." Working paper from the Institute for the Study of Learning and Expertise, Palo Alto, CA. Available at http://www.isle.org/~langley/papers/has.essay.pdf (accessed August 11, 2011).

Larkin, Jill, and Herbert Simon. 1987. "Why a Diagram Is (Sometimes) Worth Ten Thousand Words," *Cognitive Science* 11: 65–99.

Latour, Bruno, and Steve Woolgar. 1986. *Laboratory Life: The Construction of Scientific Facts.* Princeton, NJ: Princeton University Press.

Lave, Charles A., and James G. March. 1993. *An Introduction to Models in the Social Sciences.* New York: University Press of America.

Lazarsfeld, Paul. 1962. "The Sociology of Empirical Research," *American Sociological Review* 27: 757–67.

Lepenies, Wolf. 1988. *Between Literature and Science: The Rise of Sociology.* Cambridge, UK: Cambridge University Press.

Levi, Edward. 1949. *An Introduction to Legal Reasoning*. Chicago: University of Chicago Press.

Lewis, David. 1973. *Counterfactuals*. Cambridge, MA: Harvard University Press.

Liszka, James. 2011. "Charles Peirce's Rhetoric and the Pedagogy of Active Learning," *Educational Philosophy and Theory* 45, no. 7: 781–88.

Loewenstein, George. 1994. "The Psychology of Curiosity: A Review and Reinterpretation," *Psychological Bulletin* 116, no. 1: 75–98.

Lombrozo, Tania. 2006. "The Structure and Function of Explanations," *Trends in Cognitive Science* 10, no. 10: 464–70.

———. 2007. "Simplicity and Probability in Causal Explanation," *Cognitive Psychology* 55, no. 3: 232–57.

———. 2012. "Explanation and Abductive Inference." In *The Oxford Handbook of Thinking and Reasoning*, ed. Keith Holyoak and Robert Morrison, pp. 260–76. New York: Oxford University Press.

Lucas, Jeffrey, Kevin Morrell, and Marek Posard. 2013. "Considerations on the 'Replication Problem' in Sociology," *American Sociologist* 44: 217–32.

Mandelbrot, Benoit. 2012. *The Fractalist: Memoir of a Scientific Maverick*. New York: Pantheon Books.

March, James G. 1970. "Making Artists out of Pedants." In *The Process of Model-Building in the Behavioral Sciences*, ed. Ralph Stogdill, pp. 54–75. New York: Norton.

Markman, Keith, William Klein, and Julie Suhr (eds.). 2009. *Handbook of Imagination and Mental Simulation*. New York: Psychology Press.

Markovsky, Barry. 2008. "Graduate Training in Sociological Theory and Theory Construction," *Sociological Perspectives* 51, no. 2: 423–45.

Martin, John Levi. 2011. *The Explanation of Social Action*. New York: Oxford University Press.

Mauss, Marcel. 1973. "Techniques of the Body," *Economy and Society* 2, no. 1: 70–88.

Maxwell, James Clark. 1884. "Are There Real Analogies in Nature?" In *The Life of James Clark Maxwell*, ed. Lewis Campbell and William Garnett, pp. 347–55. London: Macmillan.

Mayer-Schönberger, Viktor, and Kenneth Cukier. 2013. *Big Data: A Revolution That Will Transform How We Live, Work, and Think*. Boston: Houghton Mifflin Harcourt.

Mayr, Ernst. 1982. *The Growth of Biological Thought: Diversity, Evolution, and Inheritance*. Cambridge, MA: Harvard University Press.

McCloskey, Deirdre. 1986. *The Rhetoric of Economics*. New York: Harvester Press.

McDuff, Elaine. 2012. "Collaborative Learning in an Undergraduate Theory Course: An Assessment of Goals and Outcomes," *Teaching Sociology* 40, no. 2: 166–76.

Merton, Robert K. 1945. "What Is Sociological Theory?" *American Journal of Sociology* 50: 462–73.

———. 1948. "The Bearing of Empirical Research upon the Development of Social Theory," *American Sociological Review*, 13: 505–15.

———. 1959. "Introduction: Notes on Problem-Finding in Sociology." In *Sociology Today*, ed. Robert K. Merton, L. Broom, and L. Cottrell, pp. ix–xxxiv. New York: Basic Books.

———. 1967. "On Sociological Theories of the Middle Range." In *On Theoretical Sociology*, pp. 39–72. New York: Free Press.

———. 1968. *Social Theory and Social Structure*. Enlarged ed. New York: Free Press.

———. 1984. "Socio-Economic Duration: A Case Study of Concept Formation in Sociology." In *Conflict and Consensus: A Festschrift in Honor of Lewis A. Coser*, ed. Walter Powell and Robert Robbins, pp. 262–85. New York: Free Press.

———. 1987. "Three Fragments from a Sociologist's Notebooks: Establishing the Phenomenon, Specified Ignorance, and Strategic Research Materials," *Annual Review of Sociology* 13: 1–28.

Merton, Robert K., and Alan Wolfe. 1995. "The Cultural and Social Incorporation of Sociological Knowledge," *American Sociologist* 26, no. 3 (Fall): 15–19.

Merton, Robert K., and Harriet Zuckerman. 1973. "Age, Aging, and Age Structure in Science." In *The Sociology of Science*, ed. Robert K. Merton, pp. 497–559. Chicago: University of Chicago Press.

Milgram, Stanley. 1976. *Environmental Psychology*. 2nd ed. New York: Holt, Rinehart, and Winston.

Mills, C. Wright. 1953. *White Collar: The American Middle Classes*. New York: Oxford University Press.

———. 1959. *The Sociological Imagination*. New York: Oxford University Press.

Mills, C. Wright (ed.). 1960. *Images of Man: The Classic Tradition in Sociological Thinking*. New York: George Braziller.

Murphy, Gregory. 2002. *The Big Book of Concepts*. Cambridge, MA: MIT Press.

Nagel, Ernest. 1961. *The Structure of Science*. New York: Free Press.

Nersessian, Nancy. 2008. *Creating Scientific Concepts*. Cambridge, MA: MIT Press.

Nightingale, Andrea Wilson. 2009. *Spectacles of Truth in Classical Greek Philosophy: Theoria in Its Cultural Context*. Cambridge, UK: Cambridge University Press.

Nisbet, Robert. 1976. *Sociology as an Art Form*. New York: Oxford University Press.

Oebler, Klaus. 1981. "The Significance of Peirce's Ethics of Terminology for Contemporary Lexicography in Semiotics," *Transactions of the Charles S. Peirce Society* 17, no. 4: 348–57.

Ogburn, William. 1930. "The Folkways of a Scientific Sociology," *Publications of the American Sociological Society* 24: 1–11.

Ogburn, William. 1947. "On Scientific Writing," *American Journal of Sociology* 52: 383–88.

Oxford English Dictionary Electronic Resource (OED). 2000. "Theorizing." Oxford, UK: Oxford University Press. Available at http://www.oed.com/view/Entry/200430?redirectedFrom=theorize#eid (accessed October 23, 2012).

Paavola, Sami. 2006. *On the Origin of Ideas: An Abductivist Approach to Discovery*. Helsinki: Philosophical Studies from the University of Helsinki No. 15.

Padgett, John, and Walter Powell. 2012. *The Emergence of Organizations and Markets*. Princeton, NJ: Princeton University Press.

Parisi, Luciana. 2012. "Speculation: A Method for the Unattainable." In

*Inventive Methods: The Happening of the Social*, ed. Celia Lury and Nina Wakeford, pp. 232–44. London: Routledge.

Park, Robert. 1929. "The City as a Social Laboratory." In *Chicago: An Experiment in Social Science Research*, ed. T. V. Smith and Leonard White, pp. 1–19. Chicago: University of Chicago Press.

Peirce, Charles S. 1868. "Questions Concerning Certain Faculties Claimed for Man," *Journal of Speculative Philosophy* 2: 103–14.

———. 1893. "Evolutionary Love," *Monist* 3, no. 2 (January): 176–200.

———. 1902. "Reasoning." In *Dictionary of Philosophy and Psychology*, ed. James Mark Baldwin, vol. 1, pp. 426–28. New York: Macmillan.

———. 1906. Lecture I of a planned course. Harvard University, Houghton Library, MS 857.

———. 1929. "Guessing," *The Hound & Horn* 2, no. 3 (Spring): 267–85.

———. 1932. Vol. 2 of *Collected Papers of Charles Sanders Peirce*, ed. Charles Hartshorne and Paul Weiss. Cambridge, MA: Belknap Press.

———. 1934a. Vol. 5 of *Collected Papers of Charles Sanders Peirce*, ed. Charles Hartshorne and Paul Weiss. Cambridge, MA: Belknap Press.

———. 1934b. "How to Theorize." In *Collected Papers of Charles Sanders Peirce*, ed. Charles Hartshorne and Paul Weiss, pp. 413–22. Cambridge, MA: Belknap Press.

———. 1935. Vol. 6 of *Collected Papers of Charles Sanders Peirce*, ed. Charles Hartshorne and Paul Weiss. Cambridge, MA: Belknap Press.

———. 1958a. Vol. 7 of *Collected Papers of Charles Sanders Peirce*, ed. Arthur W. Burks. Cambridge, MA: Belknap Press.

———. 1958b. Vol. 8 of *Collected Papers of Charles Sanders Peirce*, ed. Arthur W. Burks. Cambridge, MA: Belknap Press.

———. 1985. "Lowell Lectures of 1903 [476]. Eighth Lecture: Abduction. Part 2. Pythagoras." In *Historical Perspectives on Peirce's Logic of Science*, ed. Carolyn Eisele, vol. 2, pp. 1011–21. Berlin: Mouton Publishers.

———. 1992a. *The Essential Peirce*. Vol. 1. Bloomington: Indiana University Press.

———. 1992b. "Training in Reasoning." In *Reasoning and the Logic of Things*, ed. Kenneth Laine Ketner, pp. 181–96. Cambridge, MA: Harvard University Press.

Peirce, Charles S. 1997. *Pragmatism as a Principle and Method of Right Thinking: The 1903 Harvard Lectures on Pragmatism.* Ed. Patricia Ann Turrisi. Albany: State University of New York Press.

———. 1998a. *The Essential Peirce.* Vol. 2. Bloomington: Indiana University Press.

———. 1998b. "The Ethics of Terminology." In Charles S. Peirce, *The Essential Peirce*, vol. 2, pp. 263–66. Bloomington: Indiana University Press.

———. 2010. *Writings of Charles S. Peirce. Vol 8. 1890–1892.* Bloomington: Indiana University Press.

Peirce, Charles S., and Joseph Jastrow. 1885. "On Small Differences in Sensation," *Memoirs of the National Academy of Sciences* 3: 73–83.

Peirce, Charles S., and Christine Ladd-Franklin. 1902. "Theory." In *Dictionary of Philosophy and Psychology*, ed. James Mark Baldwin, vol. 1, pp. 693–94. New York: Macmillan.

Pinch, Trevor, and Richard Swedberg. 2012. "Wittgenstein's Visit to Ithaca in 1949: On the Importance of Details," *Distinktion: Scandinavian Journal of Social Theory* 14, no. 1: 2–29.

Plato. 1989. *The Republic and Other Works.* Trans. B. Jowett. New York: Anchor Books.

Platt, Jennifer. 1994. "The Chicago School and Firsthand Data," *History of the Human Sciences* 7, no. 1: 57–80.

———. 1996. *A History of Sociological Research Methods in America, 1920–1960.* Cambridge, UK: Cambridge University Press.

———. 2002. "The History of the Interview." In *Handbook of Interview Research*, ed. Jaber Gubrium and Jaames Holstein, pp. 33–54. London: SAGE.

———. 2011. Interview on the Pilot Study. Los Angeles, August 21.

Polya, George. 1950. "Let Us Teach Guessing." In George Polya, *Collected Papers*, vol. 4, pp. 504–11. Cambridge, MA: MIT Press.

———. 1954. *How to Solve It: A New Aspect of Mathematical Method.* 2nd ed. Princeton, NJ: Princeton University Press.

———. 1959. "Ten Commandments for Teachers." In George Polya, *Collected Papers*, vol. 4, pp. 525–33. Cambridge, MA: MIT Press.

———. 1979. "George Pólya Interviewed on His Ninetieth Birthday," *Two-Year College Mathematics Journal* 10, no. 1 (January): 13–19.

Popper, Karl. 1935. *Logik der Forschung.* Vienna: Julius Springer.

———. 1959. *The Logic of Scientific Discovery.* London: Hutchinson & Co.

Ragin, Charles. 2000. *Fuzzy-Set Social Science.* Chicago: University of Chicago Press.

Ragin, Charles, and Lisa Amoroso. 2011. *Constructing Social Research: The Unity and Diversity of Method.* 2nd ed. Los Angeles: SAGE.

Reed, Isaac, and Mayer Zald. 2014. "The Unsettlement of Inquiry in the Social Sciences." In *Theorizing in Social Science,* ed. Richard Swedberg, pp. 85–105. Stanford, CA: Stanford University Press.

Reichenbach, Hans. 1938. *Experience and Prediction: An Analysis of the Foundations and the Structure of Knowledge.* Chicago: University of Chicago Press.

———. 1951. *The Rise of Scientific Philosophy.* Berkeley: University of California Press.

Reisberg, Daniel (ed.). 2013. *The Oxford Handbook of Cognitive Psychology.* New York: Oxford University Press.

Richards, Ivor Armstrong. 1936. *The Philosophy of Rhetoric.* Oxford, UK: Oxford University Press.

Ricoeur, Paul. 1977. *The Rule of Metaphor: Multi-disciplinary Studies of the Creation of Meaning in Language.* Toronto: University of Toronto Press.

Rinehart, Jane. 1999. "Turning Theory into Theorizing: Collaborative Learning in a Sociological Theory Course," *Teaching Sociology* 27 (July): 216–32.

———. 2012. "Young Minds Bloom: Teaching with My Mouth Shut." Gonzaga University, Spokane, WA. Available at http://magazine .gonzaga.edu/2012/young-minds-bloom-teaching-with-my-mouth -shut (accessed October 17, 2012).

Robinson, Richard. 1950. *Definition.* Oxford, UK: Oxford University Press.

Ross, W. D. 1949. *Aristotle's Prior and Posterior Analytics.* Oxford, UK: Clarendon Press.

Rousseau, Jean-Jacques. 1953. *Confessions*. Trans. J. M. Cohen. London: Penguin Books.

———. 1992. *The Reveries of the Solitary Walker*. Trans. Charles Butterworth. Indianapolis, IN: Hackett Publishing.

Sacks, Oliver. 2012. *Hallucinations*. New York: Random House.

Sartori, Giovanni. 1970. "Concept Misformation in Comparative Politics," *American Political Science Review* 64, no. 4: 1033–53.

Sartre, Jean-Paul. 2004. *The Imaginary: A Phenomenological Psychology of the Imagination*. Trans. Jonathan Webber. London: Routledge.

Scaff, Lawrence. 2011. *Max Weber in America*. Princeton, NJ: Princeton University Press.

Schickore, Jutta, and Friedrich Steinle (eds.). 2006. *Revisiting Discovery and Justification: Historical and Philosophical Perspectives on the Context Distinction*. Dordrecht: Springer.

Schleifer, James. 1980. *The Making of Tocqueville's* Democracy in America. Chapel Hill: University of North Carolina Press.

Sebeok, Thomas., and Jean Umiker-Sebeok. 1981. "'You Know My Method': A Juxtaposition of Charles S. Peirce and Sherlock Holmes." In *The Sign of Three*, ed. Umberto Eco and Thomas Sebeok, pp. 11–51. Bloomington: Indiana University Press.

Sen, Amartya K. "Description as Choice," *Oxford Economic Papers* 32, no. 3 (November): 353–69.

Simmel, Georg. 1919. "Aus Georg Simmels Nachgelassenem Tagebuch," *Logos* 8: 121–51.

———. 1950. *The Sociology of Georg Simmel*. Ed. and trans. Kurt Wolff. New York: Free Press.

———. 1959. "The Problem of Sociology." In *Georg Simmel, 1858–1918*, ed. Kurt Wolff, pp. 310–36. Columbus: Ohio State University Press.

———. 1997. "Sociology of the Senses." In *Simmel on Culture*, ed. David Frisby and Mike Featherstone, pp. 109–19. London: SAGE.

Simon, Herbert. 1966. "Scientific Discovery and the Psychology of Problem Solving." In *Mind and Cosmos*, ed. Robert Colodny, pp. 22–40. Pittsburgh: University of Pittsburgh Press.

———. 1991a. *Models of My Life*. New York: Basic Books.

———. 1991b. "The Scientist as Problem Solver." In Simon Herbert, *Models of My Life*, pp. 368–87. New York: Basic Books.

Simon, Herbert, Patrick Langley, and Gary Bradshaw. 1981. "Scientific Discovery as Problem Solving," *Synthese* 47: 1–27.

Skocpol, Theda. 1979. *States and Social Revolutions: A Comparative Analysis of France, Russia, and China*. Cambridge, UK: Cambridge University Press.

Small, Albion. 1896. "Review of Arthur Fairbanks, *An Introduction to Sociology*," *American Journal of Sociology* 2, no. 2: 305–10.

Smith, Edward, and Douglas Medin. 1981. *Categories and Concepts*. Cambridge, MA: Harvard University Press.

Sokol, Robert. 1974. "Classification: Purposes, Principles, Progress, Prospects," *Science* 185, no. 4157 (September 27): 1115–23.

Somers, Margaret. 1995. "What's Political or Cultural about Political Culture and the Public Sphere? Toward an Historical Sociology of Concept Formation," *Sociological Theory* 13, no. 2: 113–44.

Spillman, Lynette. 2004. "Causal Reasoning, Historical Logic, and Sociological Explanation." In *Self, Social Structure, and Beliefs*, ed. Jeffrey Alexander, Gary Marx, and Christine Williams, pp. 216–34. Berkeley: University of California Press.

Stein, Maurice. 1963. "The Poetic Metaphors of Sociology." In *Sociology on Trial*, ed. Maurice Stein and Arthur Vidich, pp. 173–82. Englewood Cliffs. NJ: Prentice-Hall.

Stewart, Ian. 1998. *Nature's Numbers: Discovering Order and Pattern in the Universe*. London: Phoenix Orion Books.

Stinchcombe, Arthur. 1968. *Constructing Social Theories*. Chicago: University of Chicago Press.

———. 1978. *Theoretical Methods in Social History*. New York: Academic Press.

———. 1991. "The Conditions of Fruitfulness of Theorizing about Mechanisms in Social Science," *Philosophy of the Social Sciences* 21, no. 3: 367–88.

———. 2005. *The Logic of Social Research*. Chicago: University of Chicago Press.

Swedberg, Richard. 2009. "Tocqueville as an Empirical Researcher." In *Raymond Boudon: A Life in Sociology*, ed. Mohammed Chaerkaouie and Peter Hamilton, vol. 1, pp. 279–92. Oxford, UK: Bardwell Press.

———. 2012. "Theorizing in Sociology and Social Science: Turning to the Context of Discovery," *Theory and Society* 41: 1–40.

Swedberg, Richard (ed.). 2014. *Theorizing in Social Science: The Context of Discovery*. Stanford, CA: Stanford University Press.

Tavory, Iddo, and Stefan Timmerman. 2012. "Theory Construction in Qualitative Research: From Grounded Theory to Abductive Analysis," *Sociological Theory* 30, no. 3: 167–86.

Tetlock, Philip, and Aaron Belkin (eds.). 1996. *Counterfactual Thought Experiments in World Politics*. Princeton, NJ: Princeton University Press.

Tocqueville, Alexis de. 2009. "France before the Revolution (1836)," *Journal of Classical Sociology* 9, no. 1: 17–66.

Tversky, Amos, and Daniel Kahneman. 1974. "Judgment under Uncertainty: Heuristics and Biases," *Science* 185, no. 4157 (September 1974): 1124–31.

———. 1982. *Judgment under Uncertainty: Heuristics and Biases*. Cambridge, UK: Cambridge University Press.

van Teijlingen, Edwin, and Vanora Hundley. 2001. "The Importance of Pilot Studies," *Social Research Update* (University of Surrey), no. 35. Available at http://sru.soc.surrey.ac.uk/SRU35.html (accessed July 31, 2011).

Vaughan, Diane. 1998. "How Theory Travels: Analogy, Models, and the Diffusion of Ideas." Paper presented at the meeting of the American Sociological Association, San Francisco, August.

———. 2014. "Analogy, Cases, and Comparative Organization." In *Theorizing in Social Science*, ed. Richard Swedberg, pp. 61–84. Stanford, CA: Stanford University Press.

Wallace, David Foster, and Bryan Garner. 2013. *Quack This Way: David Foster Wallace and Bryan A. Garner Talk Language and Writing*. Dallas, TX: Penrose Publishing.

Watts, Duncan. 2011. *Everything Is Obvious—Once You Know the Answer*. New York: Crown Business.

Weber, Marianne. 1975. *Max Weber: A Biography*. Trans. Harry Zorn. New York: Wiley.

Weber, Max. 1930. *The Protestant Ethic and the Spirit of Capitalism*. Trans. Talcott Parsons. London: G. Allen & Unwin.

———. 1946. "Science as a Vocation." In *From Max Weber*, trans. and ed. Hans Gerth and C. Wright Mills, pp. 129–56. New York: Oxford University Press.

———. 1949. *Methodology of the Social Sciences*. Trans. and ed. Edward A. Shils and Henry A. Finch. New York: Free Press.

———. 1972. *Wirtschaft und Gesellschaft. Grundriss der verstehenden Soziologie*. 5th ed. Tübingen: J.C.B. Mohr.

———.1975. *Roscher and Knies: The Logical Problems of Historical Economics*. Trans. Guy Oakes. New York: Free Press.

———. 1978. *Economy and Society: An Outline of Interpretive Sociology*. Trans. Ephraim Bischoff et al., 2 vols. Berkeley: University of California Press.

———. 1988. *Gesammelte Aufsätze zur Wissenschaftslehre*. Tübingen: J.C.B. Mohr.

———. 2001. *The Protestant Ethic Debate: Max Weber's Replies to His Critics, 1907–1910*. Eds. David Chalcraft and Austin Harrington. Liverpool, UK: Liverpool University Press.

———. 2004. *The Essential Weber: A Reader*. Ed. Sam Whimster. London: Routledge.

———. 2012. *Collected Methodological Writings*. Trans. and ed. H. H. Bruun and S. Whimster. London: Routledge.

Weick, Karl. 1989. "Theory Construction as Disciplined Imagination," *The Academy of Management Review* 14, no. 4: 516–31.

———. 1995. "What Theory is *Not*, Theorizing *Is*," *Administrative Science Quarterly* 40: 385–90.

———. 2003. "Imagination in Organization Studies." Talk given at Interdisciplinary Committee of Organizational Studies (ICOS), University of Michigan, Ann Arbor.

———. 2006. "The Role of Imagination in the Organization of Knowledge," *European Journal of Information Systems* 15: 446–52.

Weick, Karl. 2014. "The Work of Theorizing." In *Theorizing in Social*

*Science*, ed. Richard Swedberg, pp. 177–94. Stanford, CA: Stanford University Press.

Weiss, Robert. 1996. "Remembrance of Everett Hughes," *Qualitative Sociology* 19, no. 4: 543–51.

Whewell, William. 1860. *On the Philosophy of Discovery, Chapters Historical and Critical.* London: John W. Parker and Son.

Whitehead, Alfred North. 1929. *The Function of Reason.* Boston: Beacon Hill.

Wickelgren, Ingrid. 2012. "Trying to Forget," *Scientific American Mind* 22 (January–February): 32–39.

Wicksell, Knut. 1958. *Selected Papers in Economic Theory.* Ed. Erik Lindahl. Cambridge, MA: Harvard University Press.

Wieth, Mareike, and Rose Zachs. 2011. "Time of Day Effects on Problem Solving: When the Non-Optimal Is Optimal," *Thinking and Reasoning* 17, no. 4: 387–401.

Willer, David. 1996. "The Prominence of Formal Theory in Sociology," *Sociological Forum* 11, no. 2: 319–31.

Wittgenstein, Ludwig. 1953. *Philosophical Investigations.* Trans. G.E.M. Anscombe. New York: Macmillan.

———. 1958. *The Blue and the Brown Book.* New York: Harper.

———. 1972. *On Certainty.* Eds. G.E.M. Anscombe and G. H. von Wright. New York: Harper & Row.

———. 1980. *Culture and Value.* Trans. Peter Winch. Chicago: University of Chicago Press.

———. 1998. *Culture and Value.* Rev. ed. Trans. Peter Winch. London: Routledge.

Woodward, James. 2009. "Scientific Explanations." In *Stanford Encyclopedia of Philosophy*, ed. Edward Zalta. Available at http://plato.stanford .edu/entries/scientific-explanation/ (accessed September 28, 2013).

Young, Cristobal. 2009. "Model Uncertainty in Sociological Research: An Application to Religion and Economic Growth," *American Sociological Review* 74: 380–97.

Zashin, Elliot, and Phillip Chapman. 1974. "The Uses of Metaphor and Analogy: Toward a Renewal of Political language," *Journal of Politics* 36 (May): 290–326.

Zerubavel, Eviatar. 2007. "Generally Speaking: The Logic and Mechanics of Social Pattern Analysis," *Sociological Forum* 22, no. 2: 131–45.

Zetterberg, Hans. 2010. Conversation with the author, International Sociological Association (ISA), World Congress of Sociology, Gothenburg, Sweden, July 16.

Zhao, Shanyang. 1996. "The Beginning of the End or the End of the Beginning? The Theory Construction Movement Revisited," *Sociological Forum* 11, no. 2: 305–18.

# Index

Lightning Source UK Ltd.
Milton Keynes UK
UKHW01f1041190618
324463UK00001B/78/P

9 780691 168135